OCS Study
MMS 2002-063

Deepwater Program: Northern Gulf of Mexico Continental Slope Habitats and Benthic Ecology

Interim Report - Year 2

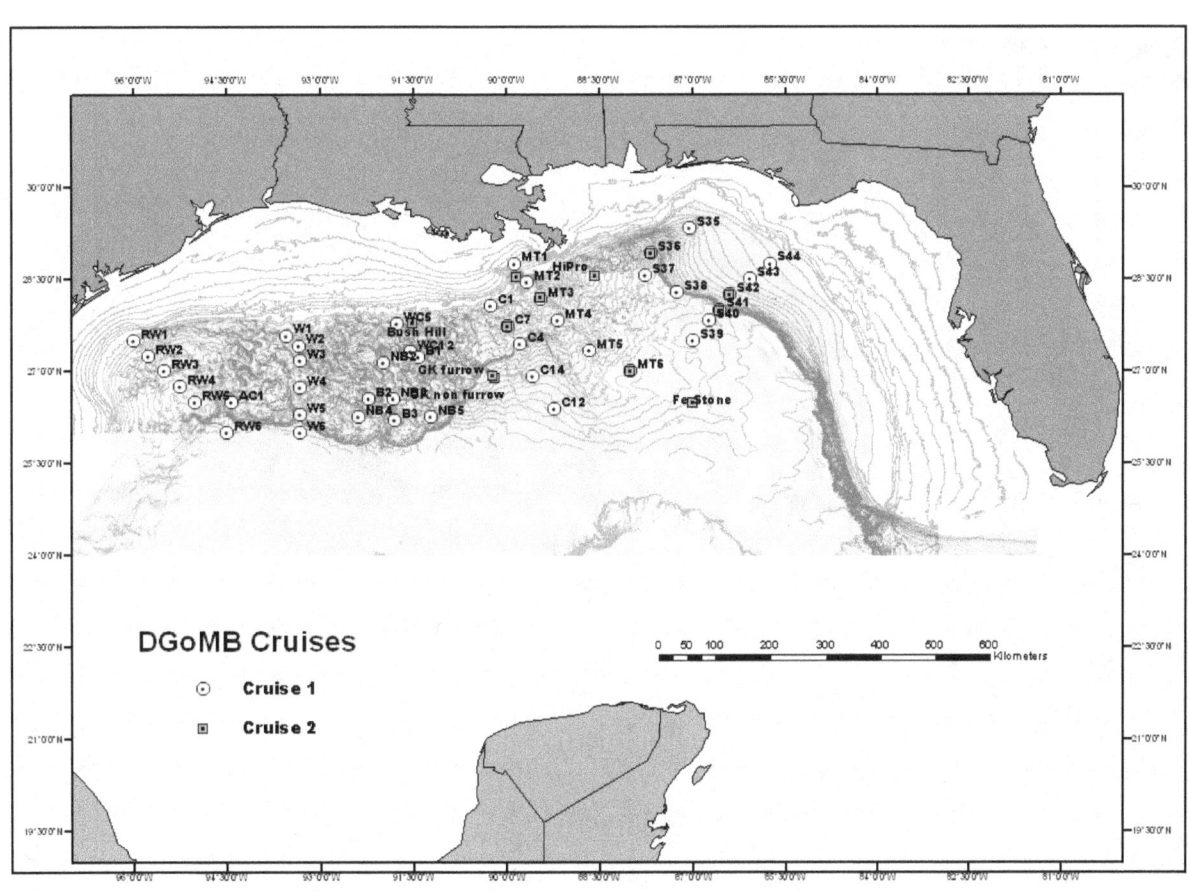

U.S. Department of the Interior
Minerals Management Service
Gulf of Mexico OCS Region

Deepwater Program: Northern Gulf of Mexico Continental Slope Habitats and Benthic Ecology

Interim Report - Year 2

Authors

Gilbert T. Rowe
Mahlon C. Kennicutt II

Prepared under MMS Contract
1435-01-99-CT-30991
by
Texas A&M University
Texas Engineering Experiment Station
College Station, Texas 77843-3146

Published by

U.S. Department of the Interior
Minerals Management Service
Gulf of Mexico OCS Region

New Orleans
December 2002

DISCLAIMER

This report was prepared under contract between the Minerals Management Service (MMS) and Texas A&M University. This report has been technically reviewed by the MMS and approved for publication. Approval does not signify that the contents necessarily reflect the views and policies of the Service, nor does mention of trade names of commercial products constitute endorsement or recommendation for use. It is, however, exempt from review and compliance with MMS editorial standards.

REPORT AVAILABILITY

Extra copies of the report may be obtained from the Public Information Office (Mail Stop 5034) at the following address:

U.S. Department of the Interior
Minerals Management Service
Gulf of Mexico OCS Region
Public Information Office (MS 5034)
1201 Elmwood Park Boulevard
New Orleans, Louisiana 70123-2394

Telephone Number: (504) 736-2519
                    1-800-200-GULF

CITATION

Suggested Citation:

Rowe, G.T. and M.C. Kennicutt II. 2002. Deepwater Program: Northern Gulf of Mexico Continental Slope Habitat and Benthic Ecology. Year 2: Interim Report. U.S. Department of the Interior, Minerals Management Service, Gulf of Mexico OCS Region, New Orleans, Louisiana. OCS Study MMS 2002-063. 158 pp.

TABLE OF CONTENTS

LIST OF FIGURES

LIST OF TABLES

EXECUTIVE SUMMARY

A research program has been initiated by the Minerals Management Service (Contract No. 1435-01-99-CT-30991) to gain better knowledge of the benthic communities of the deep Gulf of Mexico entitled "The Deepwater Program: Northern Gulf of Mexico Continental Slope Habitat and Benthic Ecology." This report provides a summary of the progress to date at the end of the second year of the program. At this stage of the program, sample analyses are in progress with only partial data sets finalized. The program is on schedule and planning is in progress for the final year's field program which includes a major extension of the sampling and analysis efforts into the deepest regions of the southern Gulf of Mexico.

Increasing exploration and exploitation of fossil hydrocarbon resources in the deep-sea prompted the Minerals Management Service of the U.S. Department of the Interior to support an investigation of the structure and function of the assemblages of organisms that live in association with the sea floor in the deep-sea. The program, Deep Gulf of Mexico Benthos or DGoMB, is studying the northern Gulf of Mexico (GOM) continental slope from water depths of 300 meters on the upper continental slope out to greater than 3,000 meters water depth seaward of the base of the Sigsbee and Florida Escarpments. The study is focused on areas that are the most likely targets of future resource exploration and exploitation. However, to develop a Gulf-wide perspective of deep-sea communities, sampling in areas beyond those thought to be potential areas for exploration has been included in the study design. A major enhancement in the program is the extension of the transects onto the abyssal plain of the central Gulf of Mexico through collaborative studies with Mexican scientists. This additional work effort will allow assessment of benthic communities structure and function throughout the basin by sampling the deepest habitats in the region.

The program is designed to gain a better ability to predict variations in the structure and function of animal assemblages in relation to water depth, geographic location, time and overlying water mass. Biological studies are integrated with measurements of physical and chemical hydrographic parameters, sediment geochemical properties and geological characteristics that are known to influence benthic community distributions and dynamics. Eight (8) hypotheses are being tested on the basis of measures of benthic community structure. It is hypothesized that community structure varies as a function of:

1) water depth,
2) geographic location (east vs. west),
3) association with canyons,
4) association with mid-slope basins,
5) sea surface primary productivity,
6) proximity to hydrocarbon seeps,
7) time (seasonal and interannual scales), and
8) association with the base of escarpments.

Measures of community structure used to test the hypotheses are variations in diversity, similarities in assemblage composition (at the species level), variations in biomass and abundance, and the mean size of individuals within specific size categories.

The underlying premise of the hypotheses to be tested is that deep-sea communities are food limited. This premise leads to the hypothesis that variations in community structure in time and space are a function of the input of food to the seafloor. In other words, community dynamics and structure are dependent on the availability and quality of food resources. Corollary hypotheses test the possibility that each independent variable is related in some way to how organic matter from multiple potential sources is utilized by the benthic community.

After defining community structure, the next set of objectives uses the information to infer the flux of organic carbon into and through the ecosystem. The conceptual model assumes that community structure and function are tightly coupled. Presently there is little reason to reject this generalization, but direct evidence for it in the deep-sea is at best fragmentary.

The conceptual model represents each of the principal size categories of the living components as standing stocks at each study site in the survey. The model includes demersal fishes, megafauna, scavengers, macrofauna, meiofauna, and heterotrophic bacteria. This model (Figure 1), of a sediment-associated food web, can be coupled with a model of fossil hydrocarbon utilization by chemoautotrophic organisms including large invertebrates that house endosymbionts. This linkage is yet to be explicitly established and is the basis for one of the hypotheses being tested. The boxes in the model represent standing stocks which have units of biomass (organic carbon per unit area) whereas the arrows represent flux between boxes and hence have units of organic carbon per unit area per unit time. For consistency, the units are mg C m^{-2} and mg C m^{-2} day^{-1}. Data from the survey portion of the program quantifies standing stocks across the survey area. Respiration rates are estimated on the basis of organism size and temperature from established relationships in the published literature. The fluxes represent transfers between components and are calculated by difference to balance respiratory losses at steady state. Burial loss of carbon is organic carbon (detrital) concentration times sediment accumulation rate. Input to the bottom is assumed to be equal to the sum of the respiration and burial losses at steady state.

The second phase of the project is designed to test the model. Direct measurements will be made of fluxes on cruises that conduct process experiments at selected locations. The model is tested based on results from process experiments completed in June of 2001 and future process experiments to be performed in 2002. Total sediment community respiration is determined by benthic lander and incubation chambers. Total respiration is partitioned by measuring bacterial activity in pressure chamber incubations at *in situ* temperatures. Uptake and respiration are determined using mixed amino acids labeled with radiocarbon. Sulfate reduction rate are measured using radio-labeled sulfate incubation of sediment. Lander/chamber flux measurements include oxygen, dissolved inorganic carbon, inorganic nitrogen, phosphate, and silicate. Scavenger domains of occupation are estimated using baited traps, time-lapse cameras and an ADCP to calculate vertical and horizontal eddy mixing and mean current direction. Stable isotopes of carbon and nitrogen are used to determine the food chain's structure and linkages. Physical and biological mixing are estimated using a suite of natural radionuclides characterized by an appropriate range of decay rates. Data from the second and third field year are used to adjust model parameters. The locations of the experimental sites were chosen based on model outputs, sampling results, and on-going testing of programmatic hypotheses. Experiments during the third field year are designed to further validate revised model rates and parameters. Additional sampling sites will be selected as needed to improve the resolution of the models and advance the testing of the hypotheses.

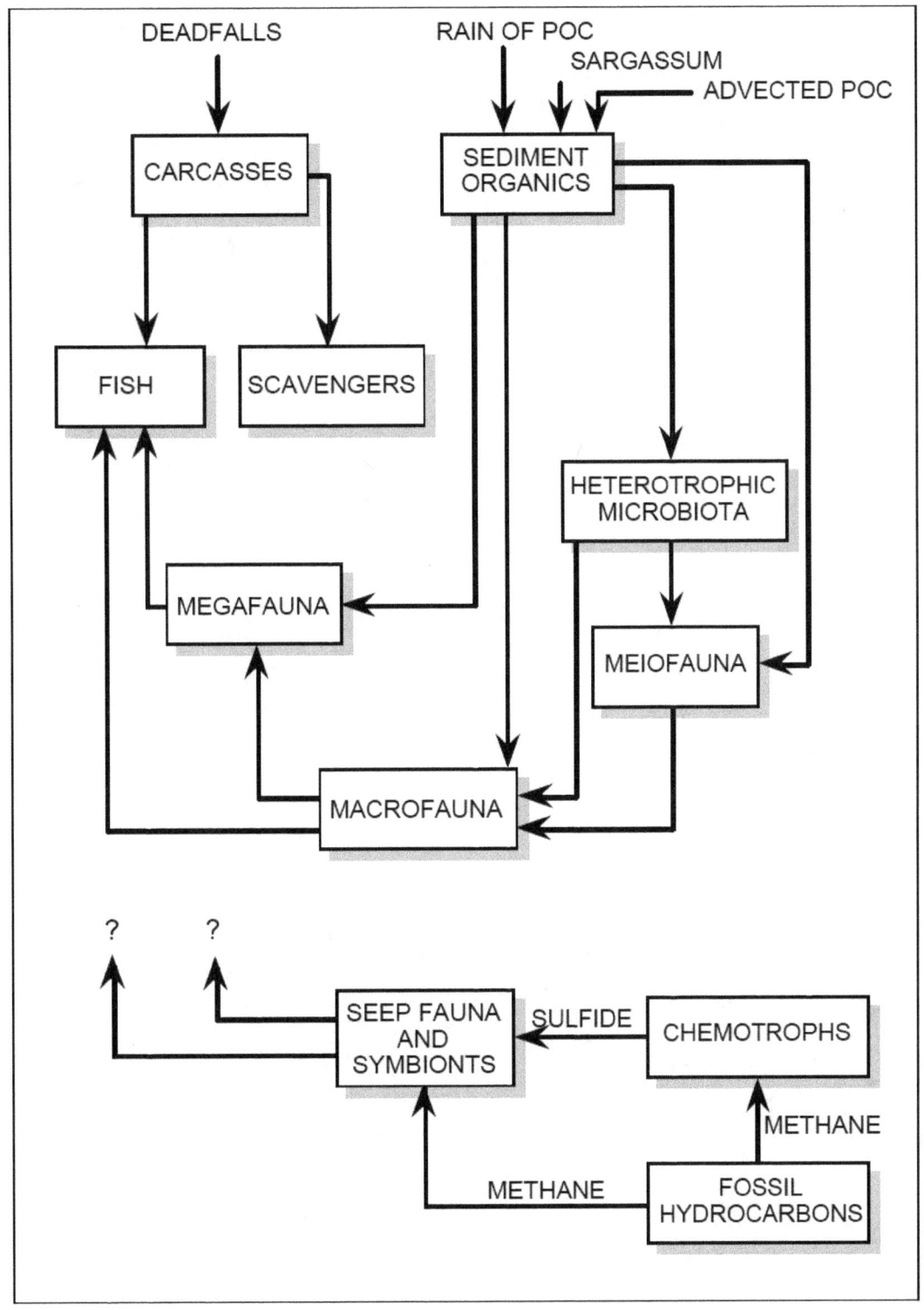

Figure 1. A general model of a sediment-associated food-web.

1.0 INTRODUCTION

The topography, geology, geophysics, currents, hydrography, chemistry and biota of the continental slope are much less well known than those of the continental shelf. The earliest information on the deep-sea biota of the Gulf of Mexico come from studies that used benthic trawling and photography (TerEco 1976, 1983). The largest study, The Northern Gulf of Mexico Continental Slope Study (NGOMCS), concentrated on geologic features, water circulation, chemistry, and biological communities (LGL and TAMU 1988). New scientific findings in the area, including chemosynthetic communities and a better understanding of the geological complexity of the region, have significantly altered our view of the GOM deep-sea (MacDonald 1998; MacDonald et al. 1996). Rapid expansion of energy industry activities into the deep-sea has occurred over the past decade. It is expected that this trend will continue and that deep-sea regions of the GOM will be the site of energy exploration and development activities for decades to come.

An MMS workshop report on the deepwater GOM concluded that there was a need for additional information on the composition and structure of benthic communities, the associated biogeochemical processes, habitat heterogeneity and physiography, trophic interactions, and the biological "health" of the region (Carney 1998). The deep-sea is a setting within which benthic communities survive and propagate in the northern GOM. The deep-sea is characterized by total darkness, low temperature, nearly featureless mud, sparse food resources, predictable biomass patterns, unusual diversity patterns, and poorly defined couplings to topography, biogeochemistry, and currents.

The DGoMB program will provide a better understanding of:

1) the present condition of biological communities in the study area,
2) the distribution and patterns of deep-sea biota,
3) the biological and physical processes that control the environmental setting, and
4) the effects that these processes have on the character of benthic and benthopelagic communities.

The program emphasizes understanding the make-up and variability of soft-bottom biological communities with a secondary effort to characterize the important biological and abiotic processes that sustain or change the observed patterns. The study will:

1) detail the composition and structure of slope biological communities,
2) infer the relationship between these communities and local conditions and forcing factors,
3) characterize the "health" and functioning of deep-sea communities, and
4) compare and contrast the GOM region with similar oceanic basins.

The DGoMB program design was developed based on historical knowledge of deep-sea communities in the GOM. The interdisciplinary nature of the scientific objectives was recognized and the study design balances the benthic survey aspects of the program with experimental (or "process") oriented studies needed to understand the deep-sea community's structure and function. A careful analysis of previous information was used to focus the study on the most relevant areas and those areas which will provide the greatest likelihood of establishing generalities about the structure and function of deep-sea benthic communities. The program will provide a predictive capability for areas not directly sampled or observed. This predictive capability is a framework for ascertaining the potential for, and the most likely impact from, fossil fuel exploration and exploitation in the deep-sea.

Each work element is nested in an integrated design that links data collection to a coherent spatial framework that provides maximum complementary information based on a detailed model of the system. Survey station results were used to choose experimental stations. Experimental stations will be a subset of reoccupied survey stations tightly linking all observations and data in space and time. Each measurement is taken to provide quantitative estimates of unknown elements of the model, to improve the quantitative accuracy of the model, and/or to test and refine the fundamental assumptions.

A review of previous studies, particularly the NGOMCS study provided valuable insights for designing the new study (LGL and TAMU 1988). The program design incorporated the following strategic conclusions:

1. **An equal sampling effort must be concentrated at different water depths to determine if "zones" exist.** Site selection emphasized equally spaced depth intervals and replication at the treatment level (sites that are mostly similar except for depth) recognizing that gradients in ecosystem properties are more likely than "zones".

2. **Depth dependence in community structure and composition must be evaluated in the context of other recently recognized confounding factors** such as seafloor topography and currents.

3. **Sampling sites must be chosen based on characteristics believed to be important in establishing biological patterns** such as detrital flux to the seafloor as influenced by near surface patterns of primary productivity.

4. **Proximity to the Mississippi River and Fan is an important spatial consideration.**

5. **Benthic communities are nestled in different topographic and sedimentologic settings** that are influenced by slope failure and varying inputs of terrigenous materials.

6. **Sampling sites must be selected to compare benthic communities associated with known physical features** such as the thermohalocline, the oxygen minimum, and high current regimes.

7. **The program should be designed to provide flexibility and allow revision and rethinking of the underlying strategy and design** on a regular basis in response to collection of new data and re-evaluation of historical data.

8. **Temporal variations in community structure and composition are important and can be quantified by reoccupying historical sites and visiting a subset of sites during each of the three planned field seasons.**

9. **An improved understanding of community structure and composition requires better and more refined measurements of biomass** for input into the conceptual model.

10. **Improved estimates of the megafaunal role in the ecosystem are important** and include a three pronged approach to surveys: trawling (with improved quantitative methodologies), photosurveys, and baited traps.

11. **The number of sites sampled and the intensity of sampling must be increased over that of previous studies.**

12. **Replication and the size of the sample must be increased over that of previous studies** to ensure that the total number of animals collected adequately samples the diversity of the communities being studied.

13. **The data must be meticulously managed** so that it will be readily available for future reassessment as our understanding of the deep-sea evolves (this includes the use of standard and accepted methods in all aspects of the program and placement of data in a GIS framework).

The program receives added value by its close linkages with previous and on-going MMS efforts in the GOM. Many members of the Team participated in programs such as the deep water literature survey and review, the northeastern GOM hydrography and chemical oceanography program, the deep water physical oceanography re-analysis program, the Mississippi-Alabama pinnacles program, and chemosynthetic community studies (Table 1.1). The methods and approaches adopted for this program are the same, or compatible with, the methods of these other programs allowing for the integration of new results with the results of other programs in the final synthesis. This will produce a holistic evaluation of the GOM deep-sea benthos and the linkages between abiotic and biotic processes that control complex ecological patterns in deep-sea benthos.

1.1   Program Objectives

The structure and function of deep-sea benthic communities is the end-result of complex interactions between and among the biota and the topography, geology, currents, hydrography, chemistry, and physical setting. The NGOMCS study attempted to describe the geology, water circulation, chemistry, and biologic communities on the northern GOM continental slope regions (LGL and TAMU 1988). The current project builds on, improves, and supplements this study. A reassessment of continental slope ecosystems, in the context of intensive oil and gas exploration and exploitation in the region, is considered essential for the management and protection of biological resources in the deep-sea.

Table 1.1 Program Team - Key Personnel*

Name	Discipline	Role	Institution
• Gilbert T. Rowe	• Deep-sea Benthic Ecology	• Project Manager	• Texas A&M University
		• Principal Scientist	
		• Chief Scientist	
		• Group Leader-Deep-sea Ecology	
• Mahlon C. Kennicutt II	• Environmental Chemist	• Deputy Program Manager Contaminant Chemist	• Texas A&M University
• Gary A. Wolff	• Data Management	• Data Manager	• Texas A&M University
• Jody Deming	• Microbiology	• Co-PI Ecology	• University of Washington
• Paul Montagna	• Benthic Ecologist	• Co-PI Ecology	• University of Texas
		• Study Design	
• Richard Haedrich	• Bottom Fishes	• Co-PI Ecology	• Memorial University
	• Megafauna	• Data Analysis	
• Richard Heard	• Macrofauna Taxonomy	• Co-PI Ecology	• University of Southern Mississippi
• John Morse	• Inorganic Geochemist	• Geochemistry Group Leader	• Texas A&M University
• William Bryant	• Geological Oceanographer	• Geology Group Leader	• Texas A&M University
• Worth Nowlin	• Physical Oceanography	• Oceanography Group Leader	• Texas A&M University
• Joan Bernhard	• Foraminifera		• University of South Carolina
• Norman Guinasso	• Physical Oceanography Field Program		• Texas A&M University
• Bob J. Presley	• Metal Contaminants		• Texas A&M University
• Terry L. Wade	• Organic Contaminants		• Texas A&M University
• Steven DiMarco	• Physical Oceanography		• Texas A&M University
• Michael Rex	• Community Structure	• Science Review Board	• University of Massachusetts-Boston
• Kenneth L. Smith, Jr.	• Community Dynamics	• Science Review Board	• Scripps Institution of Oceanography
• William W. Schroeder	• Gulf of Mexico Ecology	• Science Review Board	• Dauphin Island Marine Laboratory, University of Alabama

*Does not include taxonomists.

The overarching goals of DGoMB are to:

- **determine in greater detail the composition and structure of slope bottom biological communities and to infer relationships between biological patterns and major controlling processes and**

- **characterize the area as to its present "health" and function and compare and contrast the region with similar oceanic regions.**

Specific DGoMB objectives are to:

- **improve the conceptual model that serves as the guide for the design and overall conduct of the study and to test specific hypotheses related to the models;**

- compile and synthesize data from existing databases and on-going programs to interpret new results;

- conduct field collections to describe the distribution and structure of benthic communities on the continental slope of the GOM and elucidate the functional interactions among them in known environmental settings;

- characterize the hydrographic structure and measure the dissolved and particulate water column nutrient concentrations, primary productivity, and chlorophyll *a* at the study sites;

- characterize the sediments at the study sites including grain size and hydrocarbon, metal, carbonate, and organic carbon concentrations;

- characterize the basic attributes of the benthic microbiota and biomass at the study sites;

- characterize the soft-bottom macro- and megafauna at the study sites;

- relate variations in benthic biotic patterns to sedimentary processes and to the chemical and physical setting;

- define basic levels of animal and bacterial activity and production and describe interactions between and among benthic biota, the several ecological/biological compartments, and the abiotic environment; and

- compare and contrast the GOM benthic marine environment and communities with those in other basins of similar depth ranges and oceanic settings.

The program is to be conducted over a 48-month period of performance. Major oceanographic cruises are to be conducted, one in each of the first three years of the program. The final year of the program is dedicated to completing sample analyses begun in the first three years, data management and interpretation, model refinement, and production of the Synthesis Report. The field surveys will document the biota, the abiotic character of the slope and the important biotic and abiotic forcing factors. Study site selection criteria included consideration of anticipated zonation, water depth, distance from shore, abiotic variables, physiography and topography, geochemical environment, anthropogenic effects, and present and future leasing trends.

1.2   The Program

The program consists of four tasks:

TASK 1 - Re-examination of Existing Data and Field Study Design

All available scientific records and databases have been identified, collected, and re-examined. Previous studies of particular importance are the TerEco Corporation synthesis (1976 and 1983), the MMS NGOMCS (LGL and TAMU 1988), and chemosynthetic ecosystem studies (MacDonald 1998 and MacDonald et al. 1996). Industry data, MMS leasing history and production data, USGS Gloria data, NODC data, governmental holdings of results of various MMS physical oceanography programs (LATEX, NEGOM Deepwater), and other information will be integrated with the new findings. These data formed the basis for final recommendation of study sites to the Contracting Officer Technical Representative (COTR) and the Scientific Review Board (SRB). Historical information was used to describe the study sites to justify how each site contributes to the overall program design and to verify important features of the conceptual model.

TASK 2 - Field Sampling

The *R/V Gyre* was and will be used to conduct all cruises. Conventional sampling methodologies are used for the community structure survey and innovative experimental approaches are used for process studies and experiments. Year II and III cruises sample those sites selected on the basis of information produced in Year I and II, respectively. The goal of the sampling program is to describe the benthic communities in distinct and identifiable settings in time and space. A phased-in approach concentrated the benthic survey portion of the work in Year I allowing ample time to process samples and analyze data. Year II and III provide infilling with additional survey stations based on programmatic results to better test hypotheses. Experimental stations address key questions related to processes and forcing factors and are sampled during cruises in years two and three of the program. Experimental stations have been chosen based on existing knowledge and Cruise I results. The experimental stations are a subset of survey stations providing for a close integration of all data collected. Water column sampling provides descriptive hydrography and water column chemistry (designed similar to the NEGOM program) at all sites. Seafloor sampling of sediments for benthic and benthopelagic fauna (designed similar to the GOOMEX program) is the main activity at the survey stations. Basic ecological processes such as microbial activity; sources and fates of nutrients and detrital material; feeding habits; the relative importance of feeding guilds and taxa; and the presence of potential contaminants are studied at experimental stations. A major modification of the field program has led to a revision of plans for field efforts in the third year of the project.

TASK 3 - Sample and Data Processing and Analysis

All samples and data are being processed as specified by contract. The quality of data and samples is ensured by a comprehensive data management plan (i.e., the Program Management Plan). Chain-of-custody and sample tracking activities guarantee the integrity and quality of the samples and data from shipboard collection to final synthesis. All parameters that can be reasonably measured onboard the ship (nutrients, salinity, oxygen, etc.) are measured using standard protocols. Sample and data processing include descriptive hydrography and water chemistry; sediment properties, chemical contaminants, and sediment geochemical properties; benthic microbiota, meiofauna, macrofauna, megafauna, and fishes; and measurements of basic ecological processes. Experimental stations studied in Years II and III were planned in consultation with the COTR and the SRB.

TASK 4 - Data Interpretation, Synthesis and Reporting

Two (2) narrative Interim Reports and a Synthesis Report will have been produced. This report is the second interim report. The reports will contain an assessment of historic information, the data collected, descriptions of methods and analyses, interpretations of the analyzed information, and the results and discussions of the findings. Models will be refined and recast as warranted in light of new information. The present "health" of the area will be assessed. These reports contain appropriate charts, maps, or schematics that portray faunal and habitat variability and the major forcing factors related to community structure and function in the deep-sea GOM as data becomes available. Topics to be covered in these reports include relevant historical information; the hydrography and oceanography of the region; the biological, chemical, geological, and physical processes and interactions in the water column and at the sediment-water interface; the effects of biotic and abiotic forcing factors on slope biota; concentrations and sources of hydrocarbon and metal contaminants in the area including an assessment of potential biological effects; and the likely effects of OCS petroleum exploration and development and other human activities on biotic resources in the study area. The COTR, CO, and SRB are kept informed of progress in the program by monthly status reports.

2.0 A CONCEPTUAL MODEL OF THE DEEP-SEA

A conceptual model of the deep-sea, its living and non-living components, has been constructed to represent the interacting stocks of organisms that make-up a typical benthic boundary layer community (Figure 2.1). A biological boundary layer is defined as approximately 1 m deep into the sediments, extending up through the mixed layer of the water column to approximately 100 m above bottom. This biological boundary layer thus conforms to that previously used to describe the principal interacting components of a deep-sea benthic community (Smith 1992). This conceptual model has been drawn in software called STELLA II. The software allows flexibility in reformulating the structure and internal relationships within the system. The formulation presented is a modification of the model used by Smith (1992) and represents a deep-sea food chain. The modifications consist of defining every stock variable, living or non-living, as a "box" and every process, such as predation or respiration, as an "arrow". Thus all interactions between the biota and the sources and sinks of organic matter are explicit either as "boxes" or "arrows". On the other hand, "physical" processes are not explicitly represented. These implicit factors affect the "arrows" between the "boxes". Each "box" has a "size" in terms of concentration, biomass or abundance that is the sum of the "arrows" entering the "box" minus the "arrows" leaving the "box". At steady-state, each "box" does not change with time, and thus the inputs equal the outputs or losses. An important process, respiration, has been omitted in this conceptual food chain. Each stock can be taken separately in a submodel (Figure 2.2). Macrofaunal biomass, for example, is a function of what it consumes, what consumes it, respiration, and feces production. The contents of each stock can be expressed as a differential equation. The set of differential equations of all the stocks can be used to simulate the behavior of the entire food chain over time. The problem with doing this in the deep-sea is that data to quantify the stocks and processes are sparse at best. While considerable information exists on the stocks in a few locations and a few data exist on the rates of processes in others, the locations where both stocks and fluxes are known, even in the most minimal sense, are quite limited. One exception is a study of the central North Pacific, but even this study treated the sediment dwelling biota as one functional group due to a lack of detailed information on the foodweb (Smith 1992; Smith and Kaufmann 1999).

An advantage of this model is that with adequate data it can be used to simulate how the ecosystem will function under different conditions. Previously this approach has been used in an oligotrophic upper continental slope environment off eastern Greenland (Rowe et al. 1997). Boxcore standing stocks of the components represented were coupled with measures of community respiration (using a bottom lander with benthic chambers) and laboratory measures of bacterial activity to simulate the variations in biomass over time in response to a single seasonal pulse of organic matter related to a short ice-free period. In a purely hypothetical situation, the bioenhancement of infauna due to the disposal of organic rich material, such as sewage sludge or dredge spoils, was modeled, based on a simplified rendition of the Smith (1992) model (Rowe 1998). By adding organic matter in a pulse, the community "shifted up" to higher biomass and higher respiration and the alteration predicted by the model was validated by actual data at Deepwater Dumpsite 106 on the continental rise in the northwest Atlantic Ocean. This feature of "shifting" up or down in response to different input terms will be an important tool for interpreting the response of community structure and function in the deep-sea GOM in reaction to inputs from oil and gas exploration and production activities. The two most relevant inputs at platforms are organic enrichment due to a "reef" effect and the introduction of contaminants.

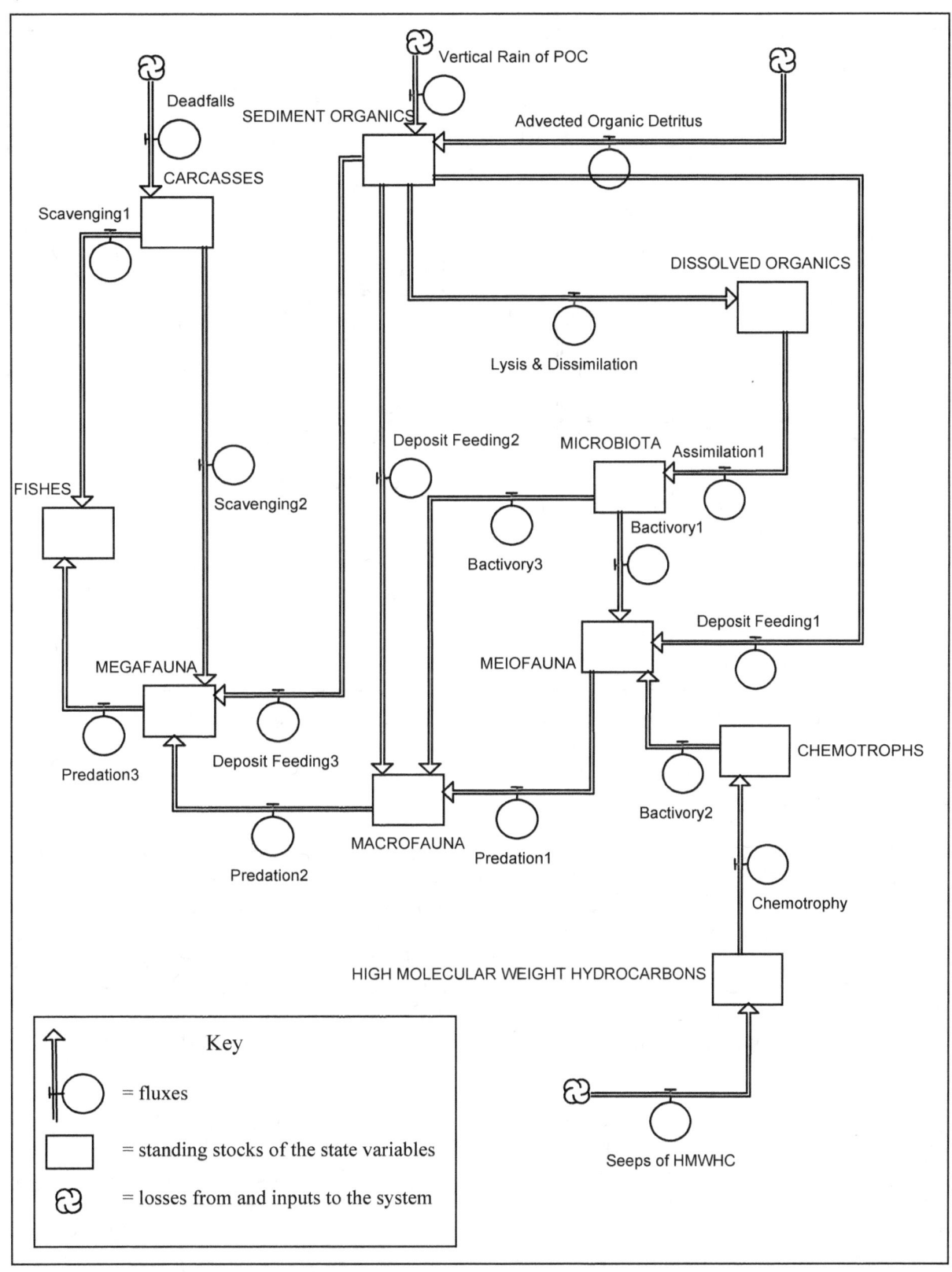

Figure 2.1. A conceptual model of the deep-sea Gulf of Mexico.

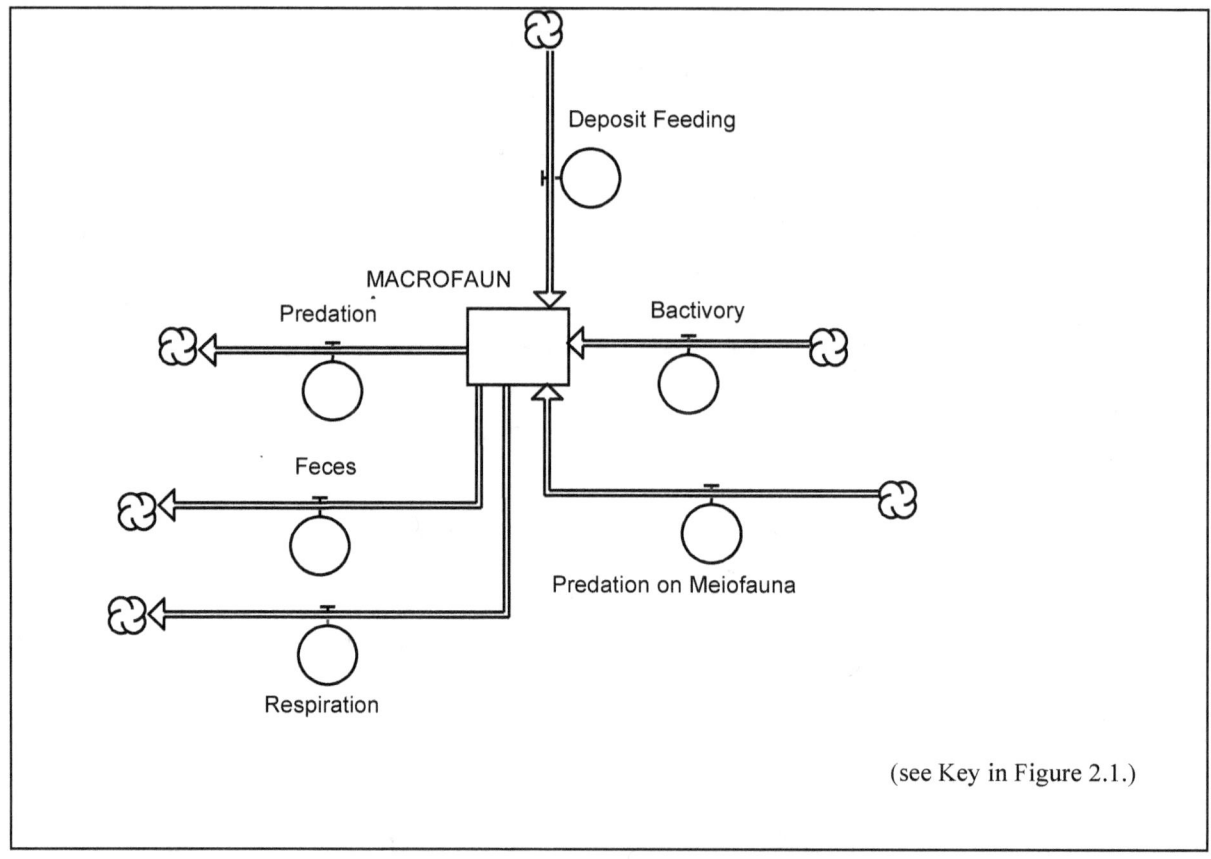

Figure 2.2. The macrofauna submodel of a system carbon food chain model.

2.1   Biotic Variables

The details of the conceptual model can be described as a number of biotic (living and non-living) and abiotic variables. In addition, the model is described in terms of various derived variables related to community structure and function. In-the-end, an understanding of the model components and their interactions are used to select the set of variables to be quantified that best describe the functioning of the system being studied. These inferences are then ground-truthed by in-the-field observations and the model is revised as needed. The biotic variables include the microbiota, meiofauna, macrofauna, megafauna, and fishes. These groups of biota make up the overall stocks of the system which are estimated through conventional quantitative sampling as described in Sections 6.0 and 7.0.

Microbiota. The microbiota are the "bottom" of the food chain. Microbiota are represented by the bacteria and protists, including benthic foraminifera. Their principal food source is thought to be dissolved organic matter, although particulate material can be directly utilized if the biota can produce exoenzymes to mobilize particles. The protists can engulf and assimilate particulate material as well. The bacteria generally have a density of about 10^9 per mL of wet sediment, measure about a micrometer in size, and can have very short turnover rates in the presence of reactive organic substrates. The protists can be much larger and occur in far fewer numbers than the bacteria. Protists are thought to be important components of ecosystems in areas of reduced oxygen. With the exception of the forams, microbiota have rarely been evaluated in the deep-sea.

Bacteria that are specially adapted to utilizing methane and sulfide are common in areas characterized by petroleum seeps (MacDonald et al. 1996; MacDonald 1998). Many of these are symbiotic, living in the tissues of large invertebrates. While these specialized associations are explicit in this model, they are presumed to be confined to "seep" areas.

Foraminifera are shelled protozoans. Foraminfera are large, often the size of metazoan meiofauna. Few studies have compared foraminiferal biomass to other benthos in the deep-sea, but biomass can exceed the meiofauna (Coull et al. 1977) and abundances commonly exceed the meiofauna plus the macrofauna (Snider et al. 1984; Gooday 1986). Although little is known regarding foraminiferal energetics, it has been shown that foraminiferal metabolism is markedly increased by organic enrichment (Linke 1992). Therefore, accurate deep-sea carbon and energy budgets should include the foraminifera.

Meiofauna. In this model, meiofauna are defined as metazoans that are retained on a 63 micron sieve. Meiofauna include nematode worms, harpacticoid copepods, and several other taxa. In some studies benthic forams are also included, but in this model, forams are considered part of the microbiota because they are single-celled organisms, rather than metazoans. Most meiofauna feed on small particles consisting of detritus, bacteria, other meiofauna, and small protozoa such as ciliates and flagellates. Turnover rates for meiofauna can be as short as a few days when temperatures are high and food is plentiful. No reliable generalizations can be made about their turnover times or growth rates in the deep-sea, but it is assumed that both are substantially slower than in shallow water due to food limitation and cold water temperatures. In shallow waters meiofauna biomass is less than that of the macrofauna, but in the deep-sea this appears to be reversed.

The finding that meiofauna biomass is higher than macrofauna biomass in the northern GOM (Pequegnat et al. 1990) indicates that meiofauna may be responsible for much of the organic matter metabolism in deep-sea sediments. Therefore, a survey of meiofauna community density and biomass is needed to characterize this energetically important group. In shallow coastal systems, meiofauna remove bacteria at a rate that equals sediment bacterial production (Montagna 1995). This indicates meiofauna are most likely responsible for maintaining bacterial populations in log-phase growth cycles and are therefore indirectly responsible for maintaining rates of nutrient recycling. Despite the apparent importance of meiofauna in deep-sea energetics, there is no knowledge of the rates at which these processes occur. Therefore, process studies are needed to assess meiofaunal consumption rates. Techniques to measure meiofaunal bacterial feeding rates on bacteria have only been used in shallow water (Montagna 1995).

Macrofauna. Macrofauna, in this model, are the invertebrates retained on a 300 micron sieve. The principal organisms are polychaete worms ($\approx$50%), bivalve molluscs, and crustaceans in the groups Isopoda, Amphipoda, and Tanaidacea. The production to biomass ratio of the macrofauna in shallow water communities is often assumed to be unity, but this can vary widely. In the deep-sea, it is assumed the ratio is much lower but there is little evidence for this one way or the other. Biomass and densities decline sharply with depth in most ocean basins. Macrofauna consume microbiota, meiofauna and organic detritus. Macrofauna are preyed upon by megafauna and fishes.

Megafauna. The megafauna are organisms that are routinely sampled by trawls with 2.5 cm stretch mesh or organisms that can be seen easily in bottom photographs, usually about 1 cm or so in diameter. They are composed for the most part of decapod crustaceans and echinoderms. Cnidaria, such as sea pens, soft corals and anemones, are also common in the megafauna. Megafauna can be suspension feeders, predators, scavengers or deposit feeders. For the purpose of the model, the swimming scavengers that consume carcasses, such as the large amphipod *Eurythenes gryllus*, are included in this group. Megafauna have been extensively observed with photographic techniques.

Fishes. Demersal fishes are defined as those species that live on or near the bottom. Fishes are both predators and feed on dead falls, megafauna and macrofauna.

2.2   Community Structure

Community structure, in the context of this model, has two interpretations. It is represented explicitly in the conceptual model as the standing stocks of the living components of the ecosystem as discussed above, and as such it represents the relative and absolute importance of the stocks in terms of biomass and rates of processes in the model. Secondly, community structure refers to the parameters that quantify the living stocks, as described below.

Biomass. A measure of the standing stock in some currency of mass per unit area of seabottom is biomass. Wet weight is a common measure. It can also be measured as dry weight, ash-free dry weight or carbon. The model currency is carbon, so the ideal measure is in terms of carbon. Biomass tends to be inversely related to depth, in a log-normal fashion. Within the entire community, the highest biomasses are found in the total bacterial counts, both in shallow and deep water. All the size fractions in the deep-sea have biomass values that are somewhat lower that 1 g C/m^2. In shallow water, each fraction can have biomasses of 10's of g C/m^2 in unusually fertile conditions. This is not expected in the deep-sea.

Abundances. A surrogate for biomass, that is often measured in ecosystem studies, is animal abundance or density. However, mean sizes can vary. In the GOM, mean size seems to decrease with depth. Common abundances for the organismal groups in the model are bacteria, $10^9/mL$ wet sed.; meiofauna, 0.25 to 1.5 x $10^6/m^2$; macrofauna, 10^2 to $10^4/m^2$; megafauna and fishes, several hundred to a thousand per hectare. The abundances of each group are hypothesized to be a function of the input of carbon and energy to the stock. If the relationship of numbers to biomass is known, these abundances can be used in the model. The NGOMCS studies used conversion factors from the studies of Rowe (1971) to calculate biomass from densities.

Diversity. Measurements of the numbers of different species are expressed as diversity values. Diversity has been assessed on macrofauna, megafauna, and fishes. Diversity indices attempt to lessen the effects of sample size, to aid comparisons between regions of differing animal densities. Common indices of diversity are Sanders Rarefaction, Hurlburt's expected species number and the information function H'(s). The GOM appears to be somewhat different from large ocean basins in that maximum diversity is not found on the deep slope or upper rise, but rather on the upper slope or outer shelf. Thus it is similar to other isolated "mediterranean" basins where diversity declines with depth down the slope. It is expected that intense inputs of organic matter will decrease diversity due to competitive exclusion. Diversity is not calculated by the model.

Zonation. The degree to which individual species and groups of species are isolated across isobaths (zonation), between geographic regions, or any other physico-chemical gradient is referred to as zonation. Zonation by groups of species as a function of depth has been measured by "rates of species change" across depth intervals or measures of percent similarity between depths. These can be measured on meiofauna, macrofauna, megafauna, and fishes. Groups of species appear to occur in zones, but considerable overlap has been observed as well, with few distinct, immutable boundaries. On the other hand, some individual species of megafauna tend to have a shallow water boundary that is sharp and severe and a deeper water boundary that is a slow decline in numbers with depth. Zonation down slope is hypothesized to be a function of competition along a gradient of declining food supplies. Zonation is not calculated by the model but can be addressed through hypothesis testing.

2.3   Community Function

The processes, or arrows, in the model encompass a wide range of interactions amongst the model's components.

Microbial activity. The respiration and the assimilation of organic substrates by the microbiota are dependent on inputs of organic matter and temperature. In the model this can be either sedimenting POC or hydrocarbons. The sedimenting POC can be derived from several sources, as indicated above. A basic assumption is that, in general, smaller organisms are consumed by larger organisms because it is more energy efficient. If the organic matter is reactive, the food web will compete for the organic matter. If the organic matter is highly refractory then it is assumed that a food chain will dominate in which the bacteria remobilize the organics in order to make it available to metazoans. Predation is represented as arrows between the living components of the model as indicated. It is assumed that large organisms will preferentially take large prey rather than small prey because it is more energy efficient. Macrofauna are assumed to be deposit feeders. Heterotrophic bacteria are assumed to consume sediment organic matter. Scavengers consume carcasses and are included in the megafauna. Fishes consume megafauna and carcasses. Respiration is one of the most important measures for each organismal group because it dominates the carbon cycle. However, respiration is not explicit in the conceptual model. Most carbon that is consumed (50 to 90%) is recycled to metabolic carbon dioxide. Respiration is estimated from animal size and temperature for the larger organisms based on literature values.

Growth, reproduction and recruitment. The rates of growth, reproduction, and recruitment are poorly known in deep-sea organisms. The model can calculate growth by fundamental or size group. Reproduction and recruitment are not well known. It is assumed that growth, reproduction and recruitment can be seasonal in some species but this kind of information for the GOM slope is inferential at best. It should be noted that in the NGOMCS study's central transect, it did appear that there were about 1.5 times as many macrofauna individuals on the upper slope in the spring than in other sampling periods, suggesting that some type of growth, reproduction, and/or recruitment had occurred, but the mechanism that gave rise to this observation is unclear.

2.4   Geochemistry

Non-living model variables include the "fuel" for the system and those processes that supply carbon and energy to the ecosystem. Inputs of carbon are critical to the functioning of the ecosystem and are often present in limiting amounts in the deep-sea. On the GOM slope, labile organic matter is transported to the communities from primary productivity (either directly settling to the site or being laterally advected), fossil sources of carbon (oil and gas to support chemosynthesis), and potentially from large animal carcasses and sinking *Sargassum*.

Sedimentary organic matter includes a suite of natural organic compounds found in deep-sea sediments. Organic matter is derived mostly from the slow rain of particulate organic matter (POM) originating from dead cells, crustacean molts, and fecal pellets produced by plankton in the overlying photic zone. Some POM sinks very slowly but aggregates and pellets can rapidly reach the seafloor. The composition of organic matter that reaches the sediment is largely unreactive and poorly characterized. POM is extensively reworked in the water column either being remineralized or transformed to dissolved organic matter (DOM). The amount of POM that reaches the sediment, its ultimate repository, is affected by many factors but, in particular, the water depth. POM concentrations in the sediments of the deep-sea are low. Relatively refractory terrigenous-sourced organic matter is an increased percentage of the POM close to shore and river discharge points. POM is usually inversely proportional to grain size, but does not correlate well with the biomass of the living components. In spite of its meager reactivity, it is assumed to be the basis of the deep-sea food chain except at hydrocarbon seep sites.

Three sources of sediment organic matter are possible in the deep-sea and two are explicit in the model: vertical transport from the photic zone and lateral export from the continental margin. The third source is slumping of material from organic matter-rich areas up-slope and its importance is unknown.

The discovery of chemosynthetic communities with large megafaunal communities dependent, through their symbionts, on methane and sulfide derived from natural seeps has highlighted a non-photosynthetic source of carbon and energy for deep-sea GOM organisms. Hydrocarbons migrate to near-surface sediments from deep subsurface reservoirs of oil and gas. The hydrocarbons can then serve as substrates for communities of organisms adapted to methane and sulfide utilization. "Seeps" support high biomass but its influence on biota outside of the immediate vicinity of the seeps is largely unknown. Recent chemical evidence indicates that the biogeochemical influences of seeps in sediments tend to be localized (John Morse, pers. comm.). The oil and gas is often degraded by bacteria inducing anoxic conditions in the adjacent sediments producing sulfidic environments.

A poorly quantified input of organics to the deep-sea are falls of carcasses that die or are killed in the water column, usually near the surface. Carcasses can range in size from a few centimeters to a whale of several tons. The relative importance of this source of organic matter is not well established. It is known that scavengers exist that can take advantage of such sources, if and when they are available. Similarly, *Sargassum, Thallasia,* wood, etc. has been observed on the bottom as well.

There are a range of abiotic variables that have been shown to influence biotic patterns in marine environments. One type are those related to the physical texture of the sediment and include properties such as grain size, permeability, porosity, and organic and inorganic carbon content. As the substrate that supports the benthos, variations in these physical properties are important in understanding biotic patterns. In addition, it is known that influxes of organic matter and contaminants can cause changes in community structure and abundance. Introductions of labile carbon will cause opportunistic animals to flourish and others to do less well. Organic matter enhancement also leads to anoxic conditions that produce a range of toxic chemicals such as sulfides. Organisms are also known to be selectively sensitive to chemical contamination from hydrocarbons and trace metals. Some animals can tolerate exposure better than others causing shifts in populations when communities are exposed to pollution. In addition, hydrocarbons, particularly aliphatics can be metabolized by microbes and may actually enhance sedimentary microbial populations rather than exert a toxic effect, though as mentioned above, oxygen and sulfate consumption can produce toxic chemicals.

Explicit in the model is microbial biomass but functional groups of bacteria are not defined. All of the bacteria and protists are assumed to be heterotrophs, as opposed to possible chemoautotrophs in the "chemotrophs" stock. However, the terminal electron acceptors (oxidants) of heterotrophs can differ. In the oligotrophic central gyre areas of the deep-sea where sediments are oxic, all the bacteria are assumed to be aerobes. In sediments on continental margins, this is probably not true. Below the sediment-seawater interface the functional bacterial groups are defined by the terminal electron acceptor (TEA) they use (Figure 3.3). Few comparisons of the importance of the different TEA's (oxidants) have been made, but in rapidly accumulating sediments near the Mississippi delta, oxygen and sulfate were of equal importance. However, as oxygen declined and became limiting, sulfate reduction dominated heterotrophic metabolism (Rowe et al. in press). These processes are measured by examination of the porewater chemistry with depth in the sediment. These processes are important in situations where organic loading depletes oxygen in surficial sediments, thus forcing deeper living bacterial assemblages to depend on other oxidants. As the loading continues, the utilization of these other TEA's increases in intensity and rises up closer and closer to the sediment water interface. Profiles of TEA's are good indicators of organic loading to the sediment community. Ammonium is a principal excretory product of invertebrates and bacteria. The ammonium produced by the benthic community can be oxidized to nitrate by nitrifying chemoautotrophs, but it can then be used, along with nitrate diffusing in from the bottom water, as a metabolic oxidant. This can be measured with benthic chamber incubations and sediment pore water profiles of ammonium and nitrate. The importance of this process can be significant relative to oxygen consumption. Oxidized metals can also be used as oxidants. Comparisons with other oxidants is limited, but in some situations this process is thought to be important. In sediments containing even modest amounts of reactive organic compounds, sulfate reduction can become the dominant respiratory process, even greater than oxygen. This is because sulfate is the fourth most abundant ion in seawater, having a concentration that is 140 times that of oxygen at saturation. Lin and Morse (1991) have made a series of cross slope transects around the GOM in which   they   derived

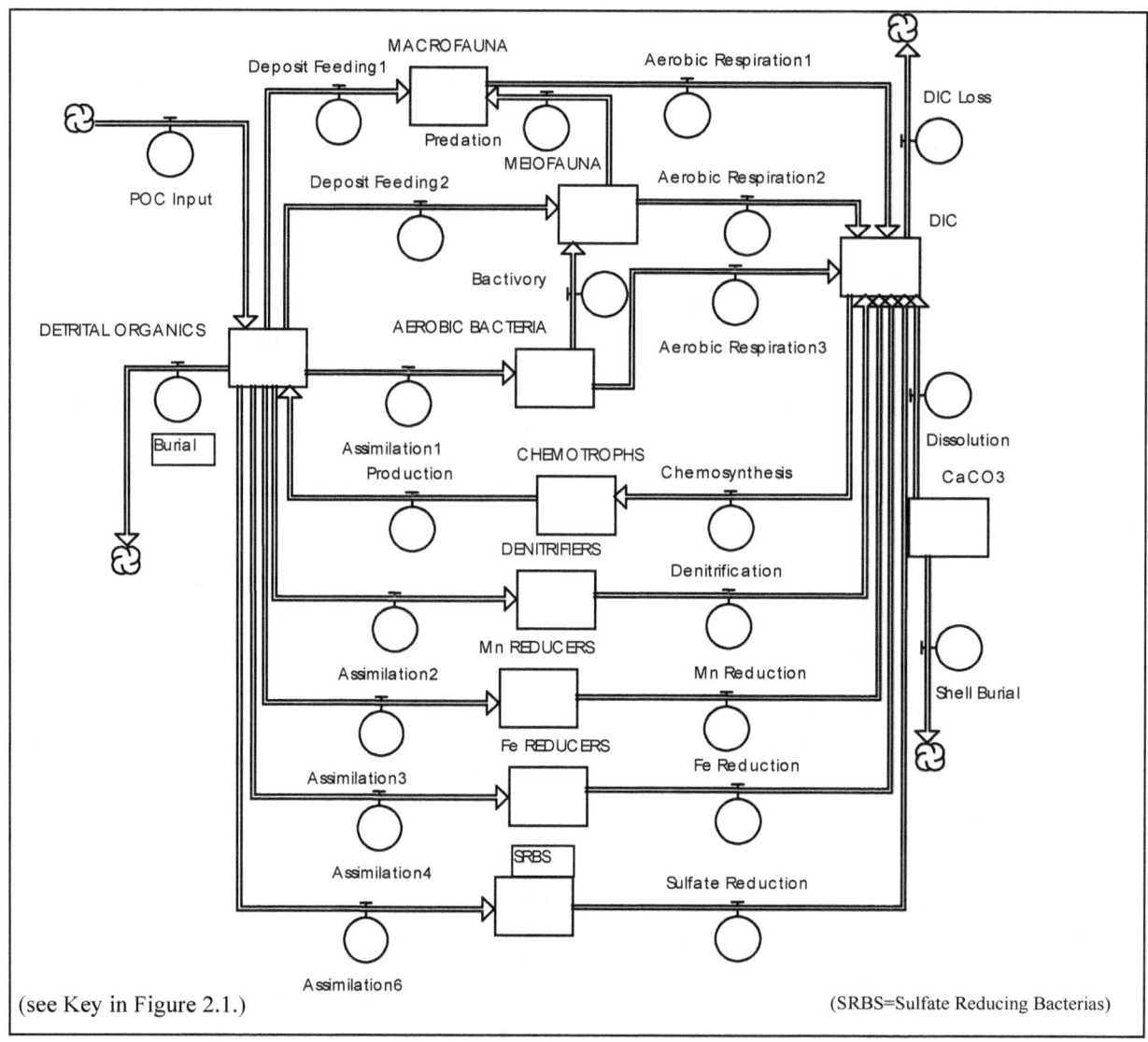

Figure 2.3. Sediment submodel of functional bacterial groups as defined by utilization of different terminal electron acceptors.

integrated sulfate reduction rates down core. Highest rates were near the Mississippi River. Lowest rates were in oligotrophic areas of the southern GOM. Methane can be produced as a breakdown product of metabolism of large carbon compounds and it can be formed when carbon dioxide is used as the oxidant. Methane can then be used as an energy source by bacteria. This methanotrophy occurs in methane seeps near hydrocarbon seeps. Therefore, characterization of the geochemical properties at a location is important for ascertaining the basic metabolic processes that are important to the base of the food chain. Significant alteration of the inputs to the system, in particular carbon, can result in large shifts in bacterial populations and metabolic strategies. In addition, the rate of sediment accumulation and the intensity of bioturbation (mixing) are important in establishing the sediment redox conditions and provide insight into the reactivity of sedimentary organic matter.

2.5   The Water Column

The currents in the overlying water column are important when considering biotic patterns. Near-bottom currents are in part responsible for establishing the sediment properties by transport to the site and also winnowing/erosion of sediments. The water column is also the media through which the overlying primary productivity is transported to the sediment. The currents serve as a mechanism for transport of larvae and juveniles throughout the system. So any model of the deep-sea must take into account the dynamic nature of the physical oceanography and the hydrography of the water masses that overlie and interface with seabottom habitats.

2.6   Community "Health"

While widely discussed, the concept of ecosystem "health" remains elusive. Due to the complex nature of natural ecosystems an overall assessment of health is difficult to define. Specific portions of an ecosystem can be characterized by parasite infestation, pathologies, reproductive success, demographics (age distribution), and the presence of measurable responses to stress (such as stress proteins and the inducement of P450 detoxification enzymes) to name just a few potential indicators of "health". However, a mechanism or approach to provide an overall integrated assessment of the community "health" has yet to be agreed to. For example, in the past it was thought that simple increases in biomass were positive for a group of organisms, but now it is recognized that these biomass increases can be accompanied by significant changes in community structure. Is this positive or negative for the community and is the community "healthy"? Acute deterioration of a community, such as massive mortalities or disappearance of species, is easily recognizable, but over longer time frames it has become clear that some of the more intractable issues related to sublethal effects are often difficult to quantify or even recognize in the early stages of change. For example, loss of biodiversity is seen as a deterioration in ecosystem health, but the natural processes that also effect biodiversity are not well understood.

Ecosystem "health" may be measured by such things as community structure, e.g., the classic view that a healthy benthic community is one of high diversity and high productivity. Therefore, unhealthy ecosystems share a number of properties - lessened productivity, declining biodiversity, dominance by lower trophic levels and others. It has also been suggested that systems degraded beyond a certain point cannot recover (Rapport and Whitford 1999; Rapport et. al. 1998; Rowe and Haedrich 1979; Haedrich et al. 1980; Haedrich and Maunder 1985; Snelgrove and Haedrich 1985; Haedrich and Merrett 1988; Merrett and Haedrich 1997). Therefore "health" can be inferred from community composition, abundances, and size frequencies. "Health" will be assessed by comparisons of the structure of similar ecosystems world-wide that have been subjected to varying degrees and types of disturbance.

At the individual level, "health" has been inferred from physiological responses such as disease incidence, size and condition, and reproductive state. Parasites, and the diseases they cause, are often important determinants of population health. Measurable effects include mortality, decreased reproductive effort, decreased condition, and reduced or aberrant growth. The outgrowth of these effects are increased morbidity, decreased fecundity and even effects on predator/prey relationships.

From another point of view, "health" may be a measure of response to the stresses a population experiences due to anthropogenic disturbances. As a first order indication of this exposure, inventories of chemicals in sediments and biological tissues are measured. While this is at least an indication that the potential for impact is present, simply documenting the presence of contaminants is not sufficient to infer biological effect in most instances. However, a range of biological effects criteria for sedimentary concentrations of contaminants have been used to infer the possibility of effects. Once the potential for exposure has been verified, first-order biological responses to contaminant exposure are often important variables to monitor. These include a range of responses including production of contaminant metabolites, the induction of detoxification enzyme systems, and molecular level indications of genetic damage, to name a few indicators of sublethal biological response to contaminant exposure.

3.0 PROGRAM DESIGN

The design of the sampling program involved a series of steps that relied on basic design principles, a thorough knowledge of the current understanding of the system to be observed, formulation of working hypotheses, application of appropriate statistical analyses (both univariate and multivariate), linkage of findings with model revision and update, and an objective approach to evaluate the utility of data being collected as the program acquires new data. Taking these issues into account, the program design includes those factors believed to be most important in characterizing the biological communities. Testable null hypotheses were formulated and the appropriate temporal and spatial scales and locations for sampling were chosen. All of these elements are essential for a full integration of the diverse interdisciplinary measurement program being undertaken.

3.1   General Design Considerations

Several general principles guided the development of the overall sampling plan.

First, treatments, or in this case similar stations, were chosen that will falsify the null hypothesis. That is, contrasts that don't delineate differences were avoided as unproductive. Due to resource limitations and the large geographic area to be studied, it is impossible to measure everything, everywhere. However, it is relevant to measure what are judged to be the most important variables at the most important sites.

Second, pseudoreplication was avoided, i.e., replication is at the treatment level. A treatment is a factor level, or combination of factor levels, applied to a sampling unit. Sampling units are stations or replicate samples within stations where all other variables but the variable to be tested are as similar as possible. The generic form of all null hypotheses is that the treatment level effect equals zero, i.e., the stations themselves are not fundamentally different by other than the variable being tested. For example, if each treatment is only represented by a single station, then in the end you only know that the stations are different, not why the stations are different.

Third, station locations were optimized to test more than one hypothesis. This is a cost reduction technique. For example, stations along a transect to test for depth differences can be paired with stations in specific habitats to test a second hypothesis.

Fourth, confounding factors were minimized. A common problem is that more than one variable is changing at a given station. For example, two stations could differ by water depth, distance from shore, and distance from the Mississippi River. In the end, you don't know which variable (or if an interaction of the variables) is causing the observed differences and thus generalities are difficult, if not impossible, to discern. Therefore, stations are chosen where comparisons can be based on differences in a single or related set of variables.

Fifth, balanced sampling designs were used. An uneven distribution of sampling effort causes distortion of sample means when there is a difference in the number of observations between the datasets being contrasted.

Sixth, a design of appropriate power was used. Power is the ability to detect change. The first five design considerations primarily protect at the α level against Type I errors (rejecting the null hypothesis when it is true). But, type II errors protected at the β level must also be considered (accepting the null hypothesis when it is false). Replication must be sufficient to detect the amount of change that is expected given variations in the variable of interest. A large multi-factorial design with little replication has many interactions terms that are often significant, thus limiting the interpretation and robustness of tests for the most important effects. In this case, previous studies suggest that a minimum of five replicate boxcores were needed at each station to adequately sample within-station heterogeneity.

Finally, there will be a meta-analysis (or synthesis) in the end. Most programs measure values for hundreds of dependent variables at hundreds of observational points (be they spatial, temporal, or random replicates). When assembled in its entirety, this meta-data set contains information that does not exist within the individual analyses. In-the-end, all of the stations and replicates are only surrogates for the environmental factors that regulate biological processes leading to the observed patterns of faunal composition. Therefore, measurements are made synoptically at locations or subsamples (replicates) are taken within a location so that a meta-data set can be created for the synthesis and integration of the overall study results.

3.2   Working Hypotheses and Station Selection

A sampling design is most effectively developed from a series of testable null hypotheses. The hypotheses are derived from the conceptual model which describes the current understanding of the system being observed (i.e., deep-sea communities). Hypotheses are then used to select stations so that the hypotheses are testable with sufficient power to detect differences in the dependent variables being measured (i.e., abundance, biomass, diversity, analyte concentrations, etc.). The null hypotheses were based on the current understanding of deep-sea benthic community structure and function and knowledge of the types of habitats that occur in the GOM.

The following characteristics are judged to represent a significant portion of the deep-sea GOM habitat and will be used to identify one area as being different from another:

1) water depth (transects perpendicular to isobaths);
2) geographic location - juxtaposition to the Mississippi River (east-west transects) and distance from shore;
3) physiographic position - in a basin, in a canyon, on an escarpment, and in a low relief area;
4) influx of organic carbon - primary productivity derived carbon, petroleum seep and chemosynthetic derived carbon;
5) energy level of the physical environment - high versus low bottom current velocity, juxtaposition to semi-permanent physical features (nitrocline, thermohalocline);
6) temporal changes -time series sampling; and
7) location of historical sampling sites.

The sampling design tests hypotheses rather than simply conducting a traditional geographic survey with closely spaced stations. This approach was adopted to establish generalities about communities in the study area and because the area to be covered is so large that sampling everywhere is cost prohibitive. The hypothesis testing allows a prediction of when and where particular types of communities, both in terms of structure and function, will or will not be encountered. Hypothesis testing provides a powerful tool for either increasing or limiting sampling intensity in time and space as new data is collected and historical data is re-interpreted. Each hypothesis, as described below, explores mechanisms believed to explain much of the variation in community structure and function in the deep-sea GOM. Some mechanisms are well established, others are not.

Based on the above considerations the following kinds of contrasting environments or habitats were sampled for comparisons:

- Depth.

  - Water depth is probably the single most important gradient in determining faunal compositions and forcing factors in the study area (Hypothesis H_{O1}). Comparisons were made along a series of transects. **Stations: RW1-RW6, W1-W6, C1-C12, MT1-MT6, S35-S44 (see Figures 3.1-3.3).**

- Nutrients (organics)

  - The input of organic nutrients from Mississippi River discharge causes an east to west gradient in faunal compositions and forcing factors (Hypothesis H_{O2}). Comparisons were made along isobaths at similar distances from shore at varying distances from the Mississippi River. **Stations: RW1-RW6, C1-C12, S37-S42 (see Figures 3.1-3.3).**

- Basins.

  - The common mesoscale basins found on the slope, unless influenced by seeps, have the same faunal compositions and forcing factors as the "normal" slope because the entire slope is draped in a similar Holocene "blanket" of silt and clay within which the biological communities live (Hypothesis H_{O3}). Comparisons were made within and outside of basins at comparable water depths and distances from the Mississippi River and shore. **Stations: WC12, B1-B3, NB2-NB5 (see Figures 3.3 and 3.4).**

- Canyons.

- Faunal compositions and forcing factors are the same in or out of submarine canyons (Hypothesis H_{O4}). Comparisons were made between stations within and outside of canyons at comparable depths and distances from the Mississippi River and shore. **Stations: MT1-MT6, W5, W6, RW6 (see Figures 3.1-3.4).**

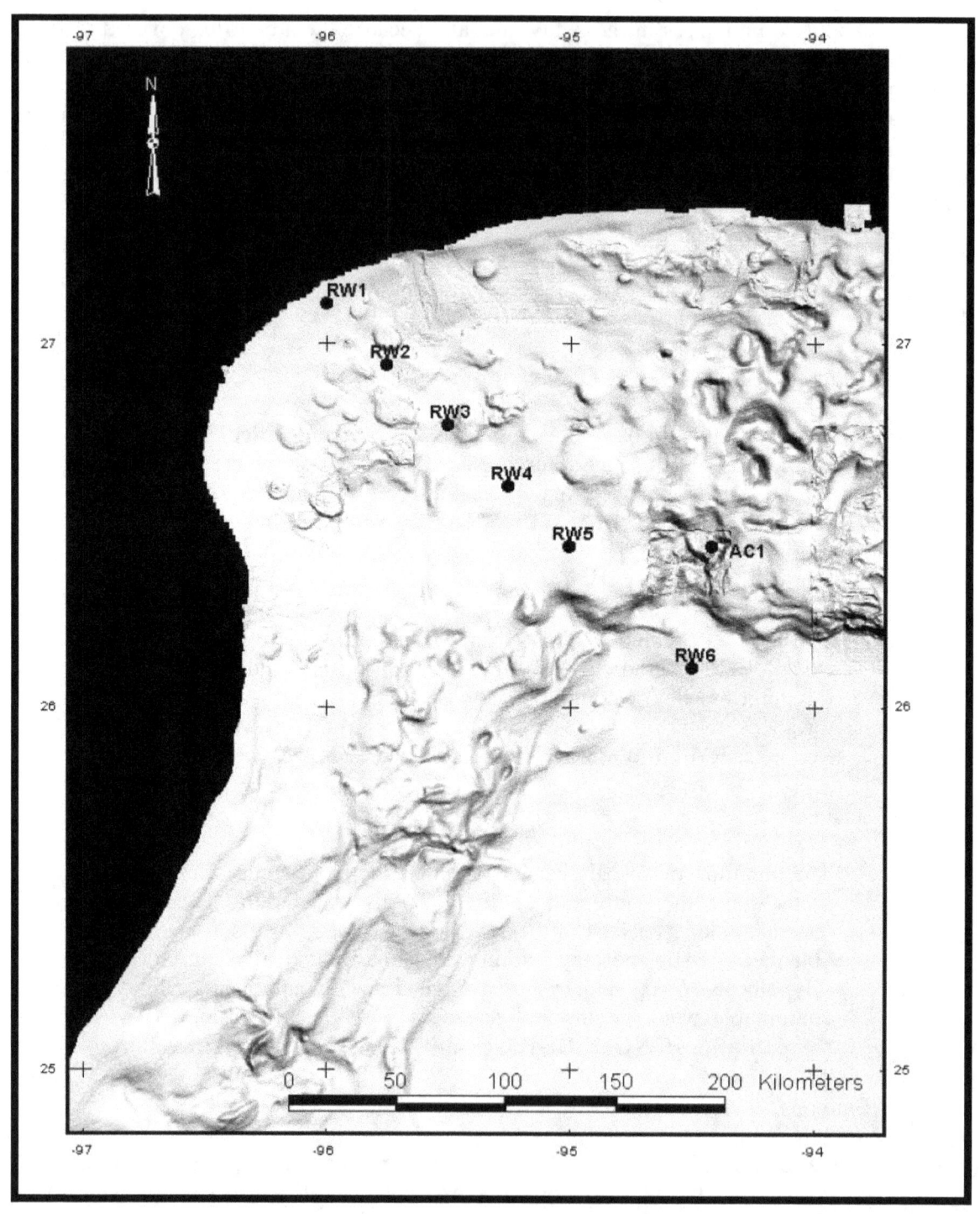

Figure 3.1. Benthic survey stations in the northwestern GOM (for regional context see Figure 4.1).

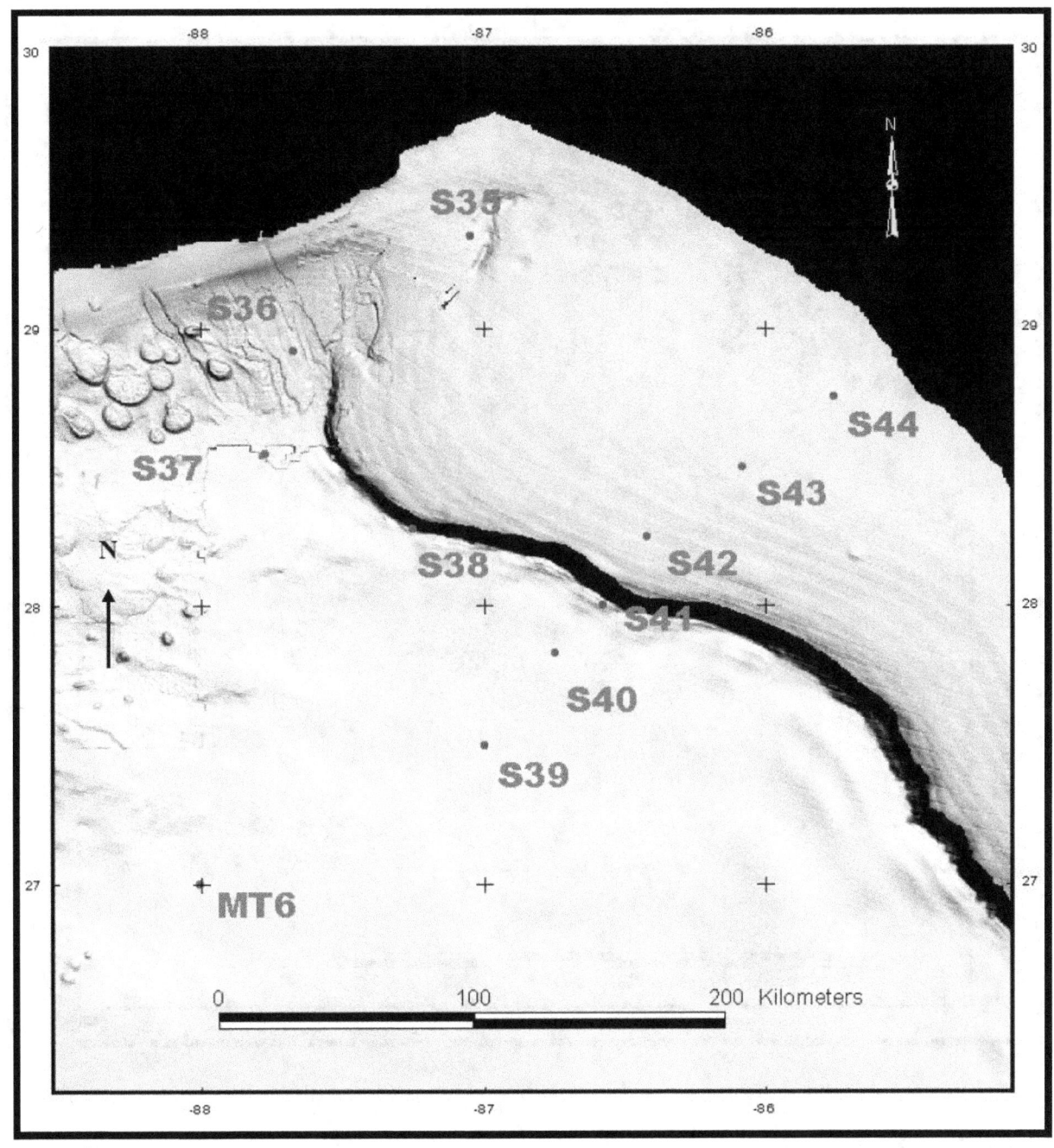

Figure 3.2. Benthic survey stations across the Florida Escarpment (for regional context see Figure 4.1).

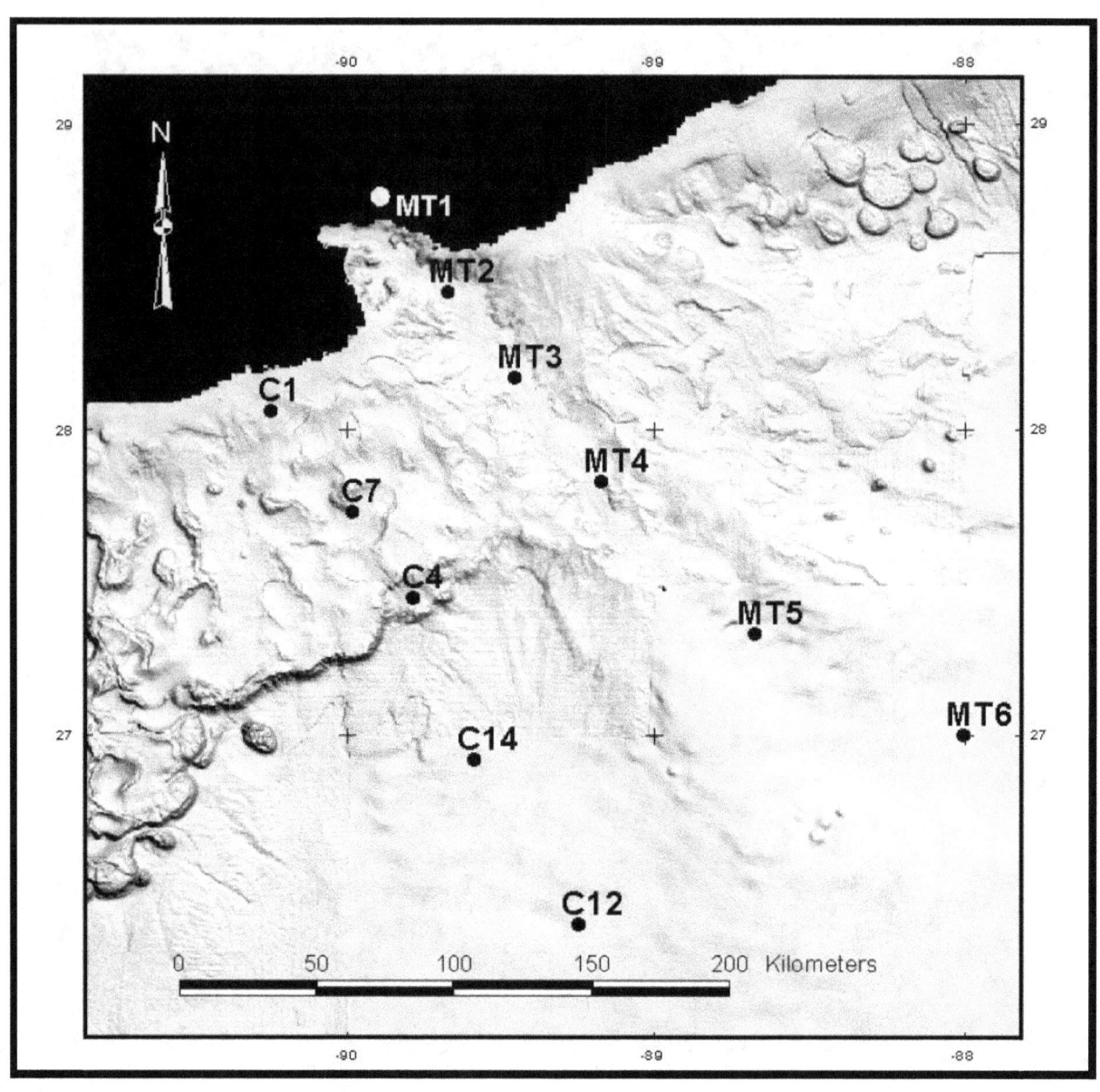

Figure 3.3. Benthic stations along the Mississippi Trough (MT1-MT6). Historical sites from the NGOMCS study are also included (C1-C14; for regional context see Figure 4.1).

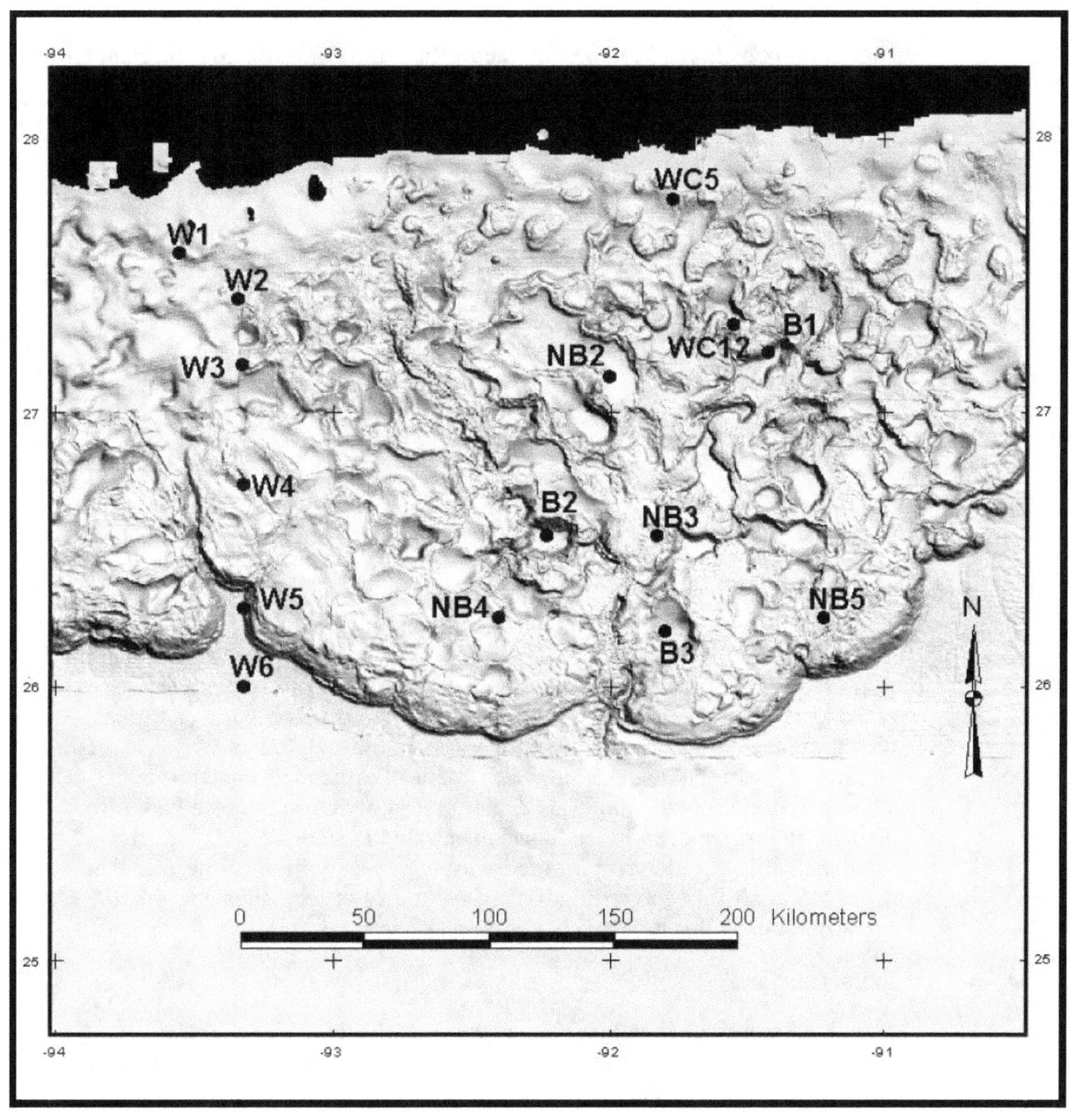

Figure 3.4. Physiographic settings for benthic survey stations in the Central GOM. Historical stations from the NGOMCS study are also included (W1-W6, WC-5, and WC-12; for regional context see Figure 4.1).

- Steep Escarpments.

  - Faunal compositions and forcing factors are the same on the "normal" slope as they are at the base of the Sigsbee Escarpment (Hypothesis H_{O5}). Comparisons were made between stations on the slope and at the base of the Sigsbee escarpment at similar water depths. **Stations: S39-S42 (see Figure 3.2).**

- Productivity.

  - Cyclonic and anticyclonic features in the surface waters consistently alter surface primary productivity and this results in differing seafloor fauna compositions and forcing factors (Hypothesis H_{O6}). Comparisons were made between stations that underlie areas of historically documented differences in sea surface primary productivity, holding other variables as constant as possible. **Stations: RW1-RW6, S35-S36 (see Figures 3.1 and 3.2).**

- Hydrocarbon Seeps.

  - Hydrocarbon seeps have a major effect on energy and carbon supplies contributing to different faunal compositions and forcing factors (Hypothesis H_{O7}). This is tacitly true since chemosynthetic fauna are restricted to seep sites. Rather than a direct test, inputs of chemosynthetic carbon to the foodweb will be recognized by stable isotopic tracer studies. Data produced from the chemosynthetic community studies will also be contrasted with equivalent non-seep data. Explicit testing by paired stations will not be attempted. Questions of "how close is close" are still difficult to resolve even in studies concentrated at seep sites. The decision to address this question in a limited way is in recognition of the fact that the MMS is already supporting extensive studies at seep sites and that the primary focus of this program is non-seep environments.

- Temporal Changes.

  - Standing crops of benthic fauna vary with time (Hypothesis H_{O8}). Comparisons were made at a subset of survey stations sampled during each of the three planned cruise activities. In addition, to provide a longer timeframe for comparisons, historically sampled sites will be reoccupied. The intercomparibility of data between studies will be explicitly addressed to ensure whether inter- program comparisons are valid. **Stations: W1-W6, WC6, C1-C12 (see Figures 3.3 and 3.4).**

The above comparisons have been translated into testable null hypotheses (Table 3.1). A critically important part of program design is selection of the most appropriate locations to conduct the measurement program to test the hypotheses. This is especially true for this program because the area to be characterized is large, the area contains a wide range of habitats and there are several important forcing factors that tend to confound delineation of cause and effect relationships. As summarized in the introductory materials, the northern GOM represents one of the most complex geological and oceanographic settings in the world. The challenge is to classify wide stretches of the slope into recognizable subregions that can then be sampled to test if the extant biological communities are different from area to area. Additional factors explicitly considered during the selection of proposed sampling sites include the location of historical sampling (to extend time series observations), the current and future trends in energy resource exploration and exploitation, and possible anthropogenic effects related to proximity to existing production facilities (primarily accommodated by screening all locations for contaminants). The study stations are explicitly tied to the hypothesis testing as listed above.

Survey stations were chosen to sample the broadest possible range of conditions at depths between 300 m and 3000 m and within the EEZ boundary with Mexico (Figures 3.1-3.4). The site selection spans the range of known conditions providing the best tests of the hypotheses posed. Thus, sampling occurs along a transect just north of the Mexican border (RW1-RW6) over to one transect across the Florida escarpment (S37-S42; see Figures 3.1-3.2). This inclusive range of conditions enables us to gain an understanding of the whole GOM deep-sea benthos, rather than isolated parts. The smooth upper slope of the northern Florida slope is contrasted with the heterogeneous topography off Texas. A transect down the Mississippi Trough (MT1-MT6) provides a sampling of the effect of particulate and nutrient input from a large river (Figure 3.3). The basins on the upper slope can be categorized according to their structure and how they were formed, testing whether or not physiographic setting affects the biota (WC12, B1-B3, NB2-NB5; see Figure 3.4). Two locations at the upper end of the DeSoto Canyon (S36, S35) were chosen because one is frequented by whales and the other is characterized by high nitrate concentrations semi-permanently in the euphotic zone (see Figure 3.2).

Experimental, or "process" stations, were chosen to reflect the greatest range in community dynamics, as inferred from the benthic survey data. The survey site selection was based on inferences about where the greatest variations in community structure will be observed based on the model. The next step was to place the experimental stations where the greatest ranges in community structure are actually observed during the study. For example, a comparison of places with high and low total biomass is important. Observations of processes, such as sulfate reduction or aerobic community respiration, provide comparison of sites where biogeochemical cycling rates are different. Potential sites at mid-depths in the Mississippi Trough (C14, C12) are believed to experience high velocity current events below the Sigsbee Escarpment (Figure 3.4). The central line of the earlier slope study (C1, C7, C4, C14, C12) appears to be characterized by a seasonal signal in the biotic community (see Figure 3.3). If the statistical tests suggest that slope basins contain enhanced biomass, then rates of metabolic processes are expected to be enhanced as well making a basin a candidate for an experimental site. Experiments designed to determine the causes of bioenhancement were considered to be important. The location of experimental stations allowed the community structure documented during the survey, to guide site selection in the context of historical data. The type and placement of experimental stations was carefully considered in consultation with the COTR and the SRB.

Table 3.1. Summary of benthic survey experimental design: null hypotheses, station selection criteria, number of stations, and number of samples. (The number of samples is based on five replicates per station.)

Null Hypotheses	Design Criteria	No. Stations	No. Samples
H_{O1}: Variation in benthic fauna is explained by depth	3 Replicate transects over 7 depths; occupy historical stations and others	21	105
H_{O2}: Faunas exhibit an East to West gradient	Additional transect to H_{O1}; remove confounding geological effects and water mass effects	7	35
H_{O3}: Basin faunas are different from non-basin faunas	3 salt bottom and 3 salt surrounded basins	6	30
H_{O4}: Canyon fauna is different from slope fauna	4 Canyons to be compared to non-canyon and non-basin biota from H_{O1}-H_{O3}	8	40
H_{O5}: Fauna below escarpments different from slope	Add sta. below escarpment in addition to H_{O1}- H_{O4} in area of furrows	7	35
H_{O6}: Surface primary production explains faunal differences	Add sta. to (H_{O1}-H_{O2}) in "hot spot" defined by historical water column data	7	35
H_{O7}: Proximity to organic input causes bioenhancement	Add sta. in proximity to "geochemical anomalies" (hydrates, brine pools, methane seeps)	8	40
H_{O8}: No variation in benthic fauna over time.	6 stations (or other elements of the design, H_{O1} -H_{O7}) over 2 years	12	60

The first interim meeting in February 2001 was used to up-date the hypotheses based on Survey Cruise data, select sites to be repeated, add new sites to strengthen comparisons and identify sites for process studies. The process sites selected were MT3, S36, S42, and MT6. New sites to be added were in the furrows below Green Knoll on the top of Green Knoll, a site between the Mississippi Trough and the DeSoto Canyon, and hear the Bush Hill seep.

3.3   Dependent and Independent Variables

Based on the various hypotheses described in the previous section, a series of dependent and independent variables were chosen that will provide the set of observations at each station to test the validity of the null hypotheses. Variable selection was based on a knowledge of the system being observed, a current understanding of how the system functions, and an estimate of the relative importance of forcing factors as described in the conceptual model (see Section 4.0).

The set of variables measured at the survey stations are organized around the characteristics that define the system including physiographic setting, time, water masses, geographic location, abiotic and biotic water column properties, sediment properties, chemical contaminants in sediments, indicators of biogeochemical processes, community structure, and community function (Tables 3.2-3.4). These variables also quantify stocks and processes for input to the model.

Table 3.2. Independent variables fixed by the sampling plan design.

Physiographic Characteristics
Water Depth
Basins underlain by salt
Basins surrounded by salt
Basins subjected to slumping/erosion
Basins overlain by an undisturbed drape of Holocene silt and clay
Canyons
Escarpments
Proximity to seeps
Basin slope angle

Time
Months
Years

Water Masses
Loop Current
Consistently "cool" water between eddies
Warm eddies

Geographic Location
East vs West
Distance from shore

Table 3.3. Dependent variables to be measured.

Community Structure

Bacterial density

Bacterial biomass

Foraminiferal biomass

Meiofaunal density

Meiofaunal biomass

Meiofaunal composition to major group

Macrofaunal density

Macrofaunal biomass

Macrofaunal diversity

Macrofaunal species composition

Megafaunal density

Megafaunal biomass

Megafaunal diversity

Megafaunal species composition

Fish density

Fish biomass

Fish diversity

Fish species composition

Community Function

Bacteria growth rates

Bacteria respiration

Bacteria response to different substrates

Foraminiferal respiration[1]

Foraminiferal feeding rates[1]

Meiofaunal respiration[1]

Meiofaunal feeding rates on bacteria

Macrofaunal respiration[1]

Macrofauna growth rates[2]

Macrofauna predation rates[2]

Macrofauna predation rates on meiofauna, bacteria, and organic matter

Megafaunal respiration rates[2]

Megafaunal predation rate on megafauna, meiofauna, bacteria, and organic matter[2]

Megafaunal scavenging on carcasses[2]

Fish respiration[1]

Fish predation on megafauna[2]

Fish scavenging on carcasses[2]

Nutrient Regeneration

Denitrification rate

Sediment mixing rates (bioturbation)[2]

Sediment accumulation rate[2]

Sedimentary community oxygen consumption

Sulfate reduction rate

Foodweb studies

1-calculated based on size and temperature
2-estimated from sub-model

Table 3.4. Ancillary variables to be measured at Survey and Experimental Stations.

Water Column Profiles

- Depth
- Temperature
- Salinity
- Oxygen
- Nitrate and Nitrite
- Ammonium
- Silicate
- Phosphate
- Particulate Matter (PM)
- Particulate Organic Carbon (POC)
- Light
- Currents

Biotic Water Column Profile

- Photosynthetic Pigments
- Primary Production

Chemical Contaminants

- Hydrocarbons
- Metals

Sediment Properties

- Grain Size
- Porosity
- Elemental composition (organic carbon, nitrogen, sulfur)
- Percent inorganic carbon (TIC)
- Permeability
- Shear Strength
- Bulk Density

Geochemistry[1]

- Nutrients
- Dissolved Organic Carbon (DOC)
- $SO_4^=/Cl-$
- Dissolved Inorganic Carbon (DIC)
- $\delta^{13}C$ DIC
- Sulfate Reduction Rate
- pH
- H_2S
- O_2
- Reactive Fe
- Reactive Mn
- Acid Volatile Sulfide

[1] Composite sample at survey station, profiles for fluxes at experimental station.

3.4   Statistical Analyses

Statistical analyses to test for differences among treatment means are performed using parametric, general linear models. Prior to analysis, data are transformed, generally by natural logarithm, to achieve homogeneity of error variance, normality of residual errors, and additivity of effects. A data set of residual errors is created for each model and tested for normality. Both untransformed and transformed residuals are computed, and the datasets that are normally distributed with means of zero are used for analyses.

The models that follow describe the relationships among the independent design variables only. The measured dependent variables are described in the methods sections. The notation used follows conventions described by Kirk (1982).

3.4.1   Univariate Analyses

Univariate analyses will be used to test each hypothesis based on the following models. The stations to be used to test each hypothesis are summarized in Table 3.1.

The first two hypotheses are as follows:

H_{O1}:   There is no variation in benthic fauna with depth, and
H_{O2}:   There is no difference in fauna along an east to west gradient.

The effect of depth is tested with stations along transects. Multiple transects were necessary to replicate at the treatment level. Transects should also hold constant nuisance variables such differences in circulation, bottom complexity, or other physical factors. The effect of longitude is tested with stations on an east - west gradient along isobaths, so this design tests two major hypotheses. The experiment is a two-way completely random factorial analysis of variance (ANOVA) that is described by the following model:

$$Y_{ijk} = \mu + \alpha_j + \beta_k + \alpha\beta_{jk} + \in_{i(jk)}$$

where Y_{ijk} is the measurement for each individual replicate, μ is the overall sample mean, α_j is the main effect for transects and $j=1-4$, β_k is the main effect for depths and $k=1-7$ (300, 750, 1200, 1650, 2100, 2550, and 3000 m), $\alpha\beta_{jk}$, is an interaction term, and $\in_{i(jk)}$ is the random error for each replicate measurement and $i=1-5$.

The third hypothesis is:

H_{O3}:   **There is no difference between basin fauna and non-basin fauna.**

Geological complexity exists in the northern GOM. One expression of this complexity is basins. Basins may cause changes in current flow such that water masses are altered as they pass across the mouth of the basin or impact a sill. This could affect benthos. One station within a basin will be paired with two nearby stations already sampled for H_{O1} and H_{O2} above to test for basin effects. Station pairing is necessary to control for distance from shore and depth. For example, a station selected for H_{O1}/H_{O2} at 1200 m may have a nearby basin at 1650 m, so stations generally distant from shore and in the same water depth would be compared against the basin stations. The entire experiment is replicated at 6 different sites, so each location is a blocking effect. The experiment is a two-way completely random factorial ANOVA that is described by the following model:

$$Y_{ijk} = \mu + \alpha_j + \beta_k + \alpha\beta_{jk} + \in_{i(jk)}$$

where Y_{ijk} is the measurement for each individual replicate, μ is the overall sample mean, α_j is the main effect for replicate sites and $j=1-6$, β_k is the main effect for treatments and $k=1-3$ (basin, non-basin same distance from shore, and non-basin same depth), $\alpha\beta_{jk}$, is an interaction term, and $\in_{i(jk)}$ is the random error for each replicate measurement and $i=1-5$. Differences between sites are not of interest because they replicate the basin effect, so it doesn't matter if that test is significant. The main test of interest is a multiple comparison tests among treatment levels if there is a significant difference among treatments.

The fourth hypothesis is:

H_{O4}:   **There is no difference between canyon fauna and non-canyon fauna.**

Another form of geological complexity in the GOM is canyons. Often sediment slumping occurs in canyons in addition to alteration in near-bottom current patterns. One station within a canyon will be paired with nearby stations at similar depths that are not in a canyon. The entire experiment is replicated at four (4) different sites. The experiment is a two-way completely random factorial ANOVA that is described by the following model:

$$Y_{ijk} = \mu + \alpha_j + \beta_k + \alpha\beta_{jk} + \in_{i(jk)}$$

where Y_{ijk} is the measurement for each individual replicate, μ is the overall sample mean, α_j is the main effect for replicate sites and j=1-4, β_k is the main effect for treatments and k=1-2 (canyon and non-canyon), $\alpha\beta_{jk}$, is an interaction term, and $\in_{i(jk)}$ is the random error for each replicate measurement and i=1-5.

The fifth hypothesis is:

H_{O5}:   **There is no difference between escarpment fauna and non-escarpment fauna.**

Another form of geological complexity in the GOM is escarpments. These steep walls may be different from more gently sloping areas. One station adjacent to the base of an escarpment will be paired with nearby stations at a similar depth that are not adjacent to an escarpment. The entire experiment is replicated at 7 different sites. The sites will be chosen based on pairing stations with samples already taken to test H_{O1}-H_{O5}. The experiment is a two-way completely random factorial ANOVA that is described by the following model:

$$Y_{ijk} = \mu + \alpha_j + \beta_k + \alpha\beta_{jk} + \in_{i(jk)}$$

where Y_{ijk} is the measurement for each individual replicate, μ is the overall sample mean, α_j is the main effect for replicate sites and j=1-7, β_k is the main effect for treatments and k=1-2 (escarpment and non-escarpment), $\alpha\beta_{jk}$, is an interaction term, and $\in_{i(jk)}$ is the random error for each replicate measurement and i=1-5. Depending on exact location of samples, this design may be altered to take into account distance from shore. In that case, the same model as that used for basins (H_{O3}) will be used.

The sixth hypothesis is:

H_{O6}:   **There are no differences in benthos in areas with different amounts of water column primary production.**

The sites will be chosen based on pairing stations with samples already taken to test H_{O1}-H_{O5}. The design is nested as a completely random hierarchical design described by the model:

$$Y_{ijk} = \mu + \alpha_j + \beta_{k(j)} + \in_{i(jk)},$$

where: μ = overall sample mean, α_j = main effect of treatments and j=1-3 (high, medium, and low productivity), $\alpha_{k(j)}$ = nested effect for replicate stations and k =1-7, and $\in_{i(jk)}$ is the random error for each replicate measurement and i=1-5. The appropriate F-test for treatments is to use the mean square error for stations as the denominator. Another approach to analyze this design is analysis of covariance, where actual values indicating primary production (e.g., measured values or chlorophyll standing stock) are used as covariates.

The seventh hypothesis is:

H_{O7}:   **There is no difference in benthic fauna near and far from seeps.**

Another form of geological complexity in the GOM is organic and inorganic inputs in geochemically anomalous environments, e.g., hydrocarbon or brine seeps. Eight (8) stations are added to pair with existing non-seep stations. The station pairs will be in 4 site regions. The sites will be chosen based on pairing stations with samples already taken to test hypotheses H_{O1}-H_{O6}. The experiment is a two-way completely random factorial ANOVA that is described by the following model:

$$Y_{ijk} = \mu + \alpha_j + \beta_k + \alpha\beta_{jk} + \in_{i(jk)}$$

where Y_{ijk} is the measurement for each individual replicate, μ is the overall sample mean, α_j is the main effect for replicate sites and $j=1$-4, α_k is the main effect for treatments and $k=1$-4 (brine seep, hydrocarbon seep, control for distance from shore, control for depth), $\alpha\beta_{jk}$, is an interaction term, and $\in_{i(jk)}$ is the random error for each replicate measurement and $i=1$-5. Differences between sites are not of interest because they are replicating seep effects, so it doesn't matter if that test is significant. The main test of interest is a multiple comparison test among treatment levels if there is a significant difference among treatments.

The eighth hypothesis is:

H_{O8}:   **There are no differences in benthic fauna among different sampling dates.**

Six of the stations sampled for H_{O1}-H_{O7} will be chosen for reoccupation in years 2 and 3 so that there will be a time series for at least 3 years. In addition, attempts will be made to include several stations that were occupied in previous studies, extending the time series to 5 or 6 sampling periods. Assuming depth and site (i.e., east-west) gradients, these two factors must be incorporated into the design. The experiment is a three-way completely random factorial ANOVA that can be described by the following model:

$$Y_{ijkl} = \mu + \alpha_j + \beta_k + \alpha\beta_{jk} + \gamma_l + \alpha\gamma_{jl} + \beta\gamma_{kl} + \alpha\beta\gamma_{jkl} + \in_{i(jkl)}$$

where Y_{ijkl} is the measurement for each individual replicate, μ is the overall sample mean, α_j is the main effect for sampling periods and $j=1$-3, β_k is the main effect for sites and $k=1$-2, γ_l is the main effect term for depths and $l=1$-3 (shallow, mid-depth, deep), $\alpha\beta_{jk}$, $\alpha\gamma_{jl}$, $\beta\gamma_{kl}$, and $\alpha\beta\gamma_{jkl}$ are interaction terms, and $\in_{i(jkl)}$ is the random error for each replicate measurement and $i=1$-5.

Hypotheses will be re-evaluated as data is collected and recast as needed. Year II and III will provide the opportunity to collect additional new survey station if needed to infill the dataset to increase the power of statistical tests.

3.4.2   Power Analysis

Power analysis is performed to determine the detectable change in the population at a given power ($1-\beta$ and sample size (n) Power is calculated by:

$$\Delta = \frac{(t_\alpha + t_\beta) \, x \, SD \, x \sqrt{\dfrac{2}{n}}}{\overline{X}}$$

where Δ is the percent change in the population, SD is the pooled standard deviation, t_α and t_β are tabled values for a two-tailed test assuming a pooled estimate of variance from a large sample size, and $\overline{X}$ is the sample mean. Values of $\alpha=0.05$, and powers of 0.95, 0.80, 0.50 were used in the analysis.

3.4.3 Multivariate Analyses

A meta-analysis (or synthesis) will be performed at the end of the study. The goal of the synthesis is to merge all data sets of response variables to create one large data set. All the ANOVA's listed above can be analyzed in multivariate mode (MANOVA) to test the null hypothesis that the vector of population means equals zero. Without the jargon, test to find out if all measured variables respond to the dependent variables in the design in a similar fashion. The advantage of MANOVA is that multivariate error is controlled. That is, error rates are controlled at α across all response variables.

Once the meta-data set is assembled other questions can be queried. It can be tested if benthic fauna respond to abiotic environmental factors and which factors control distributions of responses. As stated previously, all stations and replicates are simply surrogates for the environmental factors that regulate biological processes at different scales. These scales vary greatly from small- (replicate boxcores), meso- (across transects, basins, or nearby stations) to large- (across the entire GOM). In addition, there is a temporal scale to the variation in all measurements. Multivariate analysis can be used to test the meta-data set for correlation or covariation among the independent variables that are measured. Two multivariate techniques will be employed: a parametric method (principal components analysis, PCA), and a non-parametric methods (multidimensional scaling, MDS).

Multidimensional scaling is a non-parametric multivariate technique for examining similarity or dissimilarity between stations, replicates, or other dependent variables in the experimental design. First, a similarity or dissimilarity index is computed for elements of the design (e.g., stations) and then a plot of the distance among points is created. The plot enables us to identify unknown variables that affect the similarity or dissimilarity between stations. Because the MDS procedure is based on non-parametric (Kruskal-Wallis like) models, it is very popular among European benthic ecologists, but has rarely been used among American benthic ecologists. It is most useful to summarize biotic data (e.g., community structure), but new variables are not created, nor can one reduce the variables in a dataset.

Principal components analysis is a parametric variable reducing technique that makes a new set of uncorrelated variables in order of decreasing variance. Analysis of abiotic variables can be used to summarize the co-varying environmental influences on different levels of replications, i.e., different spatial and temporal scales. Factor loading scores are generated for abiotic summaries of observations (rows), which can be used in other analyses. For example, during GOOMEX several hundred environmental variables were reduced with PCA and the new

PCA scores were shown to correlate with average macrofauna and meiofauna abundance and toxic responses. This allowed us to detect subtle sub-lethal effects within 100 m of platforms that could not be detected with univariate analysis of variance (Green and Montagna 1996). Also, the methods demonstrated functional responses of benthic fauna to abiotic variables, while separating confounding influences in the study related to differences in the natural background in which platforms were located. The same approach will be used in the deep-sea study to provide an understanding on how environmental influences regulate benthic communities.

3.5   Revision of Taxonomic Level of Analysis

Analysis of benthic infaunal communities has been widely used in environmental assessment and monitoring studies. The use of species level data is powerful, but expensive due to the level of expertise and labor intensive effort required. This has inspired efforts to determine if species level data is really necessary. For both meiofauna and macrofauna, a promising prospect is identification to only the suborder or family level. At the Group of Experts on Effects of Pollutants (GEEP) workshop, all levels of biological organization were studied from the molecular to the community, and all biological components from bacteria to macrofauna were included in both mesocosm and field experiments (Bayne et al. 1988). In the GEEP field study, diversity indices did not detect the pollution gradient, but community structure differences were distinct and species level data gave no more information for discrimination than did nematode suborder or harpacticoid family groupings (Heip et al. 1988). Macrofauna family groupings also were just as good for distinguishing the pollution gradient as was species level data (Warwick 1988). Higher level identifications were found to be just as good as species identifications to detect pollution gradients in the Southern California Bight (Ferraro and Cole 1990). During the GOOMEX study around Gulf of Mexico production platforms, it was not sufficient to analyze at the family level for either meiofauna or macrofauna to describe differences among platforms or distances from platforms (Montagna and Harper 1996). LGL data and Year I sampling data has been reanalyzed at both species and family levels to determine if a reduction in taxonomic effort is adequate to characterize communities in different environmental settings.

4.0 FIELD ACTIVITIES

The Field Program was designed to collect a range of discrete samples and deploy continuous measuring sensors at a large number of stations in the northern GOM. The Field Program includes three cruises in each of the first three years of the program. The first cruise concentrated on the benthic survey objectives of the program and the following two cruises will be a mixture of survey and experimental stations. The survey field effort (Cruise 1) included boxcoring, trawling, photosurveys, and hydrocasts. Experimental process stations include a variety of specialized sampling efforts designed to identify important processes and forcing factors at a limited number of selected survey stations.

The details of the field and laboratory methods have been provided in the original proposal and the first Interim Report and will not be repeated here.

4.1   Cruise 1

Cruise 1 was devoted to a survey of deep-sea communities of the northern GOM. Each standard survey station consisted of the following activities:

A. <u>One (1) CTD</u>: The CTD was deployed with the starboard hydrowinch using conductor cable (the CTD remains attached to the conducting cable for the entire cruise, unless problems are encountered);

B. <u>Five (5) Boxcores</u>: The boxcore was deployed with the hydraulic winch on the non-conducting cable. A pinger was attached to the wire above the boxcore at depths of 1 km and greater. Otherwise wire out and tension was adequate to determine bottom contact.

C. <u>One (1) Camera Lowering</u>: The camera system was deployed with the non-conducting cable on the starboard hydrowinch. A pinger was attached to the frame to determine bottom contact and distance to the bottom. The camera takes up to 50 exposures.

D. <u>One (1) Bottom Trawl</u>: The otter trawl was deployed with the heavy-duty winch on the fantail.

The shipboard scientific crew operated on watches of 12 hours on and 12 hours off. Between stations, the trawl samples were sorted to species and fixed in jars by those assigned to trawling. The five sievers on watch fixed and bottled the material and then assisted with the trawl sorting, displacement volume measurements (for biomass), preservation and labeling. Shipboard marine technicians analyzed samples for oxygen, nutrients, and salinities between stations.

Each watch was assigned a "watch chief" who had the duty of keeping records, notifying the Chief Scientist when problems arose, notifying the watch when the ship was on station, waking the new watch at the appropriate hour, and notifying the bridge when station activities were completed. The watch chief maintained a log in the main laboratory on the main deck that documented each activity in chronological order. Comments on the success or failure of the activity and inventory of all samples taken were kept. The watch chief and assistant ensured that the station logs on the bridge agreed with those in the laboratory. Each "watch chief" reported directly to the Chief Scientist. The "watch chief" communicated between the bridge and scientists on the deck.

4.2   Cruise 2 - Process Cruise

Plans for the first process cruise were made during the first interim meeting in February 2001. The plans were made on the basis of findings to date. Extremes of high and low densities in bacteria, meio- and macrofauna were used as station selection criteria. The sites chosen were MT3, S35, S42, and MT6. High densities characterized MT3 and S36 at 1000 and 1850 m depth in the Mississippi and DeSoto Canyons, whereas low densities were found at S42 and MT6 at 750 and 2750 m depth.

Other sites chosen for re-occupation were MT1, C7, and S41. New sites added were "HIPRO", "furrows", "Green Knoll", "Bush Hill", and "Fe Stone".

Eleven sites were occupied during Cruise II (Figure 4.2). The lander was used successfully at S42 and MT3, providing estimates of total community respiration rates measured *in situ*. Shipboard incubations were made of total community oxygen uptake, sulfate reduction, thymidine incorporation into bacteria and bacteria grazing by meiofauna at four sites: MT3, S36, S42, and MT6. The process and survey data are being processed.

4.3   Year 3 Field Activities

The revised Year 3 field program replaces the 20 day cruise scheduled for June 2002, with two 15-day trips: one in June and one in August. In addition, two shorter supplemental cruises are proposed to be completed when ship time is available between December, 2001 and May, 2002, probably in transit back to the homeport of Galveston.

Revised Cruise 3 - 2 to 4 days (return from Panama City, FL). Activities: box coring, trawling, photosurvey, CTD, and lander deployment.

Revised Cruise 4 - 2 to 4 days (return from Panama City, FL). Activities: box coring, trawling, photosurvey, CTD, and lander deployment. (Note: The strategy for these two trips will be to utilize transits from the eastern gulf back to Galveston to fill in shallow site sampling needed for hypothesis testing and model development. A small team of investigators will take the lander, box core and trawl to meet the ship, probably in Panama City, FL. However if transit ship time is not available back from Panama City, then a single trip will be substituted during which the above work will be accomplished (Figure 2.3). In this case, the trip will be in and out of Galveston.

Revised Cruise 5 - 15 days in June, 2002. Activities - combination of survey and process sampling at 6 to 8 sites indicated, with emphasis on process studies; Staffing - 20 scientists, students, and observers, with 6 berths reserved for Mexican participants. The process stations would be emphasized on the June trip.

Revised Cruise 6 - 15 days in August, 2002. Activities: the cruise would be principally devoted to survey activities (CTD, box cores, trawls and cameras), but would accommodate any process studies not completed during the June cruise. 20 scientists, students, and observers, with 6 berths again reserved for Mexican participants.

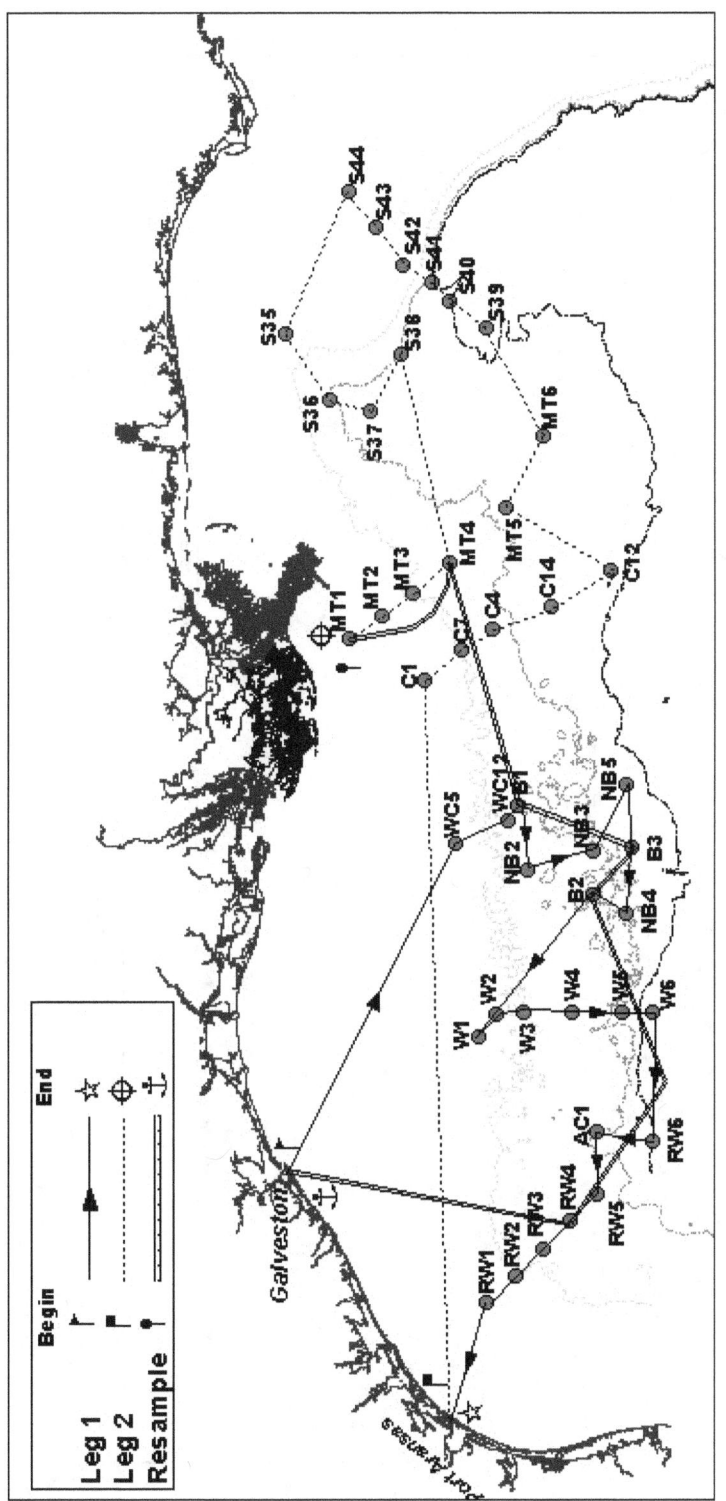

Figure 4.1. Benthic survey stations for DGoMB Cruise 1.

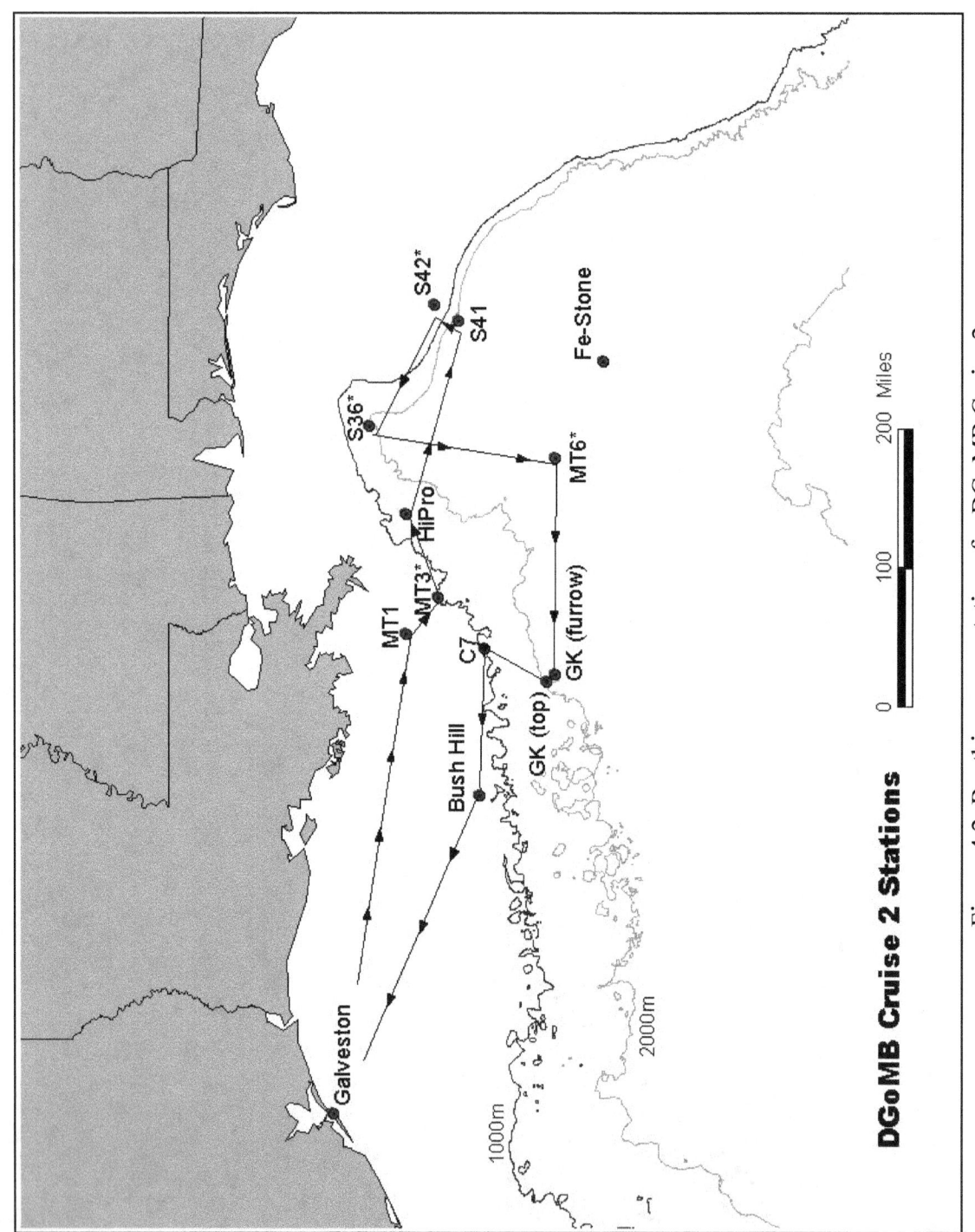

DGoMB Cruise 2 Stations

Figure 4.2. Benthic survey stations for DGoMB Cruise 2.

4-4

Table 4.1. Summary of sampling conducted during Cruise 1.

Station	Trawl	Boxcore	Camera	CTD
RW1	1	5	1	1
RW2	1	5	1	1
RW3	0	5	1	1
RW4	0	5	1	1
RW5	0	5	1	1
RW6	1	5	0	1
AC1	0	5	1	2
W6	1	5	1	1
W5	0	5	1	1
W4	0	5	0	1
W3	1	5	1	1
W2	0	5	1	1
W1	1	5	1	1
WC5	1	5	1	1
WC12	0	5	1	1
B1	1	5	1	1
NB2	1	5	1	1
NB3	1	5	1	1
B2	3	5	1	1
NB4	1	5	0	2
B3	1	5	1	0
NB5	1	5	1	1
C12	1	4	1	1
C14	1	5	1	1
C4	1	5	1	1
C7	1	5	1	1
C1	1	5	1	1
S36	1	5	1	1
S37	1	5	1	1
S38	1	5	1	1
S35	1	5	1	1
S44	1	5	1	1
S43	1	5	1	1
S42	1	5	1	1
S41	1	5	1	1
S40	1	5	1	1
S39	1	5	1	1
MT6	1	5	1	1
MT5	1	5	1	1
MT4	1	5	1	1
MT3	1	5	1	1
MT2	1	5	1	1
MT1	1	5	1	1

Table 4.2. Summary of sampling conducted during Cruise 2.

Station	CTD	B.C.	P.B.C	S.B.C.	Camera	Trawl	Lander	ADCP
MT1	1	5	0	0	1	1	0	0
MT3	1	5	4	1	0	0	1	1
HiPro	1	5	0	0	1	0	0	0
S42	1	5	3	0	0	1	1	1
S41	1	4	0	0	1	0	0	0
S36	1	5	3	0	0	0	1	1
MT6	1	5	3	0	1	0	0	1
GKF	1	5	0	0	1	0	0	0
GKT	1	1	0	1	1	0	0	0
C7	1	5	0	0	1	0	0	0
BH	1	5	0	0	1	0	0	0
Total	11	50	13	2	8	2	3	4

B.C= Boxcores sampled
P.B.C. = Process Boxcore
S.B.C. = Special Boxcore (stable isotope analysis)

5.0 PROGRAM STATUS AND PRELIMINARY RESULTS

Preliminary results are presented for each work element and the progress to date on each task is summarized. Any conclusions are preliminary and based on partially complete data sets. In general interpretations are kept descriptive and overall synthesis will only be possible when the entire data sets are complete.

5.1   Task 1 - Re-Examination of Previous Studies

Several sources of information were readily available to review and assess. These can be categorized as theses and dissertations of students of Willis E. Pequegnat; the MMS-supported slope study overseen by LGL Ecological Research Associates, Inc. (NGOMCS); and the peer-reviewed literature. Practically all of this material has been included in a review of the deep GOM environmental information conducted by Continental Shelf Associates under contract with the MMS. DGoMB personnel participated in that review (G. Rowe, W. Nowlin, W. Bryant, D. Biggs, and M.C. Kennicutt II). That report should be consulted for specific details on individual studies.

All megafauna, macrofauna, megafauna, meiofauna and sediment raw data files from NGOMCS were supplied to DGoMB by LGL Ecological Associates, Inc.. The files have been sorted by discipline and restored as individual Microsoft Excel files. These files are available on the internet to DGoMB principal investigators. Megafauna and fish distributions have been plotted to assess the effect of depth and east-west gradients on species composition. Macrofaunal polychaete diversity (Ph.D. dissertation, G. Fain Hubbard) using several complementary indices has been plotted with depth by transect to consider potential internal GOM gradients (E to W, depth, etc.) and for comparison with other ocean basins.

Several conclusions were derived from earlier studies:

1. biomass and densities of the size groups studied decrease in general as a function of water depth down the continental slope, but with frequent exceptions to this rule;

2. densities of macrofauna differed between sampling dates on the C transect (for Central), with high densities in the spring and low densities in the fall;

3. three depth zones can be tentatively defined based on species composition: the upper slope, the mid slope and deep water;

4. the continental slope in the western GOM is different in species composition (macrofauna and megafauna) from the eastern GOM;

5. sediments contained contaminant levels (low or non-detectable) typical of the deep-sea environment;

6. diversity maxima are encountered on the upper slope (as opposed to the lower slope/upper rise, in other basins); and

7. biomass and densities of the different size groups studied are lower than observed on most other ocean basin margins.

5.2   Task 2 - Field Sampling

For an update on field activities, see Section 4.0 Field Activities. Summaries of the samples collected on Cruise 2 and 2 are provided in Tables 5.1 and 5.2

5.3   Task 3 - Sample Data Processing and Analysis

Standard survey data were collected at each site during each DGoMB cruise: physical and chemical properties of the water column, geological characteristics of the sediments, geochemistry of the sediments, and kinds and numbers of organisms present (Tables 5.1 and 5.2). The status of these datasets are described along with preliminary interpretations.

5.3.1   Physical Oceanography

The physical oceanography preliminary report consists of two parts. The status of QA/QC and processing of the physical and filter data are reviewed. Secondly, a few plots of processed data are presented as illustrations of the types of information now available.

The status of QA/QC and data processing are as follows:

- Filter data from the first cruise have been received and QA/QC has been performed.

- Filter data from cruise 2 is being processed. Samples for total suspended particulate material and pigments have been analyzed. POC samples are expected to be completed soon.

- QA/QC and processing of all continuous profile data from Cruise 1 have been completed.

- The continuous data from the CTD unit for Cruise 2 have been received. QA/QC is completed on these data, with the exceptions of data from the OBS backscatter and continuous dissolved oxygen sensors. Correlations between percent light percent transmission and TSM (total suspended material) for Cruise 2 and the conversions of vertical profiles of percent transmission to profiles of TSM are being processed.

- QA/QC of the bottle nutrient, oxygen and salinity data from Cruise 1 have been completed. All data from this cruise have been merged into a single cruise file.

- Cruise 2 bottle-trip data files for the CTD upcasts are being processed.

- Shipboard ADCP data from Cruise 1 are processed and QA/QC has been performed.

- The QA/QC of shipboard ADCP data from Cruise 2 is in the process of being performed.

Table 5.1. Samples collected during DGoMB Cruise 1.

Biology	Samples	Water Column	Samples	Sediment	Samples	Geochemistry	Samples
Bacterial	201	Depth	44	Grain Size	212	Nutrients	209
Meiofaunal	208	Temperature	44	Porosity	212	Dissolved Organic Carbon (DIC)	209
Macrofaunal	212	Salinity	44	Elemental composition (organic carbon, nitrogen, sulfur)	212	$SO_4^=/Cl^-$	209
Megafaunal	43	Oxygen	44	Percent inorganic carbon (TIC)	212	Dissolved Inorganic Carbon (DIC)	209
Fish	43	Nitrate and Nitrite	44	Permeability	212	$\delta^{13}C$ DIC	209
"Trash"	43	Ammonium	44	Shear Strength	212	Sulfate Reduction Rate	209
		Silicate	44	Bulk Density	212	pH	209
		Phosphate	44	Hydrocarbons	212	H_2S	209
		Particulate Matter (PM)	44	Metals	186	O_2	209
		Particulate Organic Carbon (POC)	44	**Pore water**		Reactive Fe	209
		Light	44	O_2, H_2S, Fe and Mn	209	Reactive Mn	209
		Currents	44	Total CO_2 (DIC)	209	Acid Volatile Sulfide	209
		Photosynthetic Pigments	44	Sulfate and chloride	209		
		Primary Production	44	pH	209		
				Nutrients	209		
				Dissolved organic C (DOC)	209		
				Sediment Solids			
				C stable isotopes	209		
				Porosity	209		
				CHNS	209		
				Reactive Fe and Mn	209		
				Carbonate carbon	209		
				Metals	209		
				Hydrocarbons	209		
				Biologic	209		
				Radioisotopes			
				SO_4^{2-} reduction rate			

4 bacterial aliquots (0, 5, 10, 15) per sample
2 meiofaunal aliquots per sample
filtered samples (POC, pigments, and PM) at three (3) different depths (bottom, chl max or mid, and surface water)

Table 5.2. Summary of samples collected during DGoMB Cruise 2.

Biology	Samples	Water Column	Samples	Sediment	Samples	Geochemistry	Samples
Bacterial (0,5,10,15 cm)	113	Depth	11	Grain Size	49	Nutrients	47
Foraminiferal (times sampled)	24	Temperature	11	Porosity	49	Dissolved Organic Carbon (DIC)	47
Meiofaunal (0-1; 1-3)	111	Salinity	11	Elemental composition (organic carbon, nitrogen, sulfur)	49	$SO_4^=/Cl^-$	47
Macrofaunal	49	Oxygen	11	Percent inorganic carbon (TIC)	49	Dissolved Inorganic Carbon (DIC)	47
Megafaunal	2	Nitrate and Nitrite	11	Permeability	49	$\delta^{13}C$ DIC	47
Fish	2	Ammonium	11	Shear Strength	49	Sulfate Reduction Rate	47
"Trash"	0	Silicate	11	Bulk Density	49	pH	47
		Phosphate	11	Hydrocarbons	49	H_2S	47
		Particulate Matter (PM)	11	Metals	46	O_2	47
		Particulate Organic Carbon (POC)	11	**Pore water**		Reactive Fe	47
		Light	11	O_2, H_2S, Fe and Mn	4	Reactive Mn	47
		Currents	11	Total CO_2 (DIC)	4	Acid Volatile Sulfide	47
		Photosynthetic Pigments	11	Sulfate and chloride	4		
		Primary Production	11	pH	4		
ADCP deployed	4			Nutrients	4		
Survey Camera	8			Dissolved organic C (DOC)	4		
				Sediment Solids			
Lander	2			C stable isotopes	2		
				Porosity	47		
				CHNS	47		
				Reactive Fe and Mn	47		
				Carbonate carbon	47		
				Metals	46		
				Hydrocarbons	45		

Table 5.2. Summary of samples collected during DGoMB Cruise 2 (Cont).

Biology	Samples	Water Column	Samples	Sediment	Samples	Geochemistry	Samples
				Biologic			
				Radioisotopes	9		
				SO_4^{2-} reduction rate	10		
				BMIC sampling	5		
				BAMS	5		
				Foraminifera ATP	4		
				Bacteria T-Thymidine uptake	4		
				Meiofauna T-Thymidine uptake	4		
				Megafauna respiration	1		

Vertical profiles of properties measured at two CTD/rosette stations on Cruise 2 are shown in Figures 5.1 and 5.2. Station MT1 is an example of a relatively shallow water station which does not reach the base of the main thermocline. Notable are the chlorophyll maximum at 50-70 m (as seen in the fluorometer voltage) and some evidence of a weak nephloid layer near 100 m, as seen in the percent light transmission. The latter may indicate transport of water off the continental shelf at that depth. A deep station, GKF, is shown in Figure 5.2. Again, the chlorophyll maximum is clear. In this case there appears to be a pronounced near-bottom nepheloid layer.

A scatter plot of temperature versus salinity for DGoMB Cruise 1 is shown in Figure 5.3. The variance is small below about 16°C, indicating reasonable data quality. The scatter plot of nitrate versus phosphate for Cruise 1 is shown in Figure 5.4 and indicates the expected linear relationship.

Plots of sigma-theta versus the discrete water sample properties salinity, dissolved oxygen, nitrate, phosphate, and silicate are shown in Figures 5.5 to 5.9. In each figure, values from DGoMB Cruise 1 are plotted on the left side of the graph. The curves shown indicate the mean and $\pm$ 2.3 standard deviations based on a combination of data from DGoMB Cruise 1, LATEX A, and NEGOM. These limits would include 98% of the points, if the data had a normal distribution about the mean as a function of density. In the right frame of each figure are displayed DGoMB Cruise 1 data (pluses) and, for comparison, data from LATEX A and NEGOM (dots). The data from DGoMB are representative of information expected from the Gulf of Mexico and are of good quality.

The shipboard ADCP measurements recorded during both legs of DGoMB Cruise 1 are of good quality. Comparisons of the near-surface (40-60 m) currents measured simultaneously by the 38 and 150 kHz instruments are favorable. No large gaps exist in the data set; however, short gaps due to GPS dropout and computer down time for data backups exist. The short gaps do not affect the overall data quality.

Based on TOPEX/ERS-2 sea surface height anomaly (SSHA) plots, the Loop Current was hammer-shaped during leg 1 of Cruise 1, intruding northward of 27°N and westward to 89°W. The SSHA field for June 10, 2000 is shown in Figure 5.10. Thus, the Loop Current was east of the study region during that leg. However, two Loop Current Eddies were present in the western Gulf and their presence is seen in the ADCP vector fields. Current vectors at a vertical bin centered at 12.4 m depth are shown in Figure 5.11. The weaker of the two eddies was centered at 91.5°W, 24°N. The leg 1 Cruise 1 track passed through the northern limb of this eddy at 26°N between 90°W and 91°W. The stronger eddy was centered at 94.5°W, 26°N. The anticyclonic current field is clearly seen in the horizontal vector stick plots along the cruise track. Particularly strong southward currents (of order 100 cm/s) are seen along the eastern side of this eddy at around 93.5°W.

During leg 2 of Cruise 1, the stronger LCE drifted west about 0.5° of longitude. The SSHA field for June 10, 2000 is shown in Figure 5.12. The anticyclonic structure of the stronger eddy is again seen in the leg 2 ADCP data. ADCP vectors for a vertical bin centered at 11.6 m during leg 2 are shown in Figure 5.12. The westward movement of the eddy is also seen in the data as the strongest southward currents are located at 94°W and are reduced in amplitude about 50-70 cm/s. The cruise track of leg 2 Cruise 1 was well north of the weak LCE, centered at that time near 92°W, 23°N.

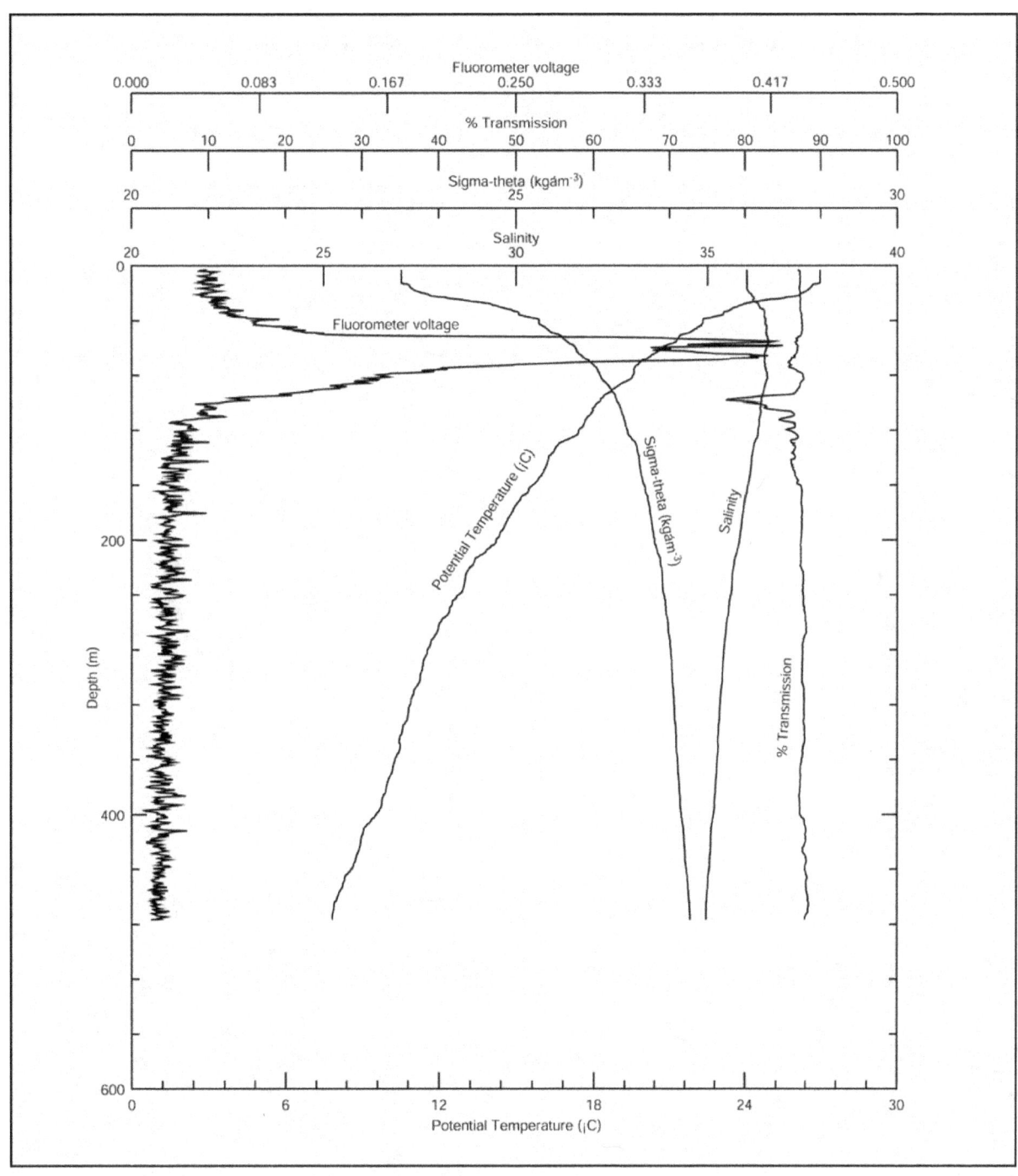

Figure 5.1.   Vertical profiles of temperature, salinity, percent light transmission, fluorometer voltage, and sigma-theta for DGoMB station MT1.

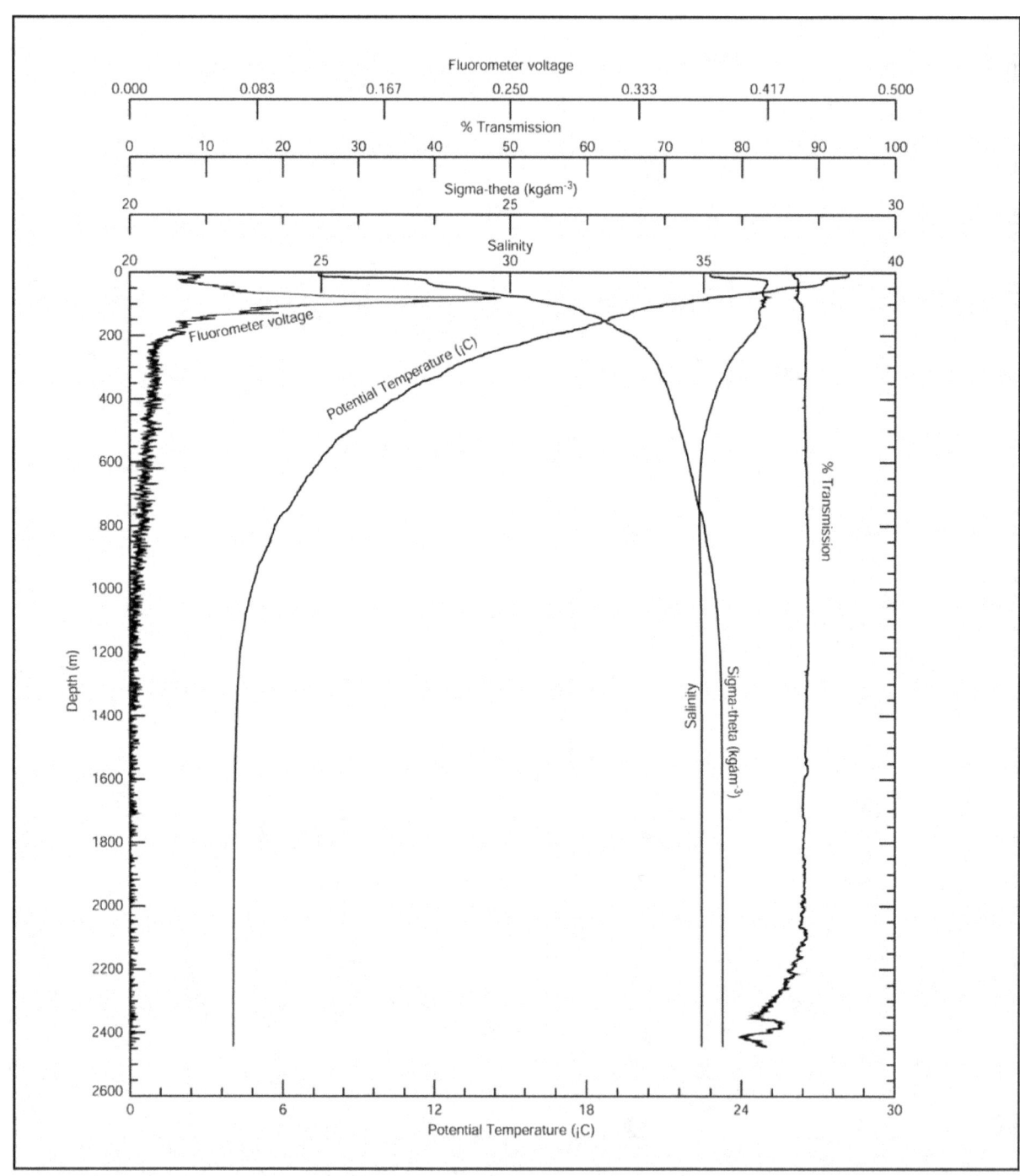

Figure 5.2. Vertical profiles of temperature, salinity, percent light transmission, fluorometer voltage, and sigma-theta for DGoMB station GKF.

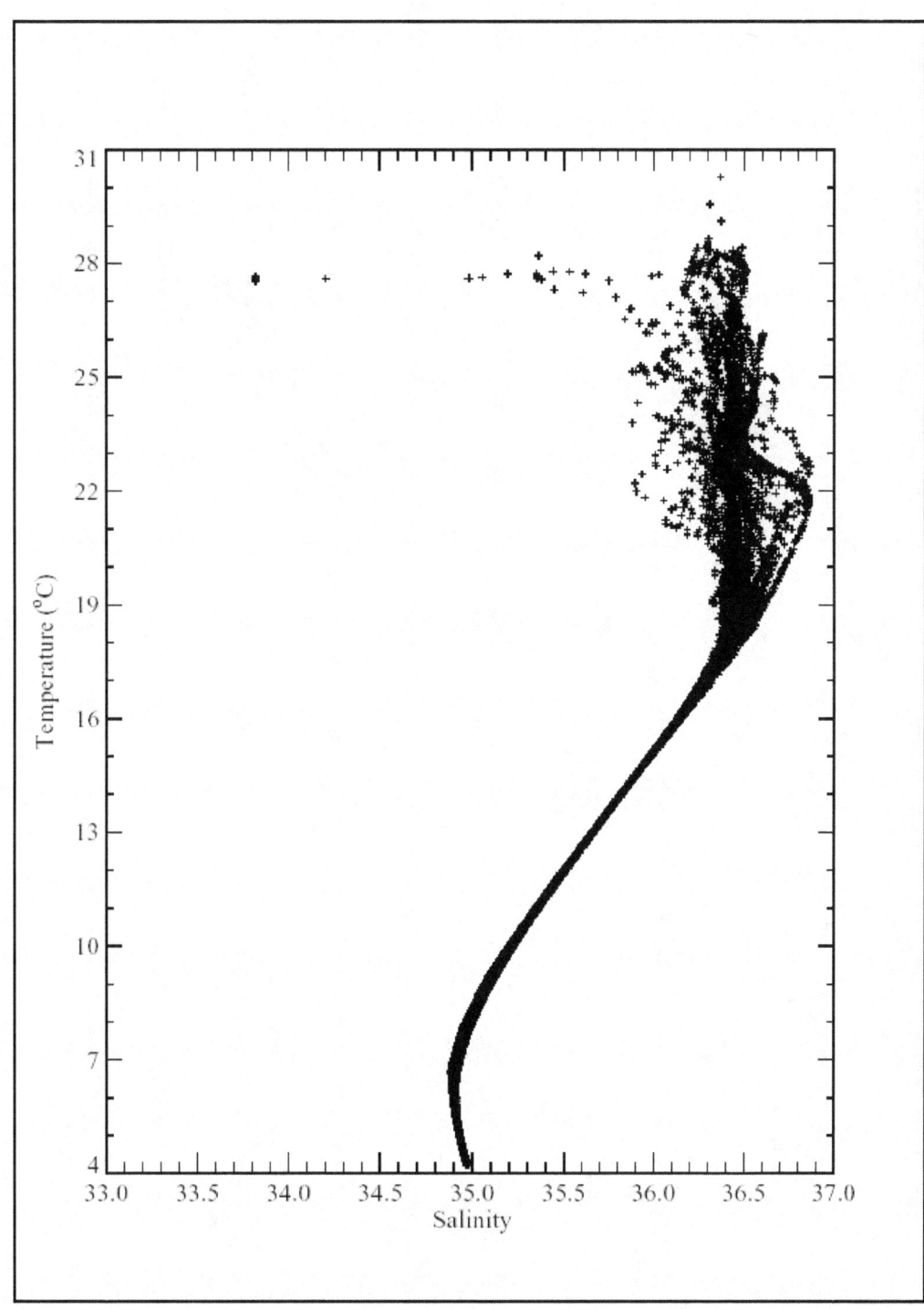

Figure 5.3. Scatter plot of temperature versus salinity for DGoMB Cruise 1.

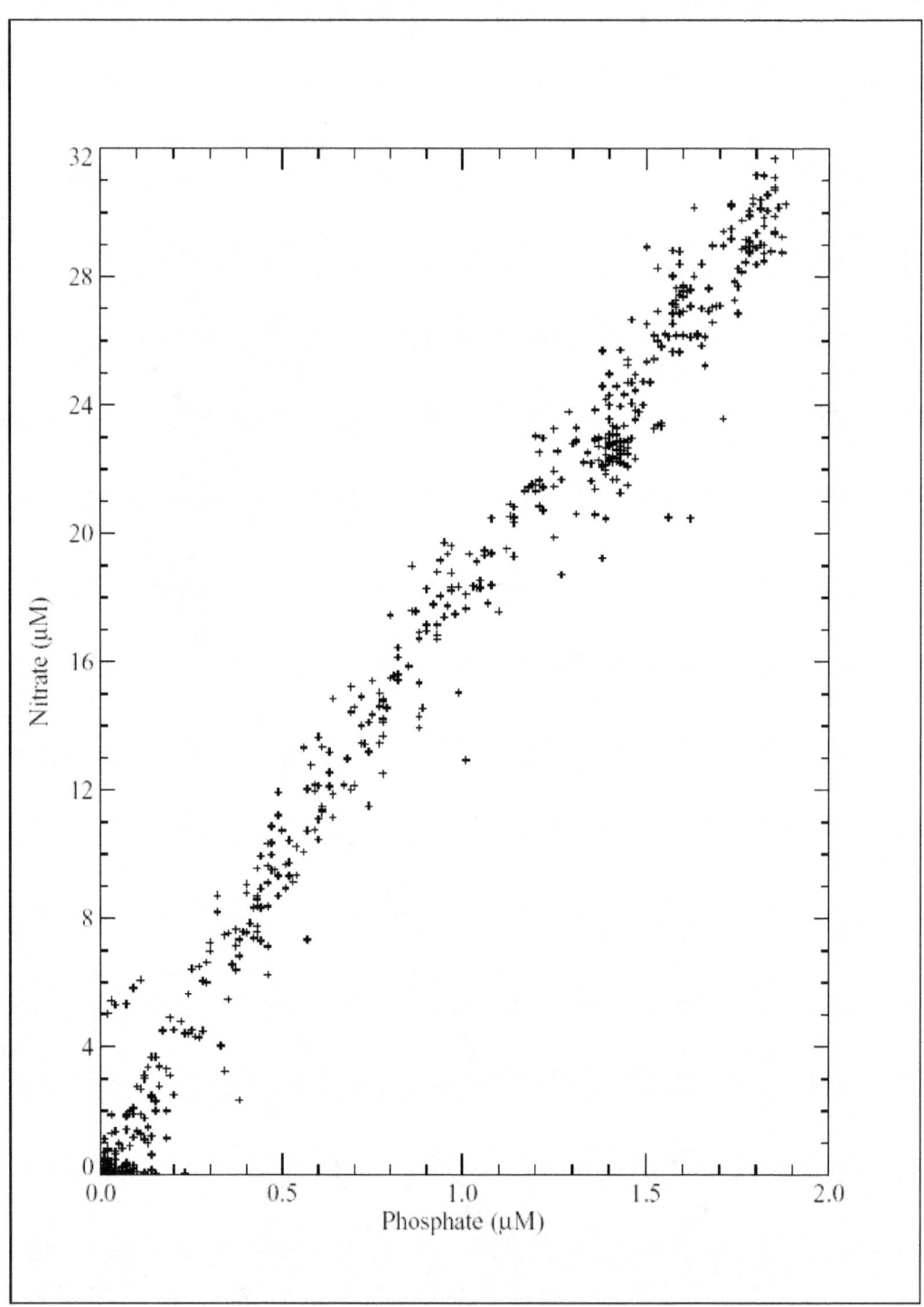

Figure 5.4. Scatter plot of nitrate versus phosphate for DGoMB Cruise 1.

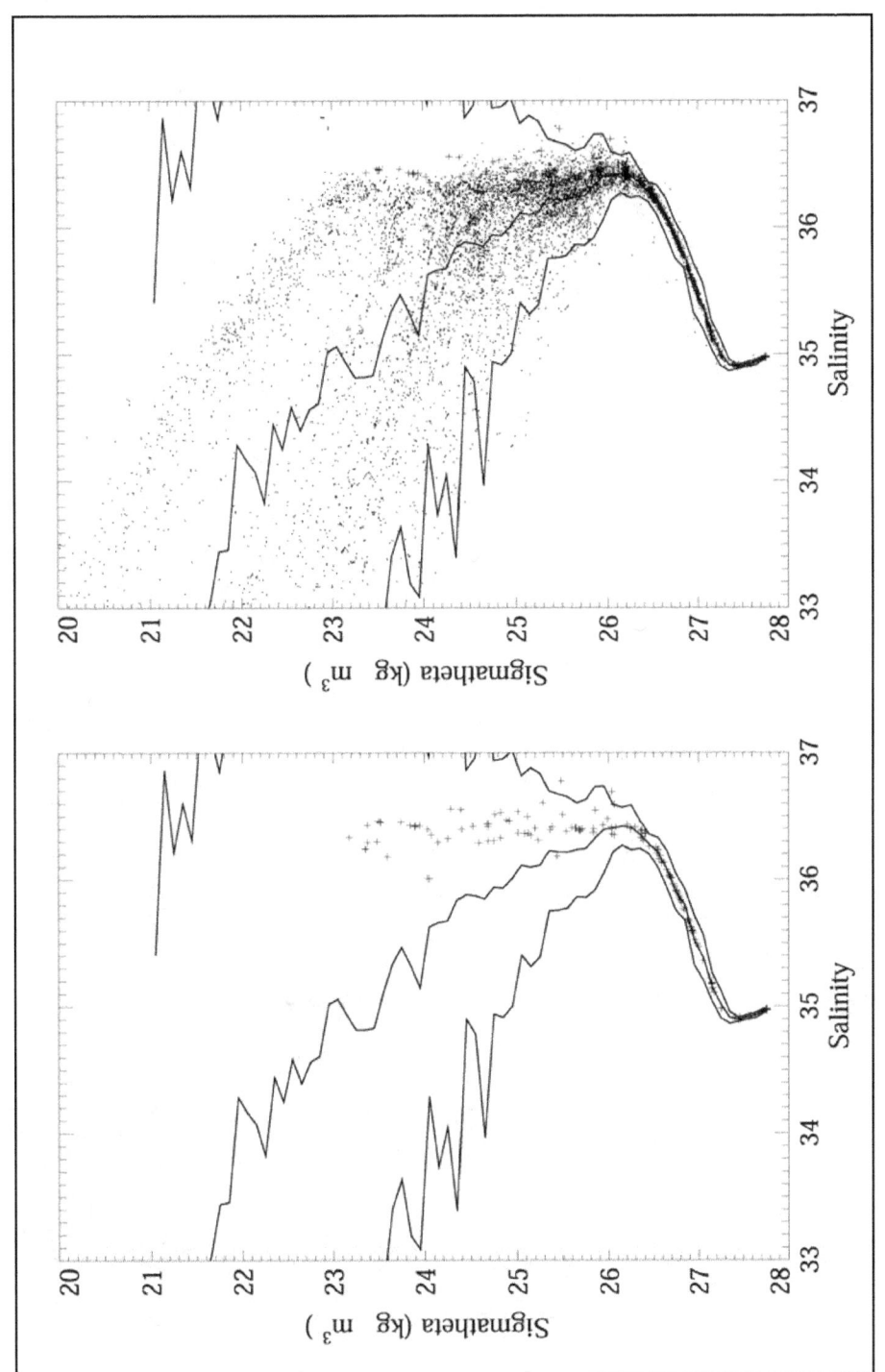

Figure 5.5. Bottle salinity versus sigma-theta for (left) DGoMB Cruise 1 and (right) a combination of DGoMB Cruise 1 (pluses) and data from LATEX A and NEGOM (dots). Curves shown are mean and $\pm$ 2.3 standard deviations based on a combination of data from DGoMB Cruise 1, LATEX A, and NEGOM.

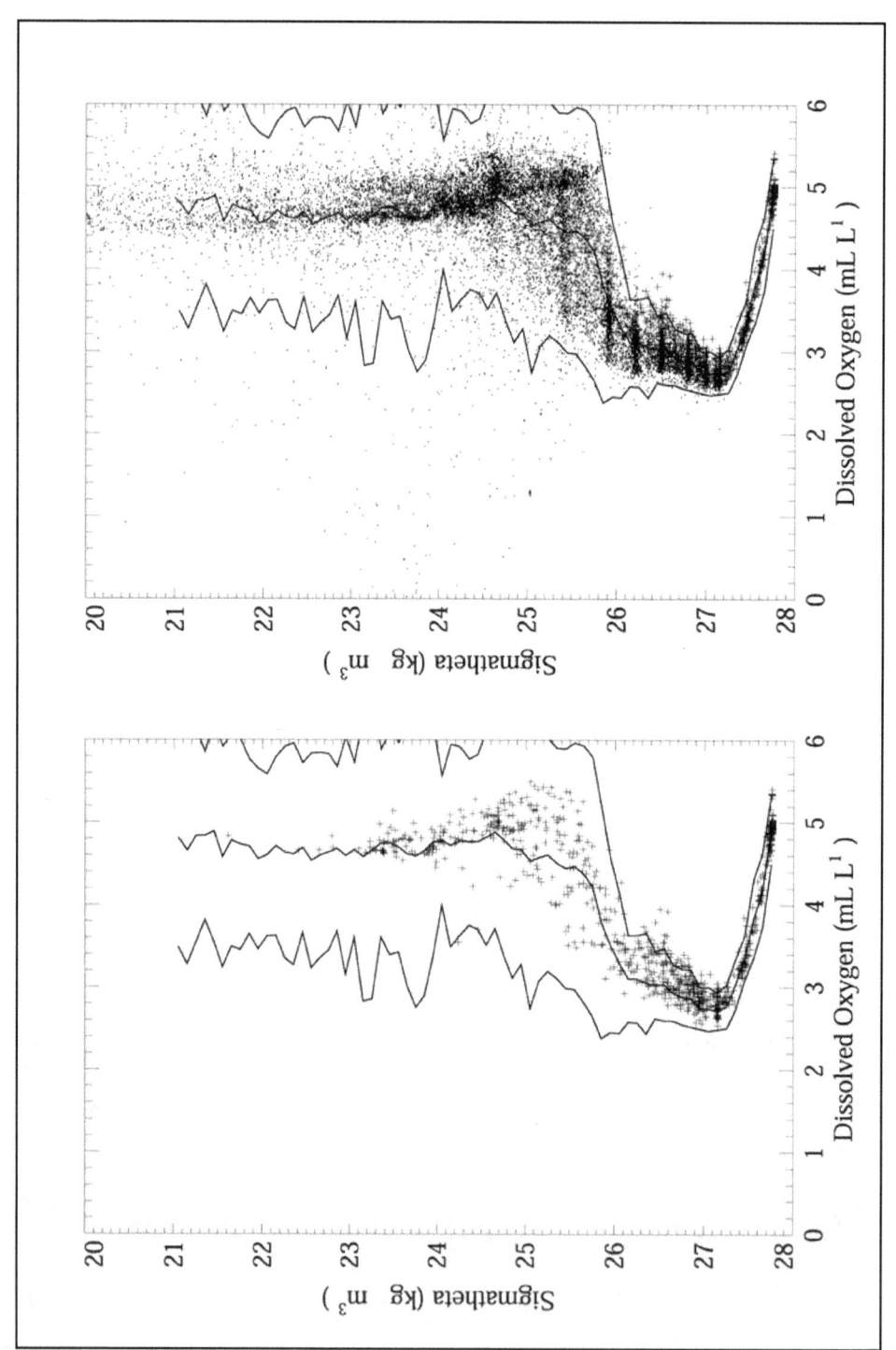

Figure 5.6. Dissolved oxygen versus sigma-theta for (left) DGoMB Cruise 1 and (right) a combination of DGoMB Cruise 1 (pluses) and data from LATEX A and NEGOM (dots). Curves shown are mean and ± 2.3 standard deviations based on a combination of data from DGoMB Cruise 1, LATEX A, and NEGOM.

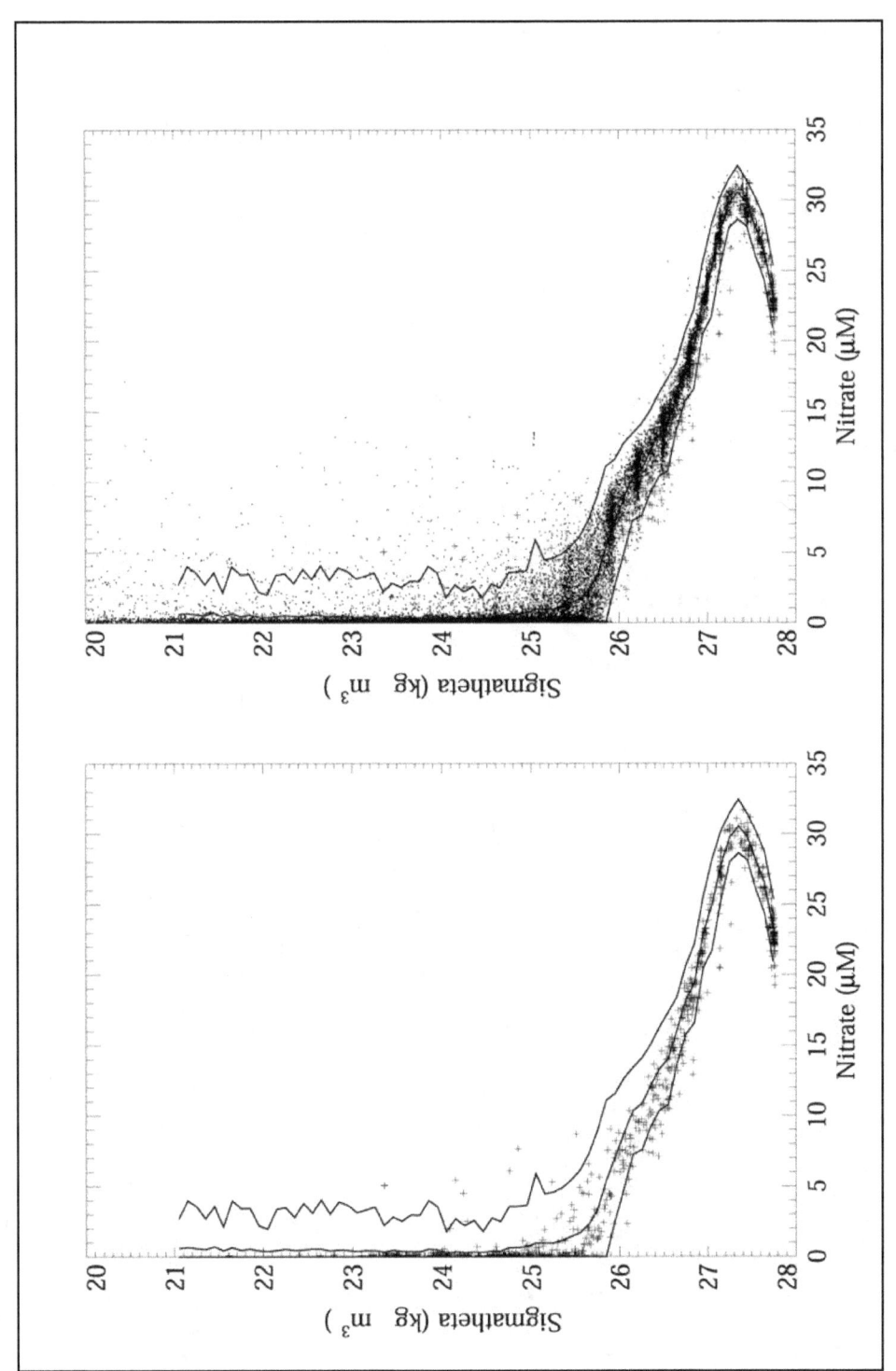

Figure 5.7. Nitrate versus sigma-theta for (left) DGoMB Cruise 1 and (right) a combination of DGoMB Cruise 1 (pluses) and data from LATEX A and NEGOM (dots). Curves shown are mean and $\pm$ 2.3 standard deviations based on a combination of data from DGoMB Cruise 1, LATEX A, and NEGOM.

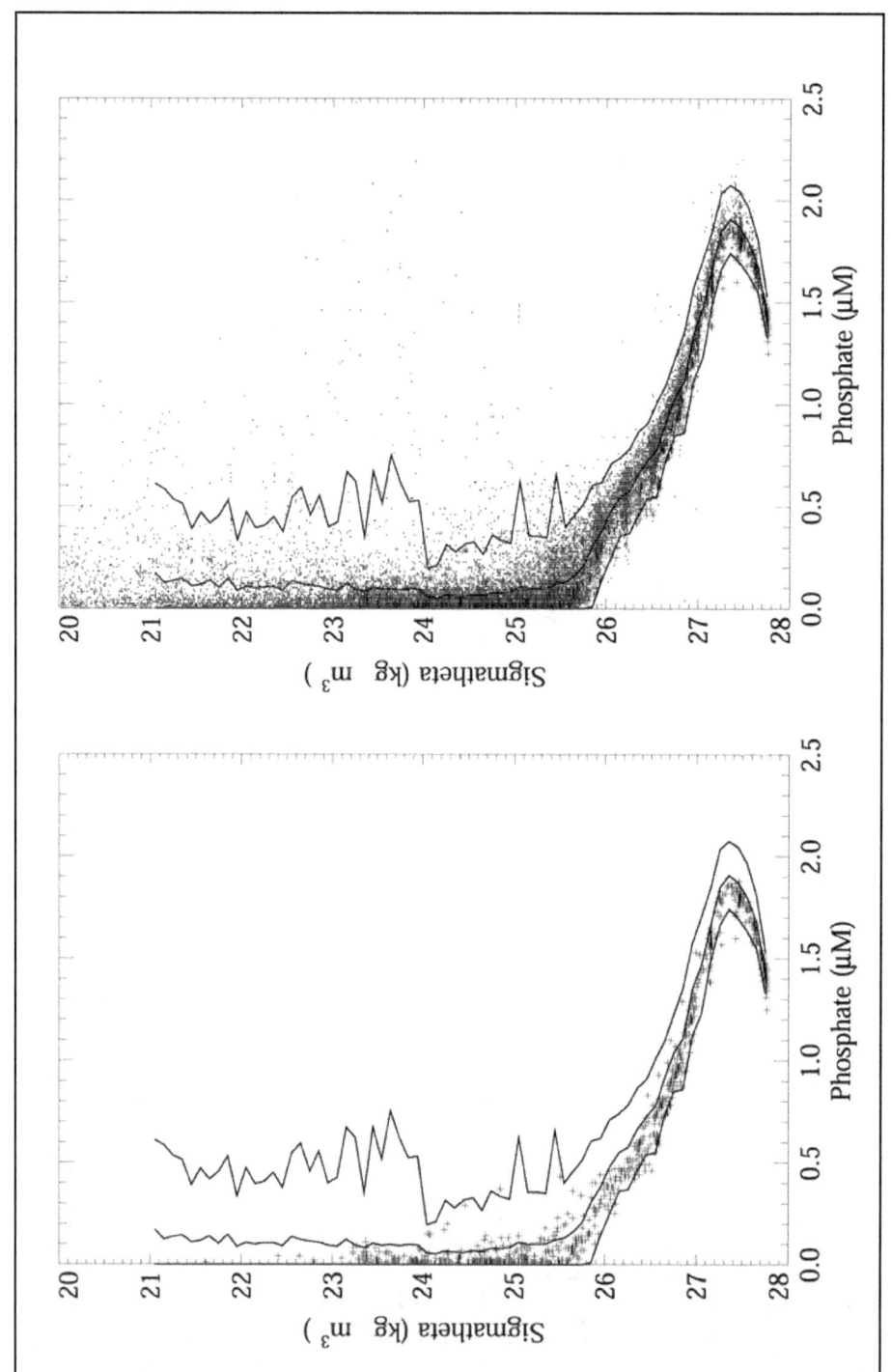

Figure 5.8.   Phosphate versus sigma-theta for (left) DGoMB Cruise 1 and (right) a combination of DGoMB Cruise 1 (pluses) and data from LATEX A and NEGOM (dots). Curves shown are mean and $\pm$ 2.3 standard deviations based on a combination of data from DGoMB Cruise 1, LATEX A, and NEGOM.

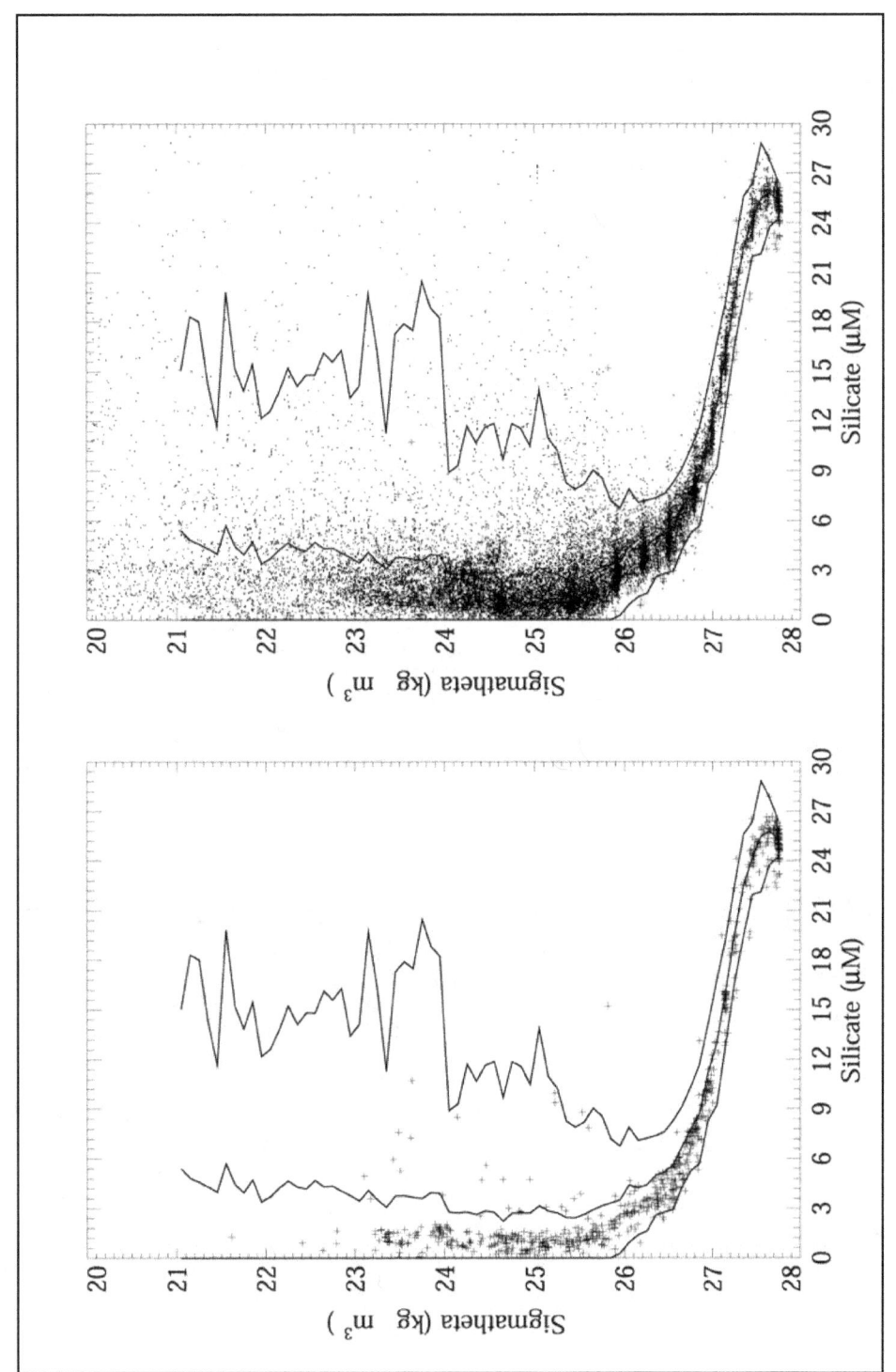

Figure 5.9.   Silicate versus sigma-theta for (left) DGoMB Cruise 1 and (right) a combination of DGoMB Cruise 1 (pluses) and data from LATEX A and NEGOM (dots). Curves shown are mean and $\pm$ 2.3 standard deviations based on a combination of data from DGoMB Cruise 1, LATEX A, and NEGOM.

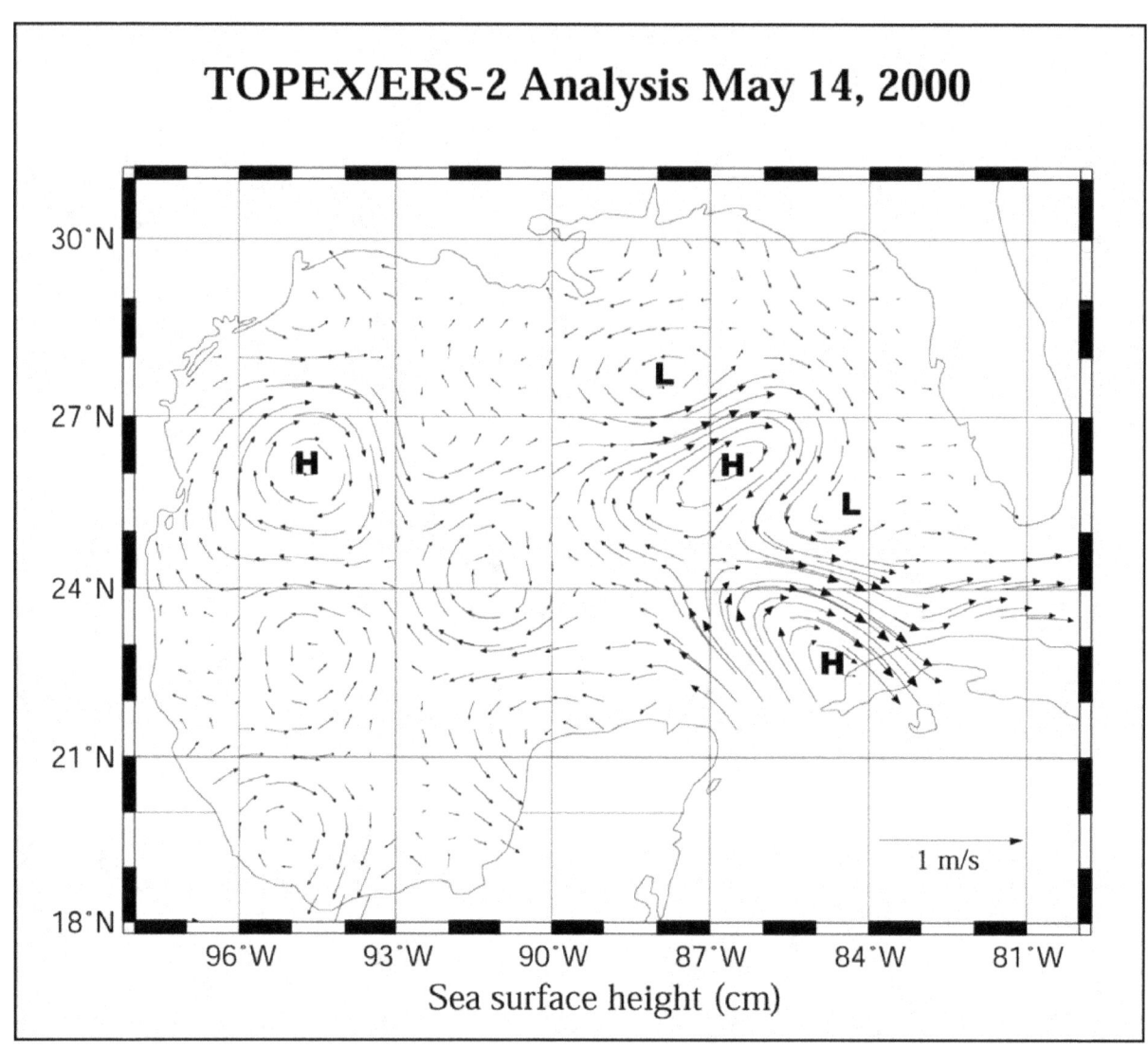

Figure 5.10. Sea surface height field for 14 May 2000 based on analyzed height anomaly of TOPEX and ERS-2 altimeter data added to mean sea surface height field. Anticyclonic (cyclonic) circulation features have clockwise (counterclockwise) currents and positive (negative) sea surface height values. Courtesy of Robert Leben (University of Colorado).

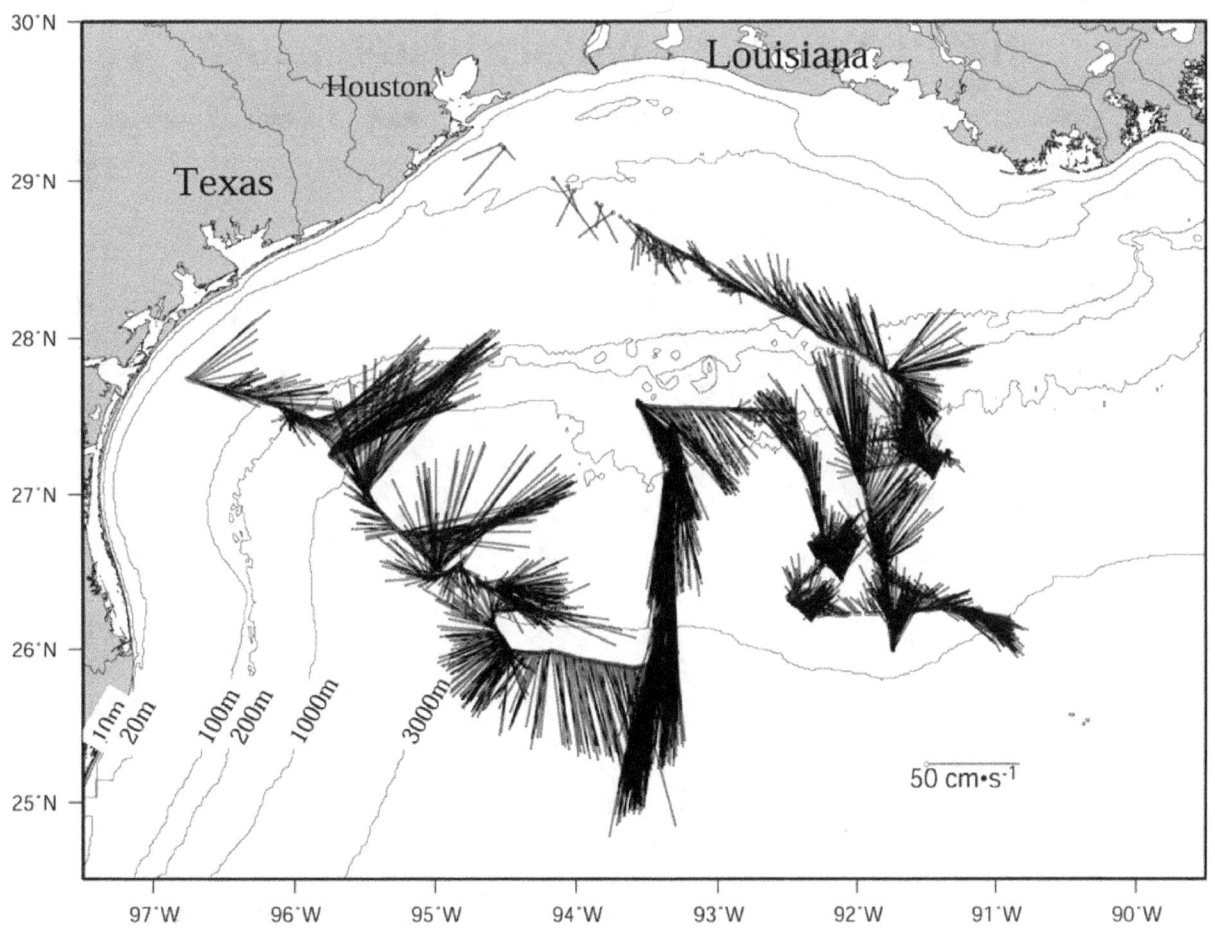

Figure 5.11. Broad-band 150 kHz ADCP current vectors at average depth of 12.4 m on
DGoMB leg 1 Cruise, 3-23 May 2000.

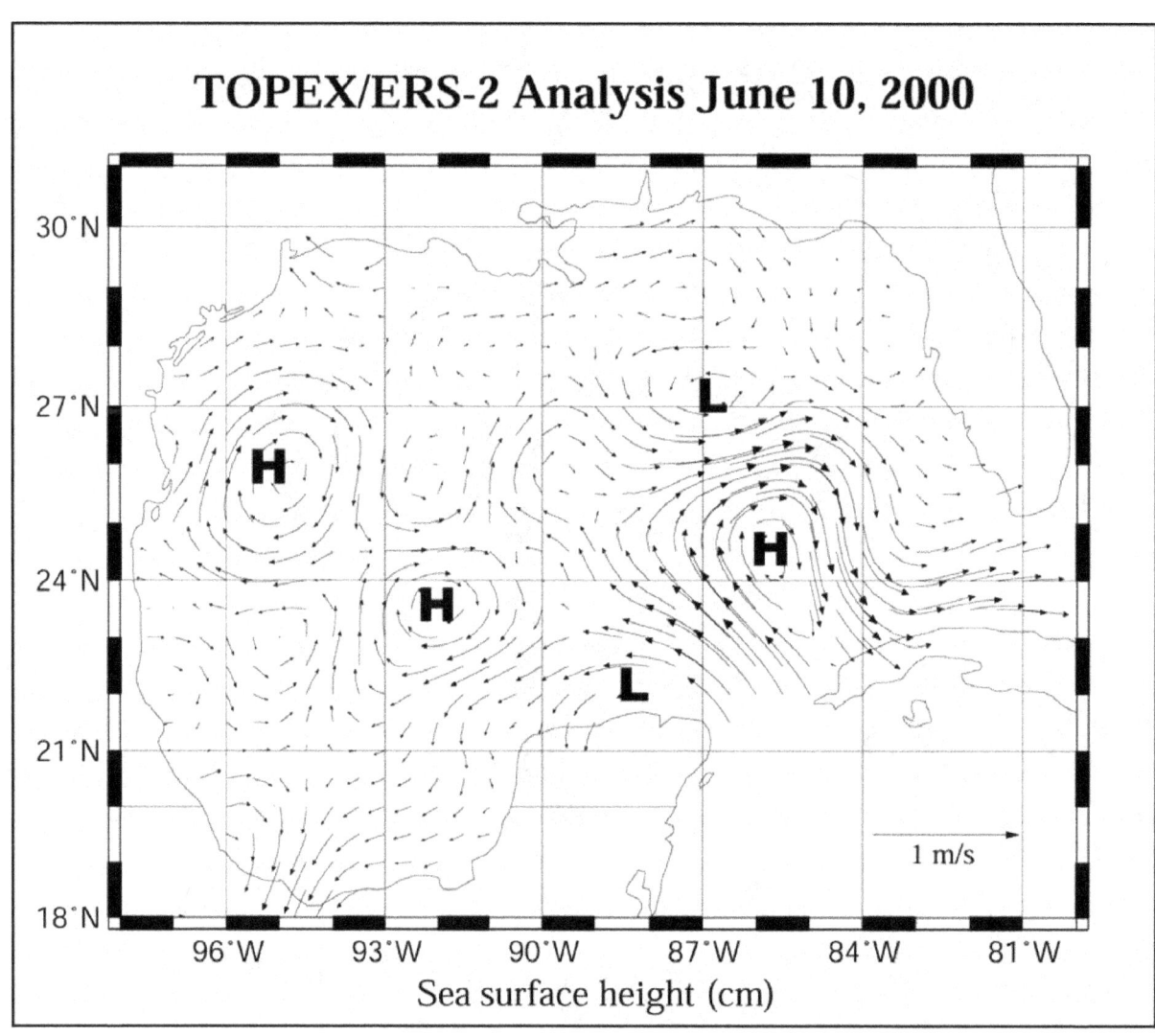

Figure 5.12. Sea surface height field for 10 June 2000 based on analyzed height anomaly of TOPEX and ERS-2 altimeter data added to mean sea surface height field. Anticyclonic (cyclonic) circulation features have clockwise (counterclockwise) currents and positive (negative) sea surface height values. Courtesy of Robert Leben (University of Colorado).

During leg 2 of Cruise 1, the Loop Current did not intrude into the Gulf as far north as 27°N (see Figure 5.13), and thus did not influence directly the currents along the cruise track. However, a weak LCE centered at 90°W, 26°N and a stronger cyclonic eddy centered at 87°W, 27°N are both seen in SSHA plots and in the ADCP data.

5.3.2 Remote Sensing: Ocean Color Climatology

During Year Two, a time series of SeaWiFS chlorophyll (CHL) at each of the stations was compiled by colleagues at the University of South Florida (Andrew Remsen, Chuan Min Hu, Frank Muller-Karger). All available SeaWiFS imagery from the Gulf of Mexico for 1998 and 1999 was composited into biweekly bins and some time early in 2002, this two-year series of biweekly data files will be continued and extended for year 2000.

The average CHL concentration was extracted for each of the DGoMB stations from all 52 biweekly scenes (104 weeks) of the 1998-1999 data series. The "average" CHL for each of the DGoMB stations, in turn, is the mean of a 5 pixel x 5 pixel grid centered on the specified latitude and longitude of each of the DGoMB stations. Since each SeaWiFS pixel has 2.8 x 4.1 km resolution, the effective area around each DGoMB station that is being averaged at each biweekly interval computes to be 287 km^2.

A table that summarizes the two-year average CHL (SeaWiFS mean; μg/L) and also the standard deviation about the 2-year mean at each of these stations is shown as Table 5.3. This has been posted to the DGoMB password-protected website. Plots of the biweekly averages have also been made; composites are presented as Figures 5.14-5.17.

1) The annual cycle of CHL at the four deepest of the "deepwater stations" (RW6, W6, B3, C12) shows the pattern previously reported from analysis of the CZCS archives by Muller-Karger et al (1991) and by Melo-Gonzalez et al (2000): deepwater CHL is lowest in spring-summer and highest November-February.

2) The annual cycle of CHL at the western stations (W1-W6) and at the Louisiana Slope Stations (the cluster of 9 stations between 93W and 91W) shows the "deepwater" pattern.

3) The annual cycle of CHL at the far western stations (RW1-RW6) generally follows the "deepwater" pattern, but there are several periods of the year in which CHL at the shallower stations (RW1 and RW2) exceeds 0.5 μg/L. These maxima occur throughout the year.

4) East of 91W, however, the "typical" deepwater annual cycle in CHL is swamped by unusually high summertime CHL. In both summer 1998 and summer 1999, a warm slope eddy, that NEGOM-COH fieldwork showed, was centered over DeSoto Canyon, acted to entrain low salinity, high chlorophyll "green water" from the Mississippi River and transport this plume seaward into deepwater. High surface CHL in summertime is evident at all stations on the Mississippi Trough Transect (MT1-MT6), and at the 3 stations farthest upslope along the central transect (C1, C7, C4)

Figure 5.13.   Narrow-band 150 kHz ADCP current vectors at average depth of 11.6 m on DGoMB leg 2 Cruise, 21 May - 21 June 2000.

Table 5.3. Summary of the two-year average chlorophyll *a* concentrations (CHL) and the standard deviation about the two-year mean at each of the stations.

Station	Longitude	Latitude	Depth (m)	SeaWiFS mean	SeaWiFS std dev
RW1	96.00	27.50	300	0.33	0.21
RW2	95.75	27.25	800	0.23	0.09
RW3	95.50	27.00	1300	0.20	0.07
RW4	95.25	26.75	1600	0.21	0.10
RW5	95.00	26.50	1800	0.18	0.05
RW6	94.50	26.00	3000	0.18	0.06
AC1	94.42	26.50	2400	0.18	0.07
W1	93.55	27.58	300	0.23	0.09
W2	93.34	27.42	800	0.21	0.07
W3	93.32	27.18	1300	0.19	0.06
W4	93.32	26.74	1800	0.19	0.06
W5	93.32	26.28	2700	0.17	0.05
W6	93.32	26.00	3100	0.17	0.06
WC5	91.77	27.78	800	0.23	0.09
WC12	91.55	27.32	1300	0.20	0.07
NB2	92.00	27.13	1500	0.18	0.06
NB3	91.83	26.55	2000	0.18	0.06
NB5	91.22	26.25	2100	0.18	0.06
B1	91.42	27.22	2200	0.19	0.07
NB4	92.40	26.25	2400	0.17	0.04
B2	92.23	26.55	2600	0.18	0.05
B3	91.80	26.20	2600	0.18	0.06
C1	90.25	28.06	300	0.94	1.95
C7	89.98	27.73	1000	0.34	0.47
C4	89.78	27.45	1400	0.24	0.16
C14	89.58	26.92	2600	0.20	0.09
C12	89.24	26.38	2800	0.18	0.06
S35	87.05	29.33	700	0.60	0.70
S36	87.67	28.92	2000	0.87	1.37
S37	87.77	28.55	2300	0.43	0.42
S38	87.25	28.28	2300	0.24	0.10
S44	85.75	28.75	200	0.37	0.28
S43	86.08	28.50	400	0.39	0.44
S42	86.42	28.25	900	0.28	0.25
S41	86.58	28.00	2800	0.24	0.15
S40	86.75	27.83	3000	0.22	0.08
S39	87.00	27.50	3200	0.21	0.07
MT1	89.83	28.54	300	4.91	2.26
MT2	89.67	28.45	600	3.68	5.42
MT3	89.49	28.22	1000	1.42	1.07
MT4	89.17	27.83	1400	0.62	1.45
MT5	88.67	27.33	2200	0.25	0.19
MT6	88.00	27.00	2700	0.19	0.06

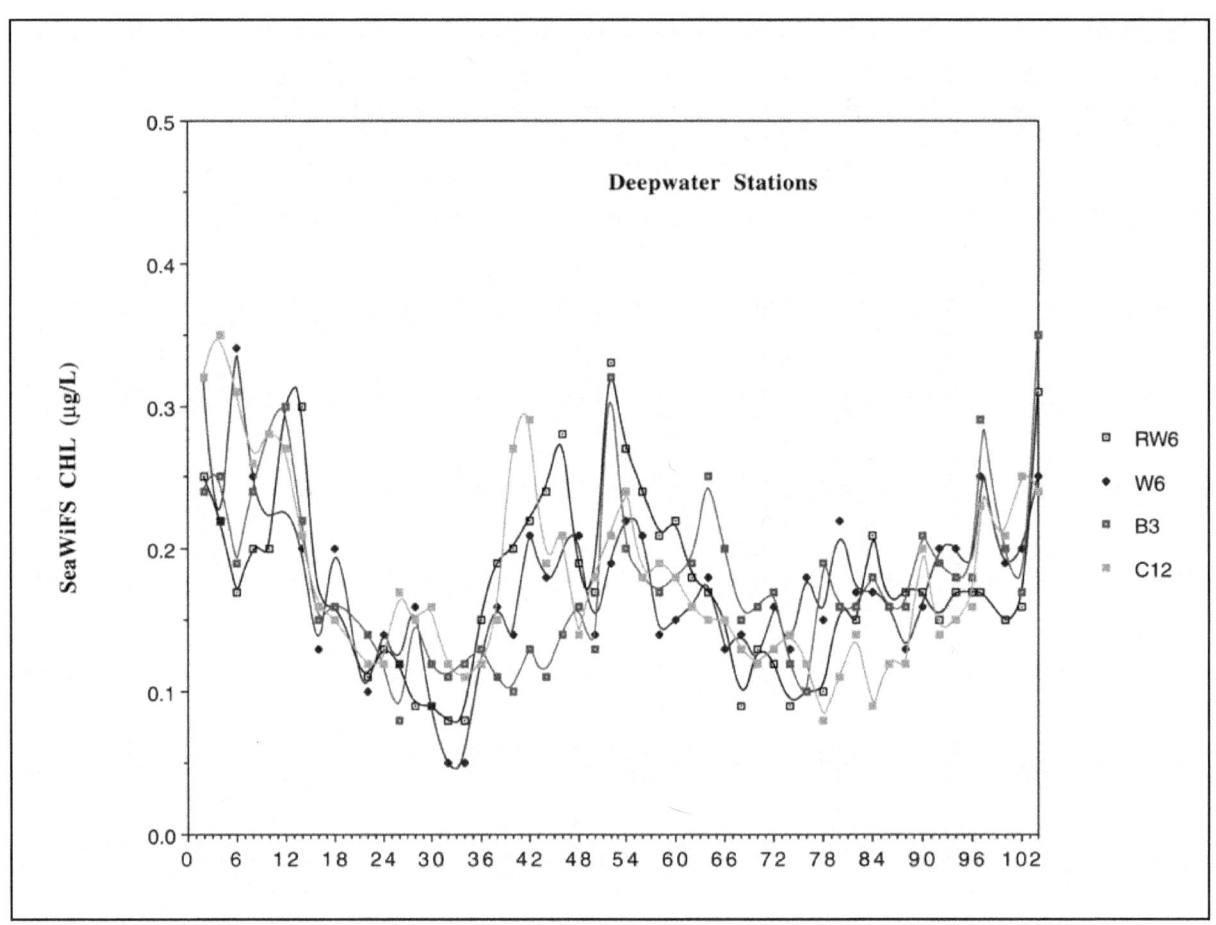

Figure 5.14. Two-year time series of SeaWiFS chlorophyll concentration at deep water DGoMB stations > 2600 m water depth in north-central and northwestern Gulf of Mexico. Data extend from January 1, 1998 through December 30, 1999. SeaWiFS data are courtesy of orbimage and NASA; data compositing and processing were done at the College of Marine Science, University of South Florida.

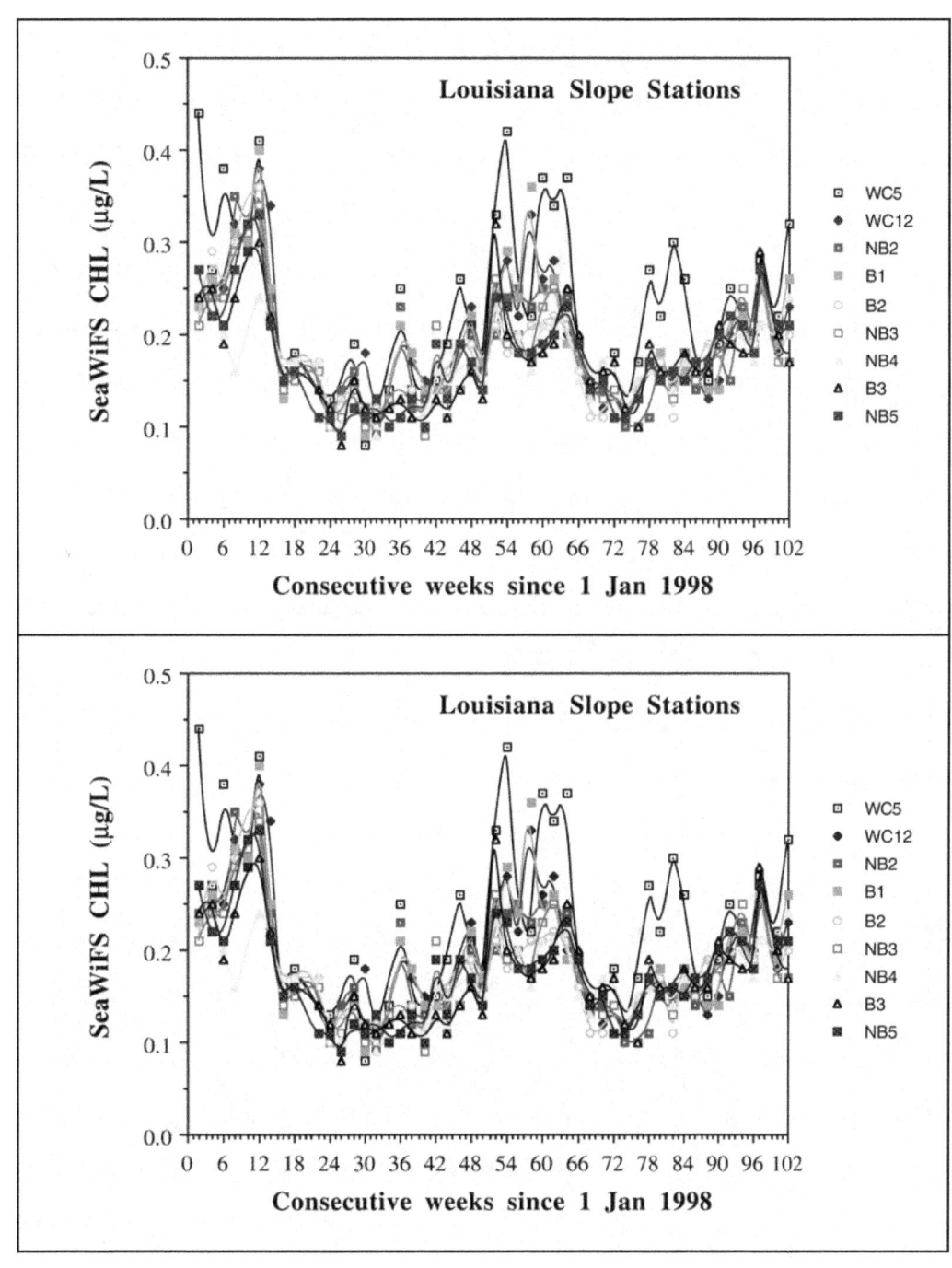

Figure 5.15. Two-year time series of SeaWiFS chlorophyll concentration for DGoMB stations along Western (W) Transect and on Louisiana Slope. Data coverage and source same as for Figure 5.14.

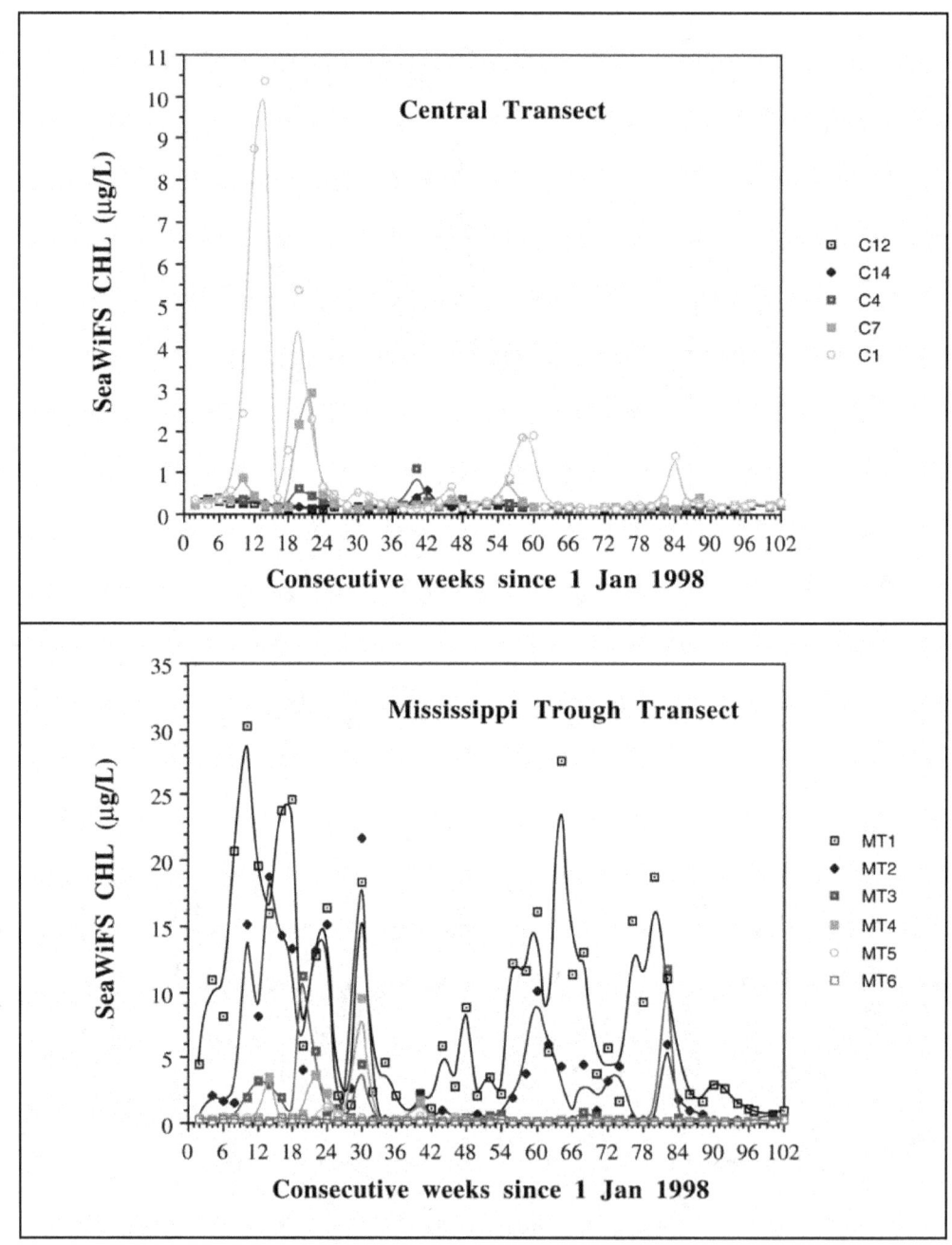

Figure 5.16. Two-year time series of SeaWiFS chlorophyll concentration for DGoMB stations along Central (C) Transect and Mississippi Trough (MT) Transect. Data coverage and source same as for Figure 5.14, but note that y-axis ranges are greater than those of Figure 5.14.

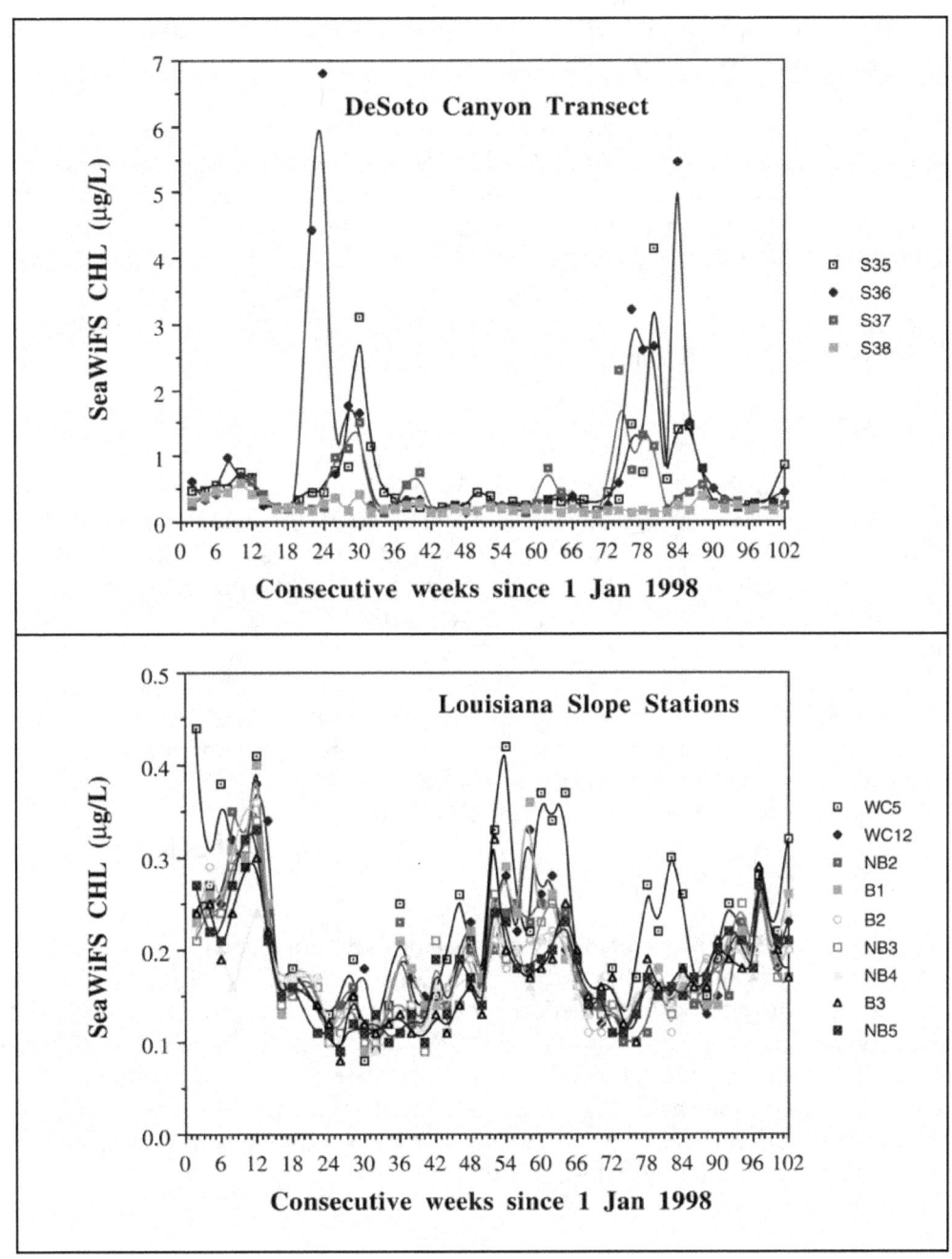

Figure 5.17   Two-year time series of SeaWiFS chlorophyll concentration for DGoMB stations in DeSoto Canyon and along Eastern Transect. Data coverage and source same as for Figure 5.14, but note that y-axis ranges are greater than those of Figure 5.14.

and at the 3 stations farthest upslope along the DeSoto Canyon transect (S35, S36, S37). High summertime CHL is evident, as well, at 3 of the stations along the eastern transect (S44, S43, S42).

5) Biweekly average CHL have been extracted at each of the 12 stations where SAIC moored current meters in April 1997 to March 1999 in support of the DeSoto Canyon Eddy Intrusion Study. There is a robust correlation between the time of year in which there was highest CHL in surface waters and the time of year in which there was highest ADCP backscatter (Scott 2001). These data indicate that traditional "nutrients-phytoplankton-zooplankton (NPZ)" paradigm seems to apply in the deepwater NEGOM, at least in the upper 90 m of the water column where the ADCP backscatter is able to image.

5.3.3 Geology

Two hundred and forty five cores, 30 to 35 cm in length, were recovered from 43 stations during the survey. Each core was analyzed at 1 cm intervals for bulk density, porosity, water content, p-wave velocity, void ratio and impedance. That analysis resulted in 48,500 individual measurements of geotechnical properties. All cores were split and photographed and shear strength measurements were attempted but the surficial sediments have shear strengths lower than our instruments could measure.

An example of the data generated is illustrated in Figure 5.18. All 5 cores at Location NB3 had very similar measurements between the geotechnical properties and depth within the cores. In contrast to the uniformity found in cores taken at Location NB3, the cores recovered at Location C7 display a wide variation in properties with depth within each core (Figure 5.19). The location of sites that have large variations in geotechnical properties between cores taken at the same location are shown in Figure 5.20.

All cores were examined for the degree of bioturbation that the cores has undergone. Figure 5.21 is a photograph of a split core taken at Location W4. The sediment at Location W4, has under gone very little to no bioturbation. In contrast, the core from Location MT5 (Figure 5.22) illustrates a high degree of bioturbation. A core from Location RW5 (Figure 5.23) illustrates sediment that has under gone slight to a moderate degree of bioturbation. Figure 5.24 illustrates the degree of bioturbation of the sediments at all locations of the year 2000 cruises. There is a very distinct and significant boundary between sediments consisting of slight to no bioturbation and those that are highly bioturbated.

5.3.4 Geochemistry

The geochemical studies consist of measurements of sediment solid phase and pore water chemical properties. They include determination of bacterial sulfate reduction rates and are interfaced with benthic lander flux measurements. As with the other components of the program, the geochemical studies are divided into a set of measurements for survey sites and a more comprehensive array of measurements at survey sites selected for the study of benthic processes.

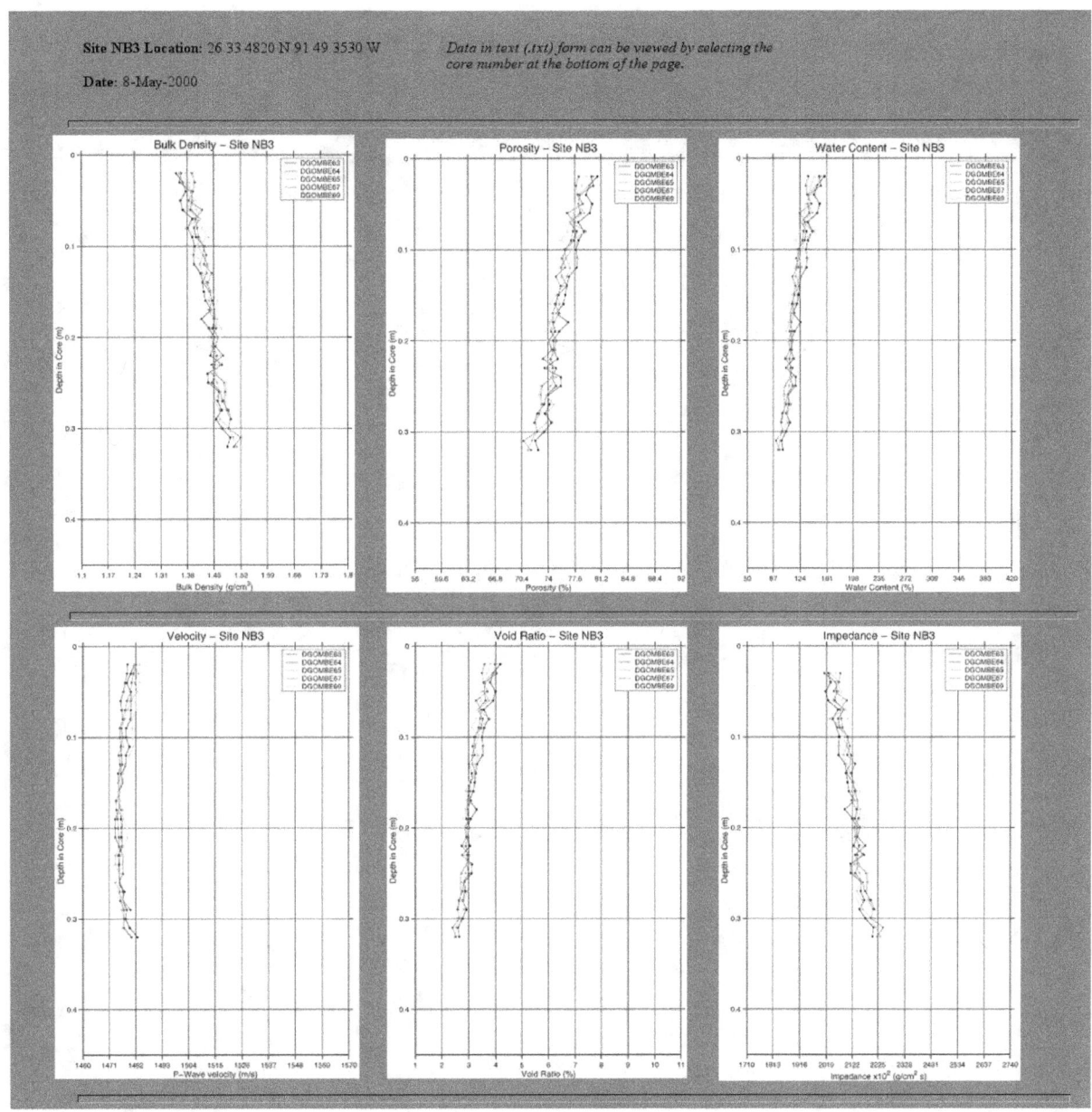

Figure 5.18. The sediment geotechnical properties of cores (5 replicates) taken at at the NB3 location. Note the compact arrangement of the various properties with depth in the core that indicate a uniformity of the sediment at location NB3.

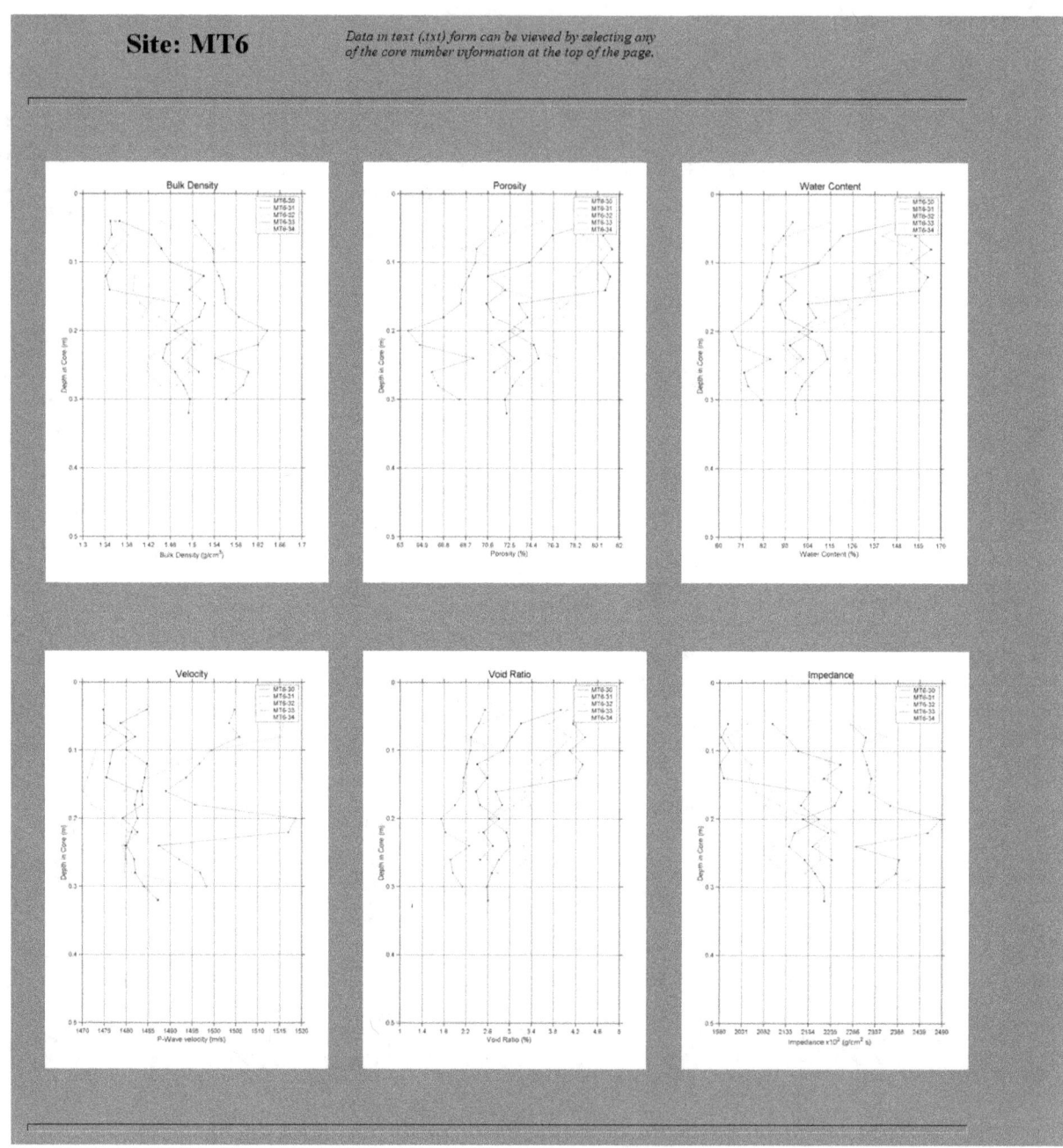

Figure 5.19. The sediment geotechnical properties of cores (5 replicates) taken at the MT6 location. Note the dispersed arrangement of the various properties with depth in the core that indicate a wide variety of sediment types at location MT6.

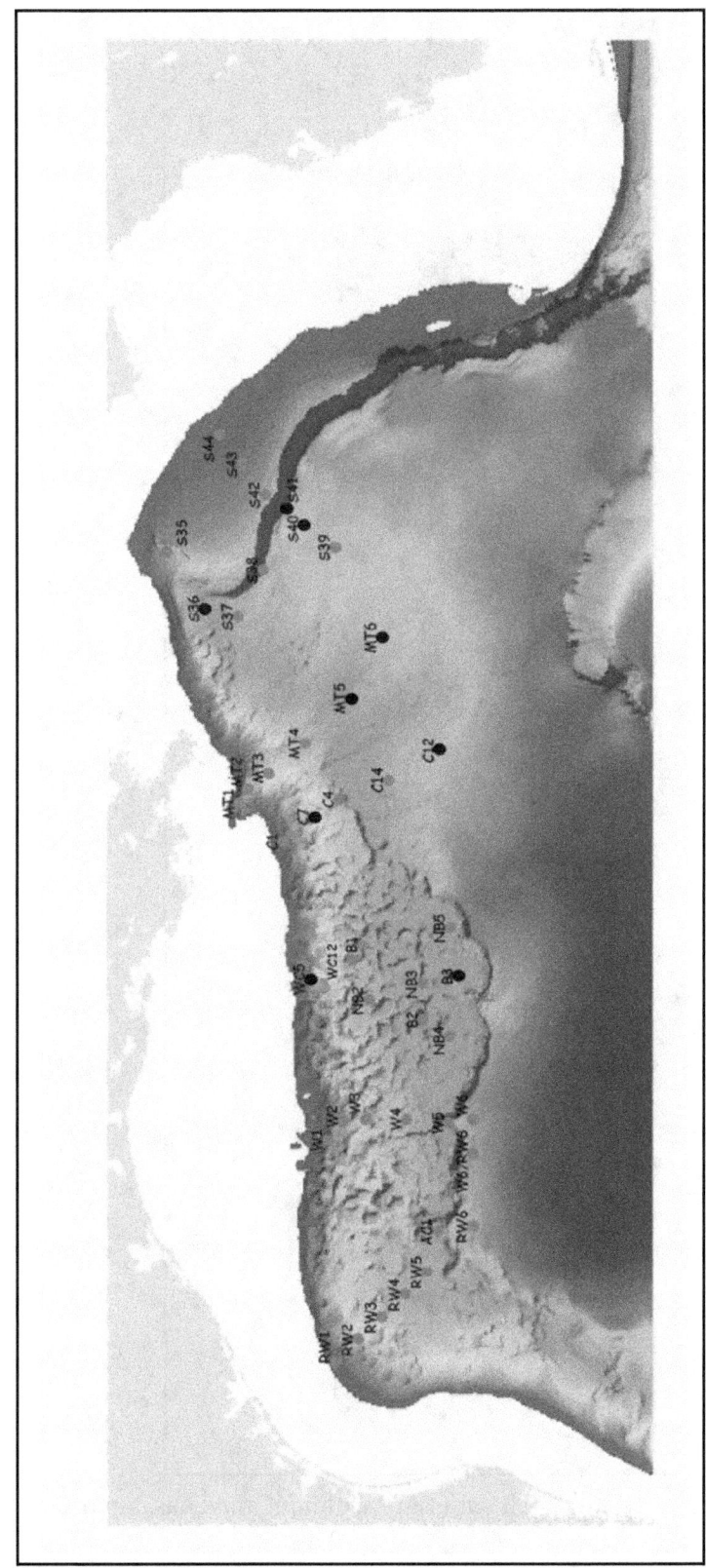

Figure 5.20. A map showing the locations of the stations that have highly variable geotechnical properties.

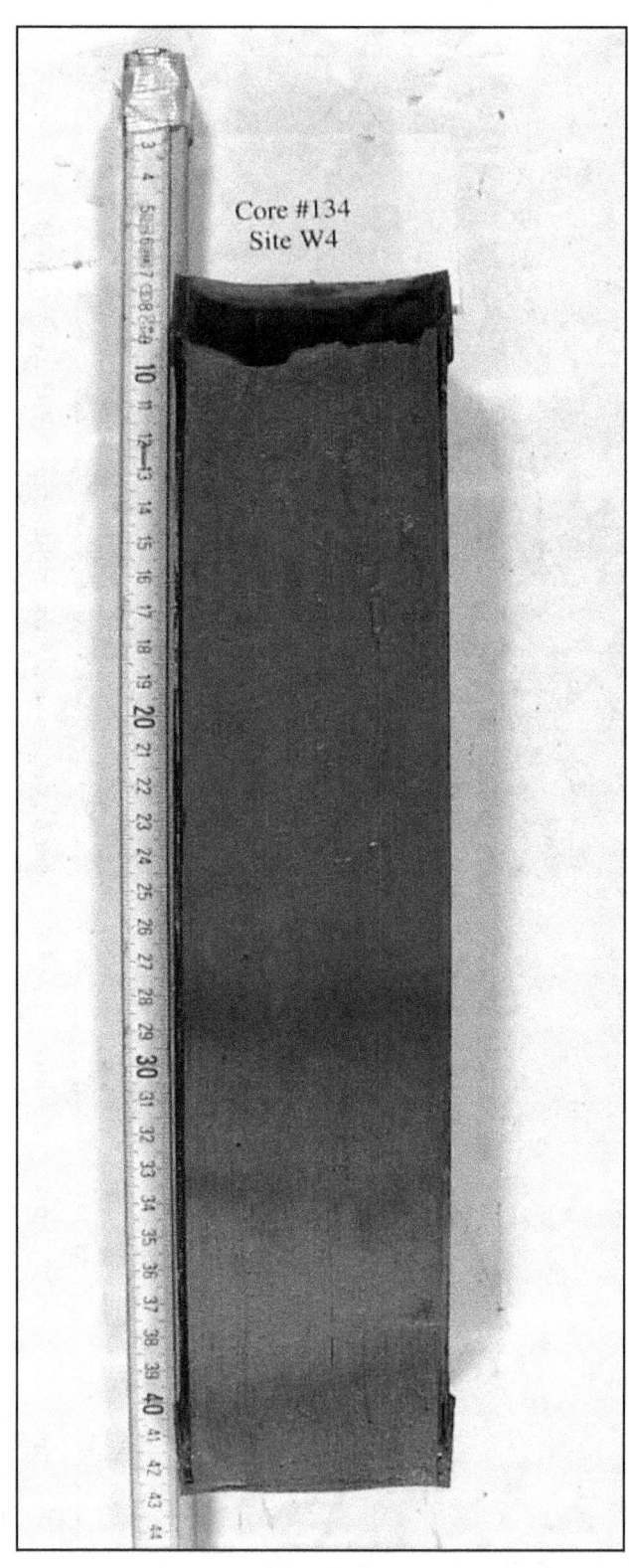

Figure 5.21. Boxcore 134 at station W4 illustrating sediment that has almost no sediment bioturbation.

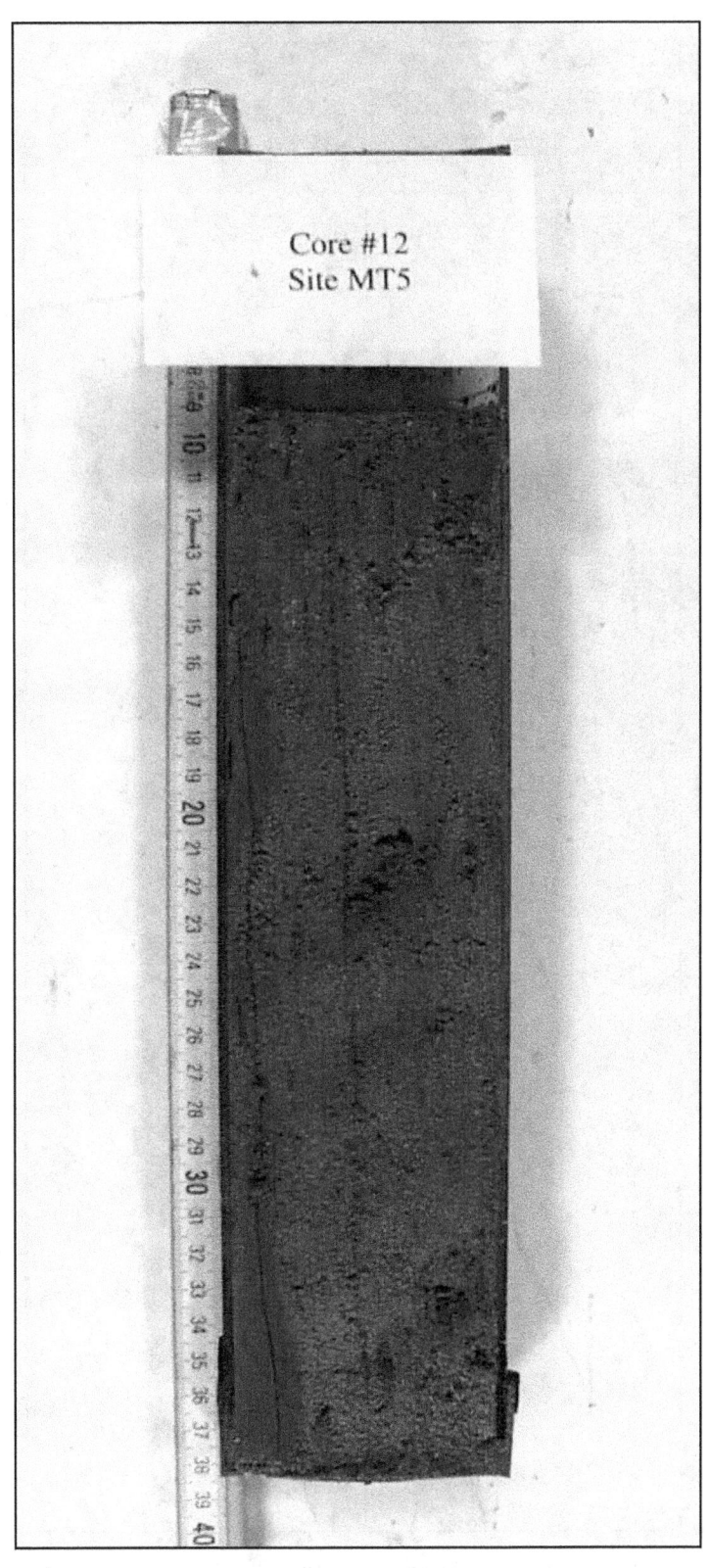

Figure 5.22. Boxcore 12 at station MT5 illustrating sediment that has undergone a slight to moderate degee of bioturbation.

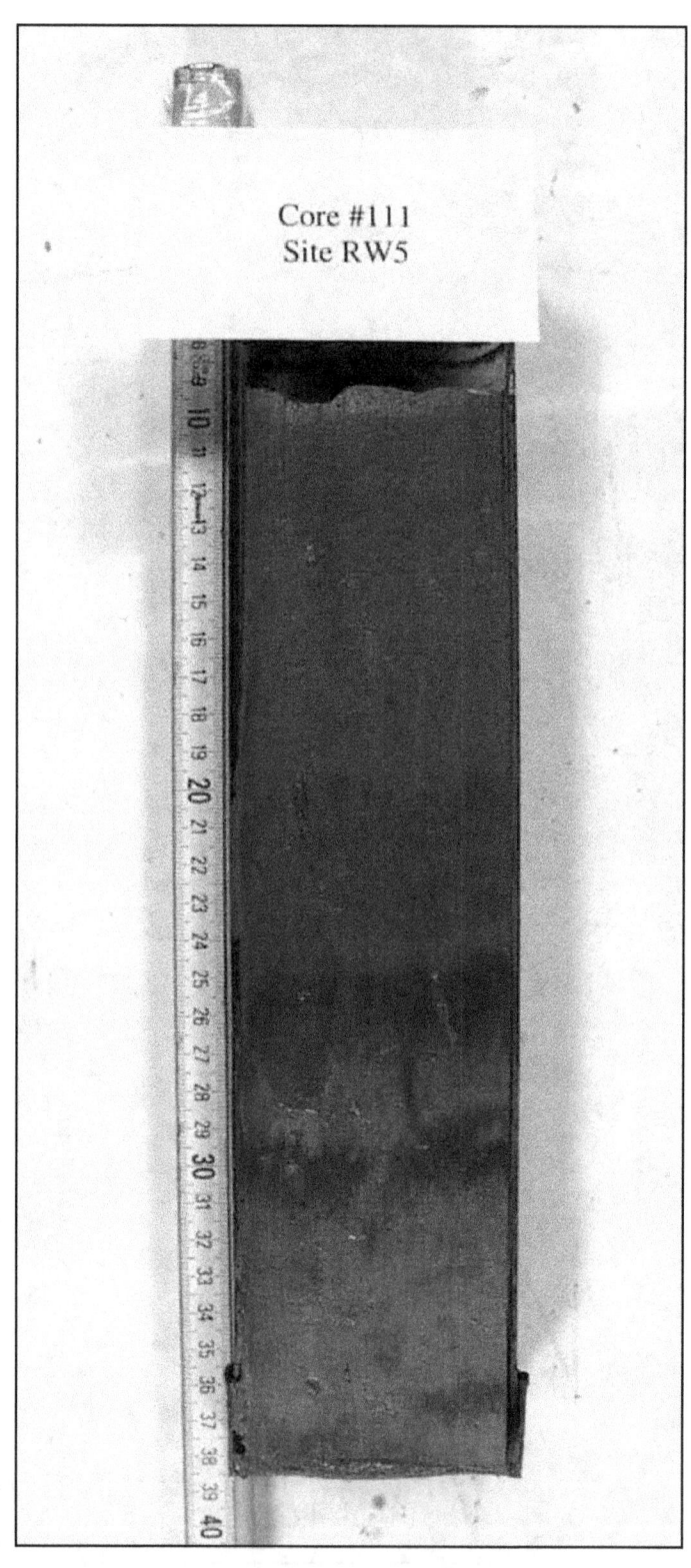

Figure 5.23. Boxcore 111 at station RW5 illustrating a high degree of bioturbation.

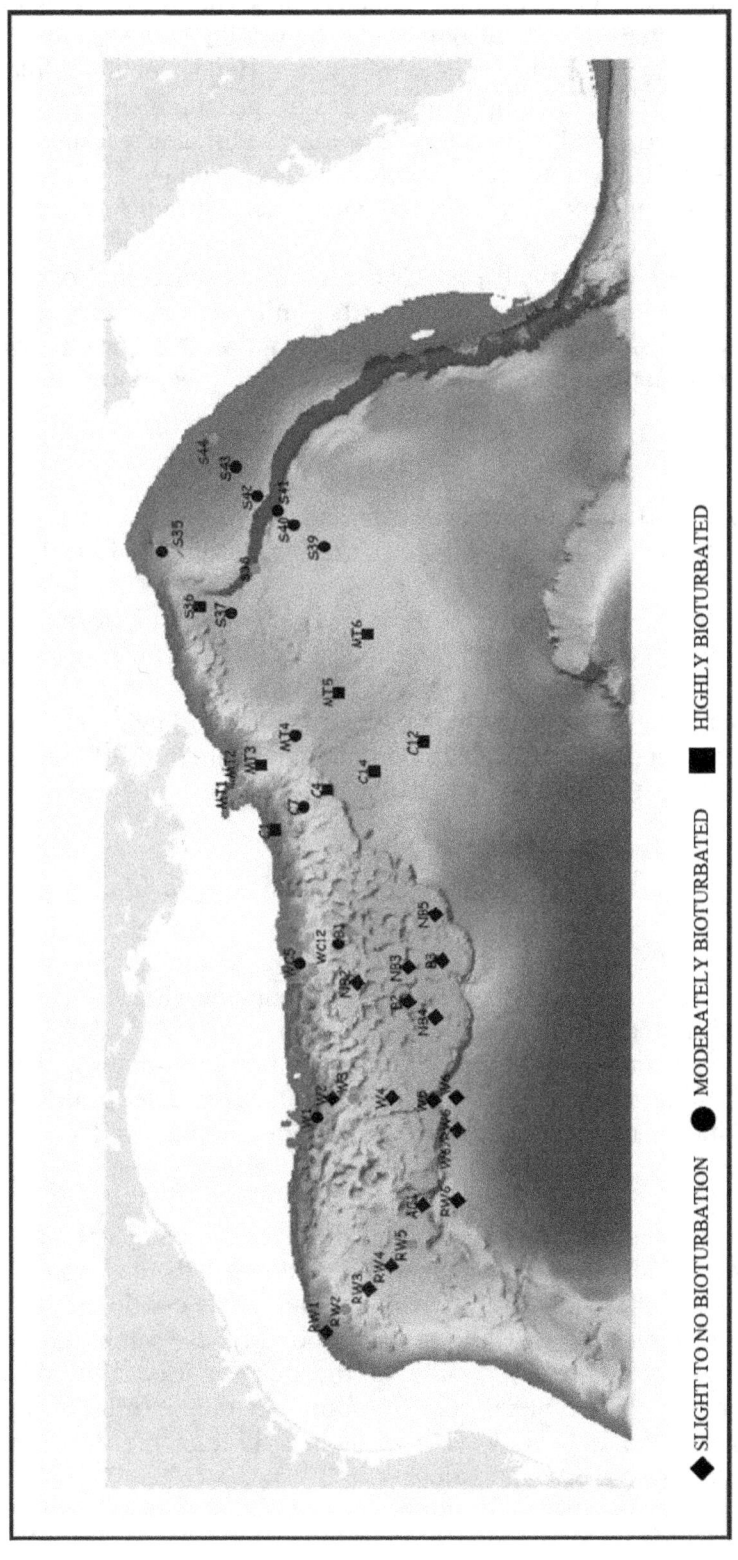

SLIGHT TO NO BIOTURBATION ◆   MODERATELY BIOTURBATED ●   HIGHLY BIOTURBATED ■

Figure 5.24. A map showing the degree of sediment bioturbation present at the survey sites.

At the survey sites selected metal and organic compounds were determined as an indication of the presence of natural and anthropogenic contaminants that might influence community ecology. Additionally, a limited number of pore water (e.g., SO_4^{2-}, DOC, nutrients) and solid phase (organic-C) bioreactive components are determined to estimate relative biologic activity. The process sites are subject to a more comprehensive set of measurements generally performed down core to provide depth profiles. Of special note are the additional measurements made with microelectrodes, sulfate reduction rate measurements using $^{35}SO_4^{2-}$, and determination of sediment accumulation and mixing rates based on a variety of radioisotopes.

All analyses associated with the survey sites from Cruise 1 have been completed. The analysis of samples from Cruise 2 are incomplete as of this report. Limited commentary will be offered on the results to date, however, it should be taken with the precaution that until the work is complete and more fully integrated with other components of the program it is preliminary.

5.3.4.1 Metals

Major and minor metal analyses of the surface sediment samples collected on the first DGoMB cruise (0-2 cm, N=43) have been completed. Much, but not all, of the analytical work on samples from the second cruise is also complete. Location maps show that some of the sampling sites are within areas with numerous offshore drilling and production platforms. This includes areas around sampling sites C1, MT1, 2, 3 and WC5. On the other hand, many of the sampling sites are many kilometers from present-day intensive petroleum development. It has been previously shown (Boothe and Presley 1989) that significant metal contamination of sediments by off-shore drilling and production is restricted to within a few hundreds of meters of platforms. Therefore it is not expect that sediments would be contaminated at the DGoMB stations.

For this study, elements were determined known to be major constituents of drilling fluids (Ba, Cr) as well as some of environmental concern which are antimony, arsenic, beryllium, cadmium, copper, lead, manganese, mercury, molybdenum, nickel, silver, tin, thallium, vanadium, and zinc. Metals were measured to assess if petroleum activities in the study area might affect the benthos. In addition, aluminum, calcium, iron and silicon were determined to facilitate recognition of sediment trace metal variations caused by natural (non-anthropogenic) differences in sediment texture and mineralogy. A total of 20 elements were determined in all sediment samples. Second cruise data for the elements which can be determined by INAA and ICP are complete and are given here. Data produced by GFAA will be available soon.

The data sets for the two cruises agree well in almost all cases with only a few differences of more that 10% between individual data points. This, along with the good spike recoveries and good results for analysis of standard reference materials gives confidence in the analytical results. Many of the trace elements were in low concentration in these samples, but all elements in almost all samples were above the detection limits of the methods used. Both Al and Fe were used for this report to normalize trace metal concentrations, as they exhibit a strong covariance. Trace metal concentrations that fall above a best fit line through the data are of interest, assuming that most of the data are background values.

Average concentrations of potential pollutant metals; Ag, Cd, Cu, Hg, Pb, and Zn; in the study area samples are similar to average crustal abundances and to average values for areas of the northern Gulf of Mexico thought to be low in pollutant metals. Average values may not, however, be the best way to evaluate this data because of the relatively small number of samples and the considerable variability in the data, some of which is due to the variable $CaCO_3$ content of the samples. It is better to compare the slope of a best fit line through the data for each element on an element versus Al or Fe scatter plot to that expected for Mississippi River Delta material. The Mississippi River is the most likely source of most of the silicate fraction of the sediments at the study sites.

When concentrations of several elements are plotted against Al (Figures 5.25 and 5.26), most data points not only lie near a best fit line but the line has almost the same slope as one drawn through data for Mississippi River Delta sediment. This is true for Be, Co, Cr, Fe, Si, Tl, V and Zn (plus K and Mg not reported here) which have positive slopes on the metal versus Al plots and for Ca and Sr (not reported here) which have negative slopes. Thus, for these metals there is no indication of additions from human activity. Rather, the metal concentrations in a particular sample are determined by the relative amounts of Mississippi River derived silicate material and plankton derived carbonate in the sediment. The picture is less clear for the other elements. Ni, Pb, Cd, As and especially Cu concentrations show more scatter on the metal versus Al plots than do the elements discussed above. Furthermore, the slopes suggest a general enrichment in these elements of 25 to 50% over Mississippi River derived material.

A few points on each of the metal vs Al plots are also far enough off the general trend line to suggest possible human influence. On the other hand, Mn concentrations are more variable and much more elevated over Mississippi Delta material than are those of any of the other elements. It is very unlikely that this Mn enrichment is due to human influence. Rather, it is due to remobilization of Mn from buried reduced sediment. The Mn then diffuses up through the sediment column and redeposits in near the surface sediment under oxidizing conditions. This phenomenon has been well documented for northern GOM sediments by Trefry and Presley (1982) and others.

Other metals have been shown to undergo the same diagenetic remobilization process that affects Mn (e.g., Presley et al. 1992) and it seems likely that this process is at work in the DGoMB area. The fact that there is not a good correlation between Ni, Pb, Cd and Cu concentrations and Mn does not mean that all have been unaffected by similar diagenetic processes. The situation is complicated by the intensity of reducing conditions, the relative amounts of available sulfide which would precipitate metals, and variable metal sulfide solubilities. In short, it seems likely that the somewhat anomalous Ni, Pb, Cd and Cu concentrations in the DGoMB area are due to natural diagenetic and transport processes rather than to human activity. In any case, all of the concentrations are well below levels that would be expected to have harmful effects on organisms.

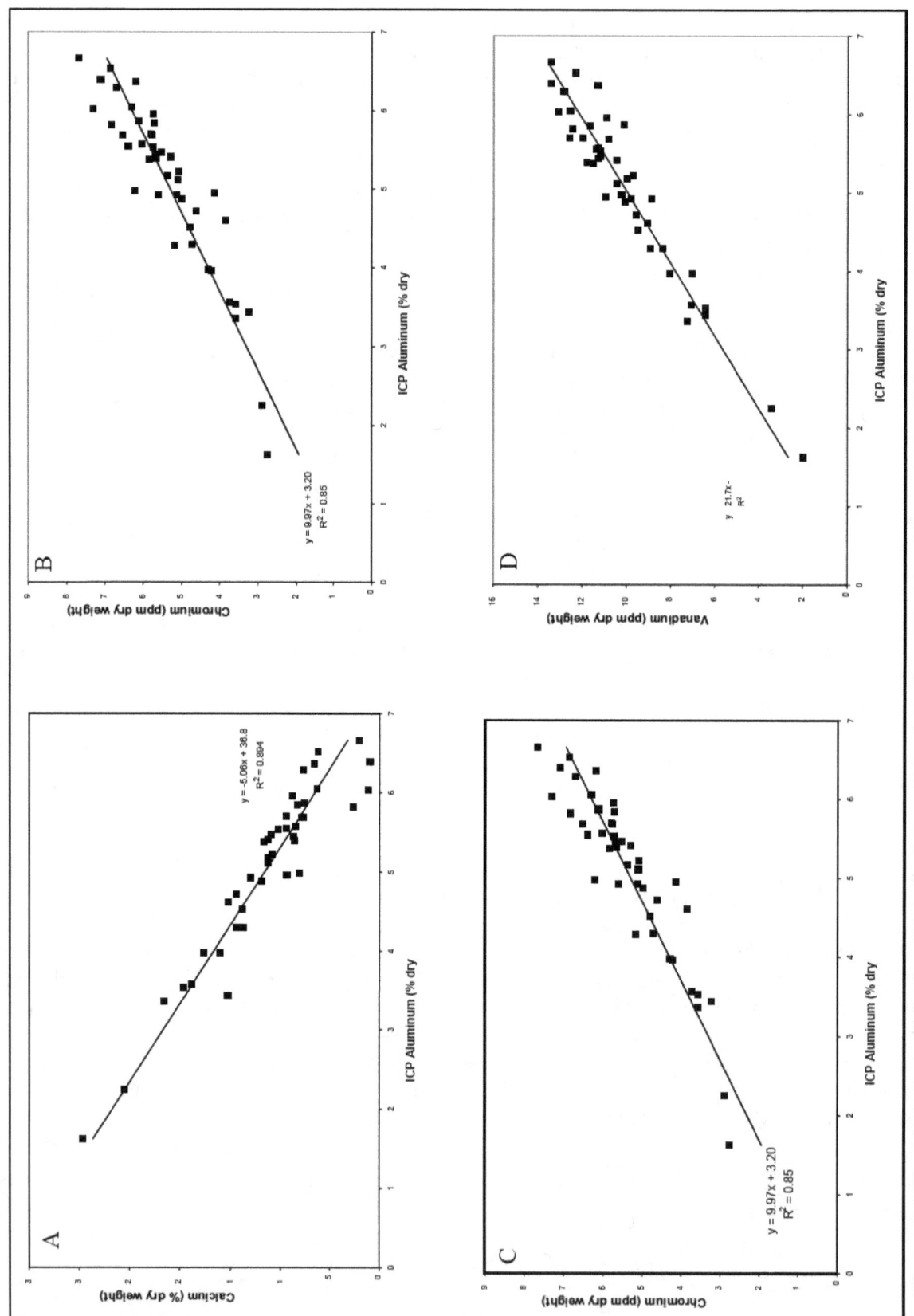

Figure 5.25. Variations in total sediment calcium (A), chromium (B), zinc (C), and vanadium (D) concentrations as a function of changes in sediment mineralogy (as indicated by sediment aluminum levels) measured by inductively coupled plasma spectrometer (ICP).

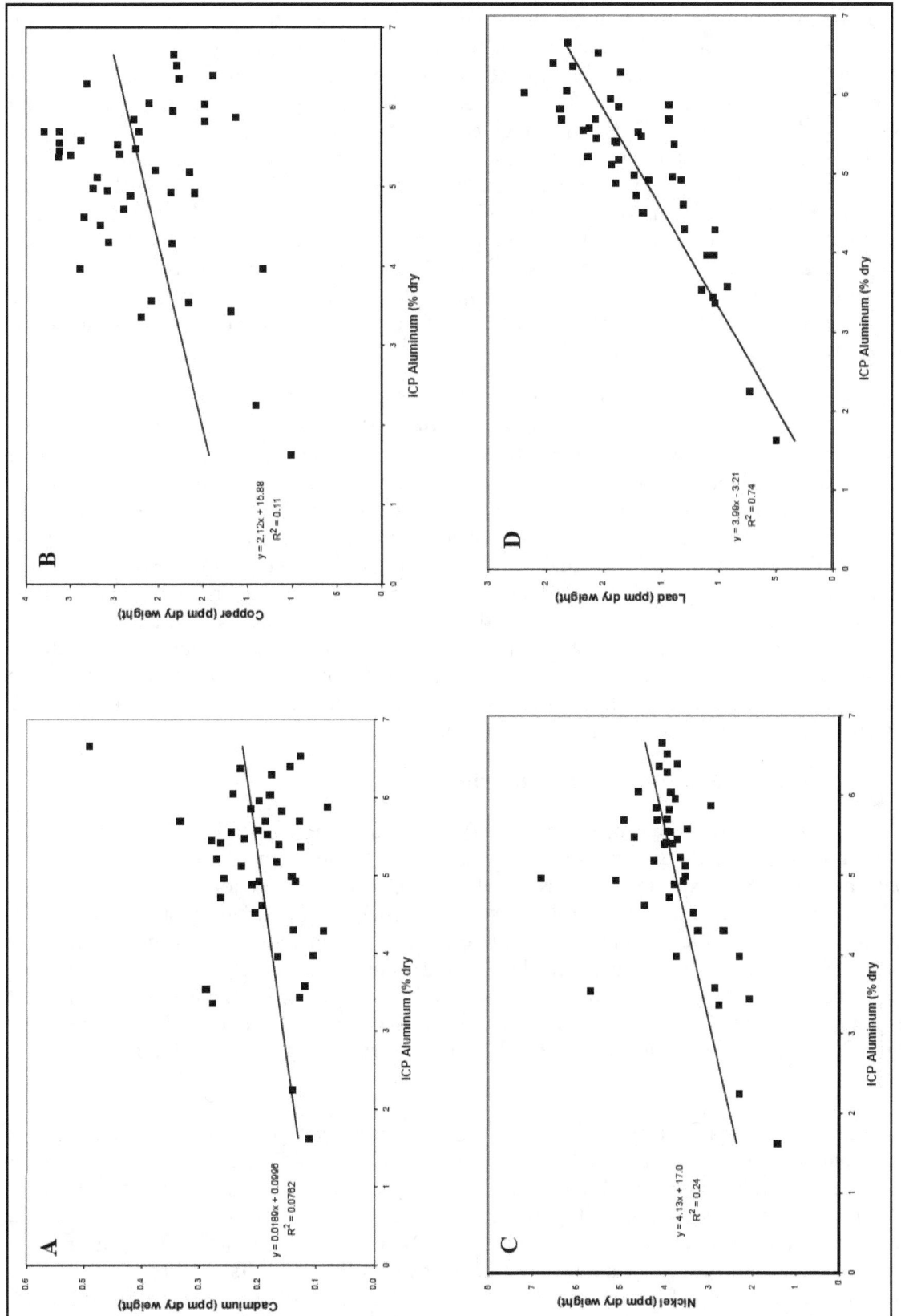

Figure 5.26.   Variations in total sediment cadmium (A), copper (B), nickel (C), and lead (D) concentrations as a function of changes in sediment mineralogy (as indicated by sediment aluminum levels).

In contrast to the elements discussed above, barium (Ba) shows a few values that are higher than those of average crustal material and average clay-rich sediments but are typical of near-platform sediments from the northern GOM. In the case of Ba, it seems likely that the enrichments, which are up to almost a factor of ten, are due to disposal of oil well drilling mud. Up to 90% of the dry weight of drilling muds can be Ba (Boothe and Presley 1985) so small amounts of mud could account for the Ba enrichments seen in the sediments. The Ba-enriched samples are from the three shallowest water sites in the Mississippi Trough (sites MT1, 2 and 3) and from site C1 and WC5 just to the west of these. All are in an area of intense petroleum exploration and development. Previous studies have found even greater enrichments of Ba near some drilling platforms in the northern Gulf of Mexico. Barium concentrations of tens of thousands of ppm have been found in many samples (e.g., Boothe and Presley, 1989). Even at the most Ba-enriched sites in the present study, the concentration is well below that thought to adversely affect organisms (e.g., Neff et al. 1969)

In summary, the samples analyzed for this project were a mixture of carbonate and terrigenous silicate materials and thus varied considerably in aluminum, calcium and iron concentrations. Trace metal concentrations also varied considerably, as would be expected with a varied mineralogy. Concentrations of the elements Al, Ca, Sr, Na, K, Mg, Be, Co, Hg, Cr, Ti, V, and Zn were as expected for coastal Gulf of Mexico sediments with equivalent Fe concentration. Copper, As, Cd, Pb, Ni and especially Mn concentrations were found to be somewhat higher than those in Mississippi Delta and shallow GOM samples but were not unexpectedly high considering the deeper water from which the present samples came. The enrichments are almost certainly due to complex natural transport and diagenetic processes, not to human activity. The strong Ba enrichments of up to almost a factor of ten in a few samples are almost certainly due to the presence of residues of oil well drilling muds discharged from the many drilling platforms in the area. Based on literature data, none of the metal concentrations in the study area sediments are high enough to adversely affect marine organisms.

5.3.4.2   Trace Organic Contaminants

Polynuclear aromatic hydrocarbons (PAH) are a major toxic component of petroleum. It is important to determine the sediment concentrations of PAH in order to see if they are present at levels that might be expected to cause biological effects. The major sources of PAH in offshore sediments include natural petroleum seepage, offshore production platform operations and spills. Previous studies around production platforms showed that sediments close to platforms (<500 m) contained discharged drilling muds and cuttings. Hydrocarbons, including PAH and trace metals (Ag, Ba, Cd, Hg, Pb, and Zn) contaminants, were associated with these coarse-grained sediments (Kennicutt et al. 1996). However, contaminant concentrations including PAHs close to platforms were below concentrations thought to induce biological responses.

Sediment samples collected on the shakedown cruise were analyzed for PAH. A total of five sediment samples were collected, four with the GOOMEX boxcorer and one with an USNEL spade corer. The total PAH concentrations ranged from 47 to 159 ng/g with a mean of 113 ng/g and a relative standard deviation of 37%. These total PAH concentrations are low. The PAH concentration in samples collected with the USNEL spade corer was 108 ng/g and was close to the mean indicating the sampler type does not bias PAH results. The relative standard deviation of 37% is expected for the combined effects of analytical uncertainty (~10%) and the natural inhomogeneity of sediments. These samples were collected at about 23.5 km (14.5 miles) southwest of Station W1 and 35.5 km (22 miles) west of Site W2. Samples collected at Site W2 had a total PAH concentration of 53 ng/g and W3 a concentration of 41 ng/g which is within or slightly below the lower end of the range of total PAH concentrations from the shakedown cruise.

A total of 43 sediment samples were analyzed for PAH from DGoMB Cruise 1. These samples represent 41 stations with two sampling sites (W6 and MT3) being analyzed in duplicate. Concentrations for total PAH ranged from not detected (ND) to 1032 ng/g with a mean of 128 ng/g and a median of 59 ng/g. There were only nine samples (21%) with total PAH concentrations above 130 ng/g and only four (9.3%) with concentrations above 400 ng/g. Two of the samples with concentrations in the highest range (OC-615, 1033 ng/g and OC-618, 404 ng/g) were collected from MT-3.

The concentration of perylene is depicted for the sampling sites in Figure 5.27. Perylene is a PAH produced by biological processes. Perylene is often detected as the major PAH in sediments from relatively pristine areas. In the sediment samples analyzed for this study, the percentage of perylene of total PAH ranged from 0 to 63%. Perylene concentrations ranged from ND (<1 ng/g) to 110 ng/g. Perylene is also produced from combustion or processing of fossil fuels (e.g., perylene is present in creosote made from the heating of coal). Due to its anthropogenic as well as biogenic origins, the total PAH data for this report is discussed both with and without perylene. Other PAH are predominantly from anthropogenic sources. The pattern of perylene concentrations (Figure 5.27) is not understood but it does not co-vary with the total PAH distribution.

The concentration of total PAH without perylene is depicted in Figure 5.28. Several sites had relatively high concentrations. These sites include MT1, MT3 (duplicate), C1, B1, and RW6. These sites, based on their PAH distribution, can be divided into two types of sites with PAH predominantly from oil and those with PAH predominantly from combustion sources. For sites MT3 (both), MT2, and B1, oil appears to be the major source of PAH. For RW6 and C1, combustion sources predominate. Combustion PAH in the sampling area may be discharged from ships or platforms (e.g. bilge pumping) or atmospheric deposition of PAH from onshore industrial areas. The ship/platform operations are the most likely sources as atmospheric deposition would be expected to produce similar PAH concentrations over large regions.

The total PAH concentration without perylene is plotted versus barium concentration in Figure 5.29. Most of the sites plot near the origin because they have low PAH and low barium concentrations. Five sites have high barium concentrations (MT2, MT1, MT3, C1, and WC5). Four of these sites also have high PAH concentrations [MT3 (duplicate), MT1 and C1]. Barium is a tracer of drilling muds from platform operations. The elevated barium and PAH at the MT1, MT2, MT3, and C1 sites are likely due to inputs from platform operations in the vicinity of these sites.

A frequency distribution for total PAH and total PAH without perylene concentrations are plotted versus cumulative percentage (Figure 5.30). The concentrations are plotted on a log scale. It is apparent that the distributions are similar "S" shaped curves. The addition of perylene causes a slight increase in concentrations over the entire range. The median concentration for total   PAH

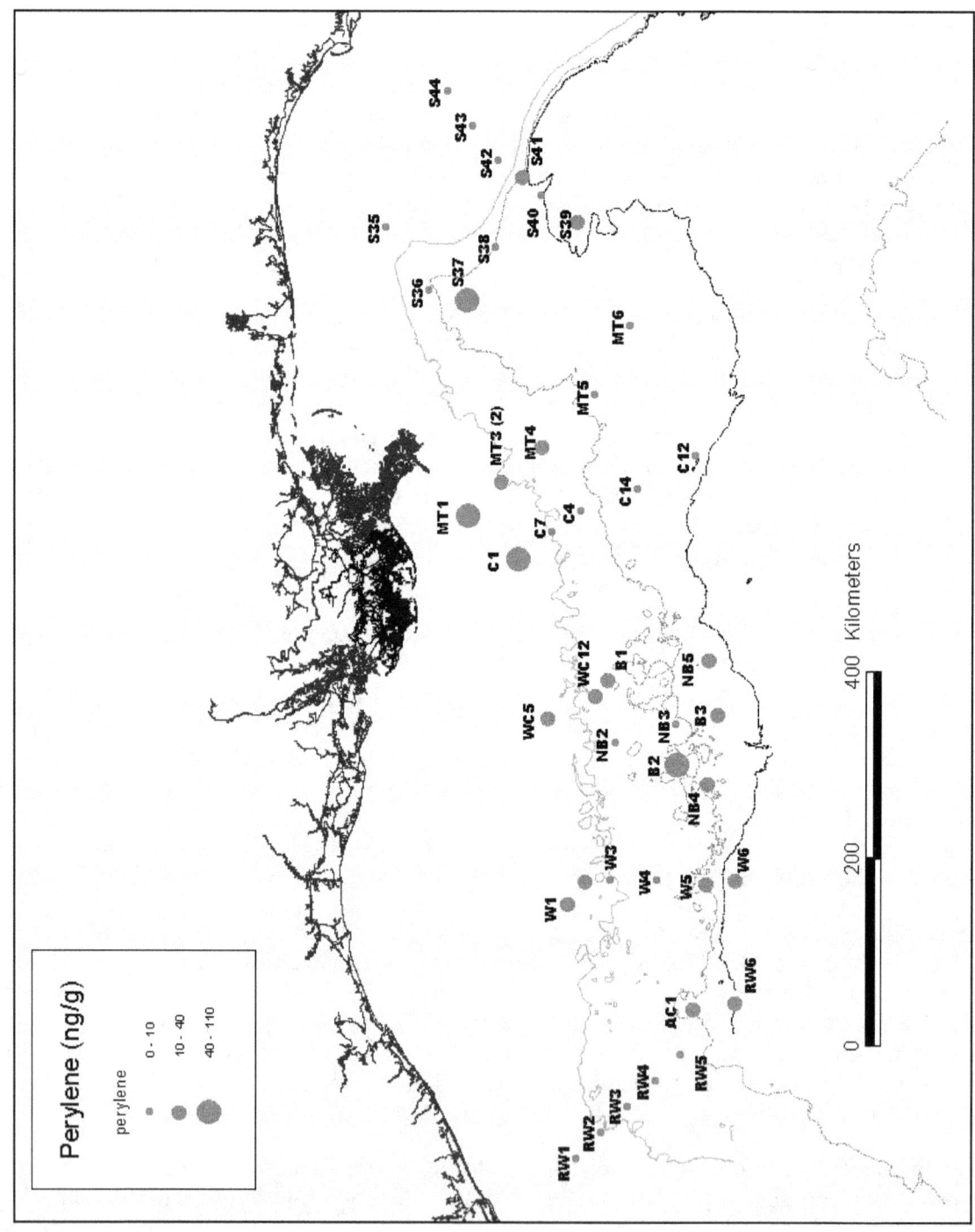

Figure 5.27. The concentration of perylene in sediments.

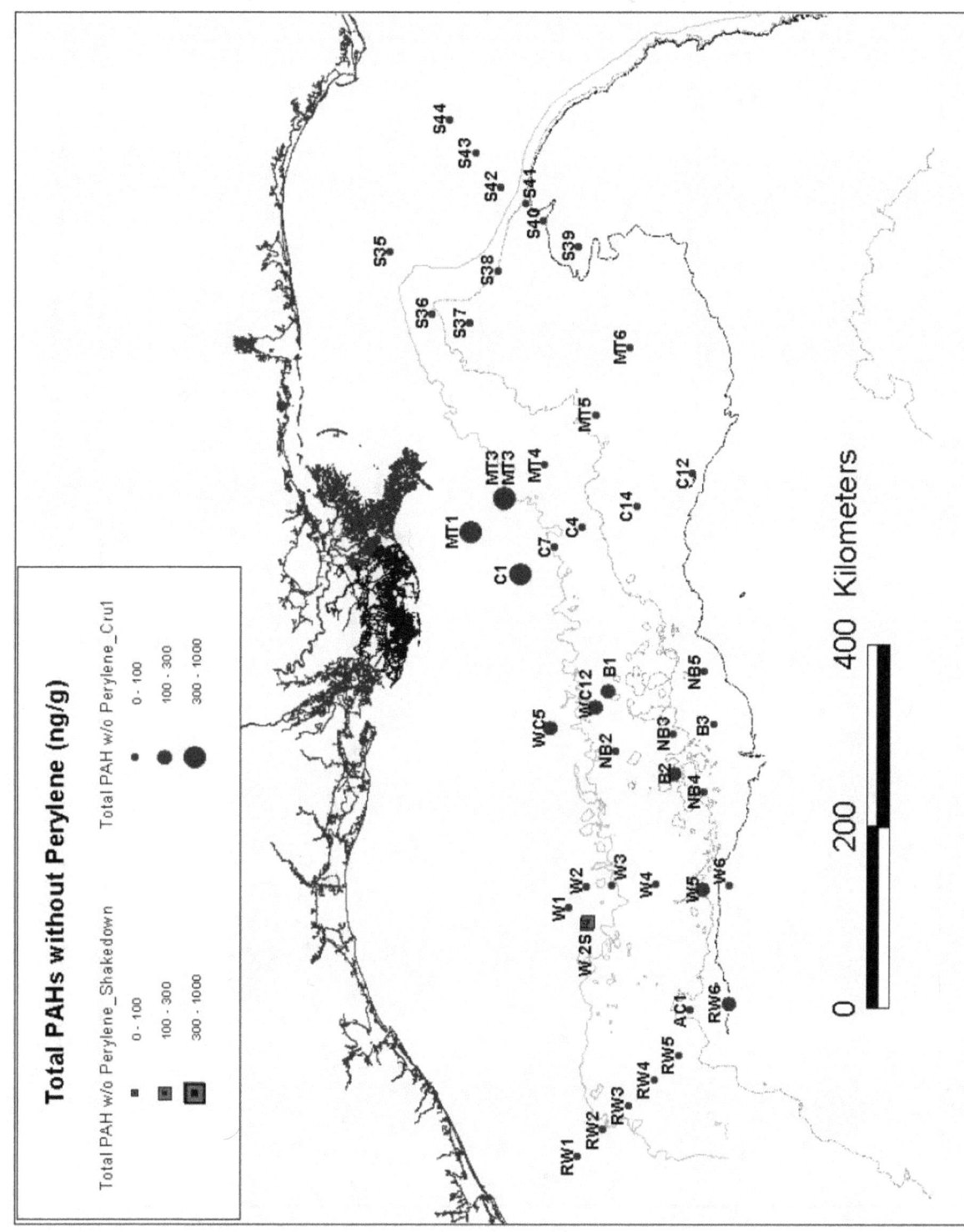

Figure 5.28. The concentration of total polycyclic aromatic hydrocarbons (PAH) without perylene in sediments.

5-41

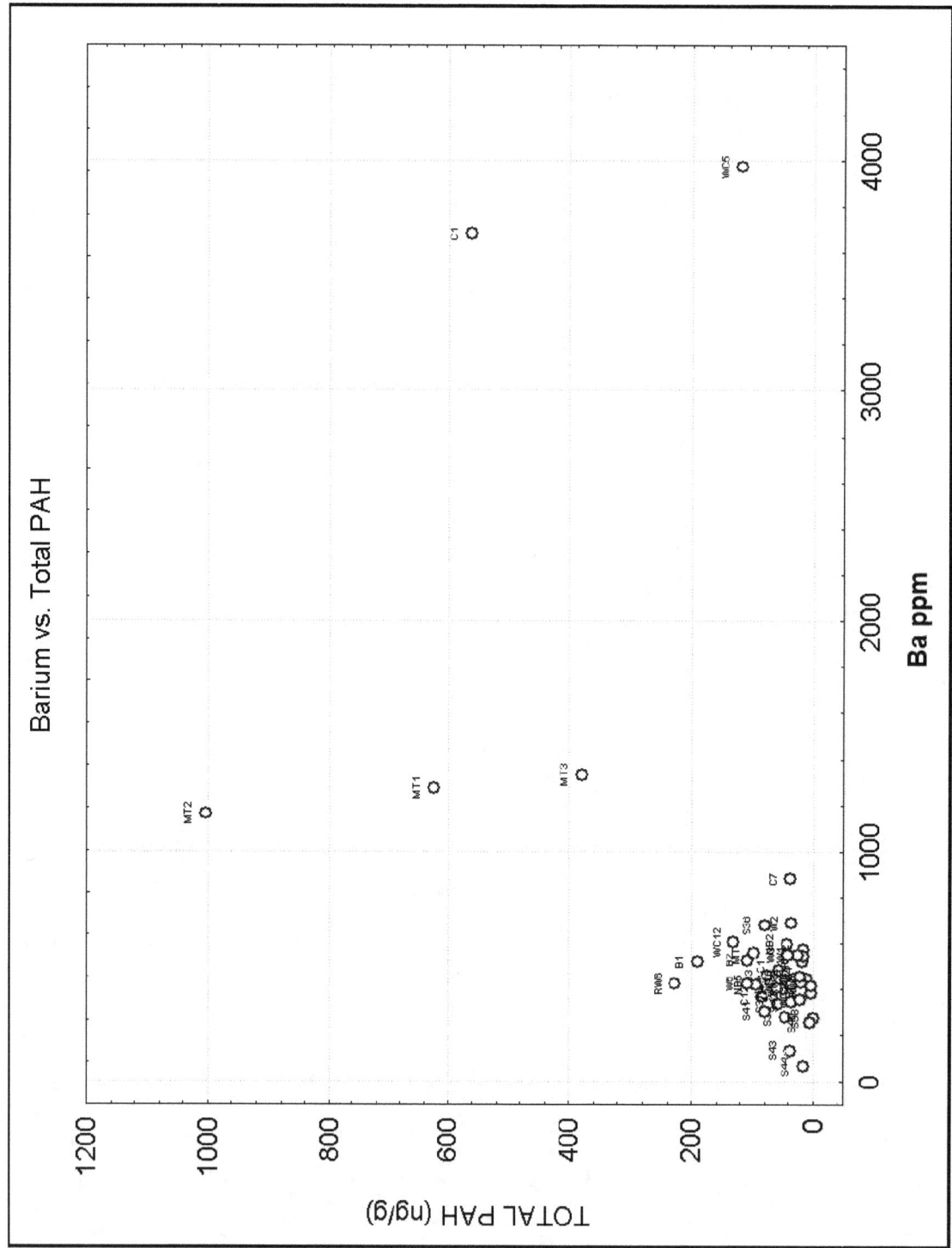

Figure 5.29. The total PAH concentration without perylene versus barium concentration.

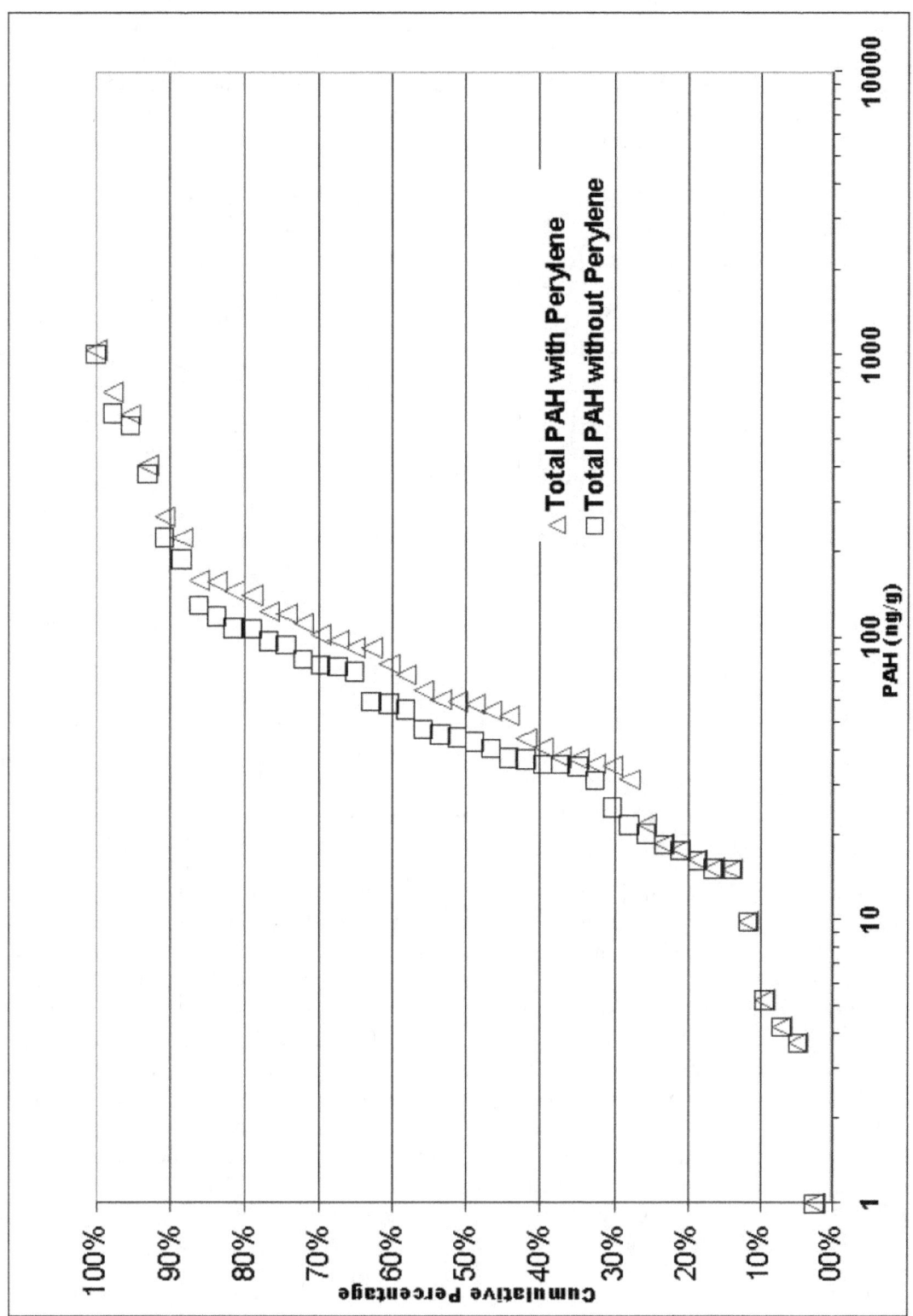

Figure 5.30. Frequency distribution of total PAH and total PAH without perylene concentrations versus cumulative percentage.

is 59 ng/g and for total PAH without perylene is 45 ng/g. This indicates the relative importance of perylene, especially at low concentrations. Similar frequency distributions for total PAH were reported for the GOOMEX program (Kennicutt et al. 1996) and the cumulative curves had similar shapes. The concentrations of PAH found in close proximity to production platforms ranged from 10 to 6400 ng/g with the highest concentrations close to the platforms. However, most concentrations were less than 1000 ng/g (Kennicutt et al. 1996). The frequency distribution for total PAH for the GOOMEX study (Kennicutt et al. 1996) is similar to the distribution found here with the exception of the few concentrations that exceeded 1000 ng/g in this study. When the frequency distributions found in this study are compared to those for nearshore studies (NOAA NS&T and EPA-EMAP-NC), the median PAH concentrations for this study is lower by about a factor of four. Total sediment PAH concentrations greater than 4000 ng/g are expected to elicit a biological effect 10% of the time (Long and Morgan 1990). The highest total PAH concentration found in sediments from this study (1032 ng/g) is four times less than the biological effects level. Therefore, it is unlikely that the PAH at any of these sites are having a major effect on the associated biota.

In summary, concentrations of PAH measured for the DGoMB project from offshore Gulf of Mexico sites are low, as expected. Perylene, a PAH with a biogenic source, is the major PAH detected at many locations. Four sites that have high PAH concentrations [MT3 (duplicate), MT1 and C1] also have high barium concentrations. This indicates that drilling operations in the vicinity of these sites is a likely source of PAH. Total sediment PAH concentrations all sites were less than 1040 ng/g. It is unlikely that the PAH concentrations found at any of these sites would have a major adverse effect on the biota living in these sediments.

5.3.4.3   Biogeochemistry

Survey samples from DGoMB Cruise 1 have been completed, but survey samples from the Cruise 2 are only partially processed at this time. The geochemical data from Cruise 1 has been provided to the central DGoMB database. Discussion will be limited to issues arising from the data that are of specific interest to the assessment of future sites and parameters to be studied in the "experimental" phase of the program.

Approximately one-third of the sites exhibited clear (>~4%) sulfate reduction, with a few sites showing extensive sulfate reduction. Unlike most sulfidic sediments, there were not accompanying elevated concentrations in other bioreactive components such as nutrients, DOC and organic-C. This raises the question as to why no readily apparent correlation exists among these chemical components. One speculative possibility is that normal infalling particulate organic carbon from overlying waters is not the dominant source of metabolizable organic matter at these sites. This area is well known for its hydrocarbon seeps that may locally form the basis of the food web for benthic communities at these sites (e.g., MMS CHEMO program). The biologic oxidation of hydrocarbon gases does not contribute dissolved nutrients. Also, their presence may not significantly contribute to total organic or dissolved organic carbon pools. It is recommended that future studies add measurements of hydrocarbon gases such as methane to the program to test this hypothesis as it could be important in determining the distribution and composition of benthic communities.

In only one sample (MT3) was the weight percent calcium carbonate relatively low (6%). In most other samples it ranged between 20% to 60%. It is interesting that there is no readily apparent pattern in the geographic distribution of calcium carbonate. This calls into question the hypothesis that there could be an east to west influence of sedimentary carbonate on benthic community structure. A possible explanation for the observation is that the carbonate is primarily derived from pelagic sources such as forminifera that are relatively evenly distributed.

Differences in mean concentrations were observed for silicate, nitrite, ammonia and urea, but averages were surprisingly constant for nitrate and phosphate (Figure 5.31a,b,c). DOC mean concentrations were also variable, but standard deviations were high. Isotopic ratios of DIC were similar at all stations except MT3.

5.3.4.4   Geochemical Processes

Results indicating the highest possible sulfate reduction rates are based on estimates, so they should be taken with extreme caution. At all stations, sulfate reduction rates were low but fall within the expected range as noted by a previous study of ~100 mmol/m^2*day (Lin and Morse 1991). S36 shows the highest rates at 132 mmol/m^2*day, while MT3 and MT6 were close to each other at 63 and 59 mmol/m^2*day respectively, and finally S42 was at 35 mmol/m^2*day.

Microelectrode cores measurements were also made at the processes stations and the data are now complete. At site MT3 a good profile was obtained with strong evidence of manganese reduction (Figure 5.32). Profiles were measured every 2 mm from water-sediment interface to 2 cm, then measured every 5 mm to 15 cm sediment depth. Values for pH were similarly profiled with typical values around 8.0. Oxygen concentrations were depleted to zero soon below the water-sediment interface. After oxygen disappears, manganese and sulfide concentrations begin to increase. Highest manganese concentrations occurred at depths of 3-8 cm. After 8 cm, manganese concentrations decrease indicating a possible layer change. No iron was detected throughout the core. At site MT6 oxygen concentrations were significantly higher in both the water column and in sediment porewaters. Oxygen was present to 8 cm in the core. This was a result of the top 2-3 cm being high in water content. The oxygen may have oxidized any reduced manganese or iron present in the core. Sulfide concentrations however co-existed with oxygen for part of the profile. A possible explanation presumes that bacterial respiration rates for sulfate reduction must have been faster than the rate of sulfide oxidation. Sulfide values were very low, and sulfide appeared around 2.5 cm. At site S36 oxygen concentrations penetrated to a depth of around 4 cm. There was slight overlap between sulfide and oxygen concentrations. The profile was similar to MT6, however, there was a small increase in sulfide concentrations between 4 and 7 cm depth. Even the highest sulfide concentrations were low, averaging around 2μM. No iron or manganese was detected. Site S42 was profiled with success and characterized by deeper oxygen penetration depths and low sulfide concentrations (>2.0 μM). Oxygen penetrated to about 3 cm, where low sulfide concentrations began to occur. This site appeared similar to the other sites. No iron or manganese was detected here either. pH was profiled using a Cole-Parmer semi-microelectrode. Hansson's buffer was used to calibrate the electrode at around 8.3. The sediment may have had adverse effects on the electrode, creating inaccurate readings. A side experiment was performed using squeezed porewater to measure pH as opposed to sediment porewater profiling.

Analyses of nutrients, dissolved organic carbon (DOC) and dissolved inorganic carbon (DIC) isotope ratios (δ^{13}C) at process stations have been completed, but DIC concentration and elemental analyses of sediments are yet to be completed. Site MT3 was most active, showing

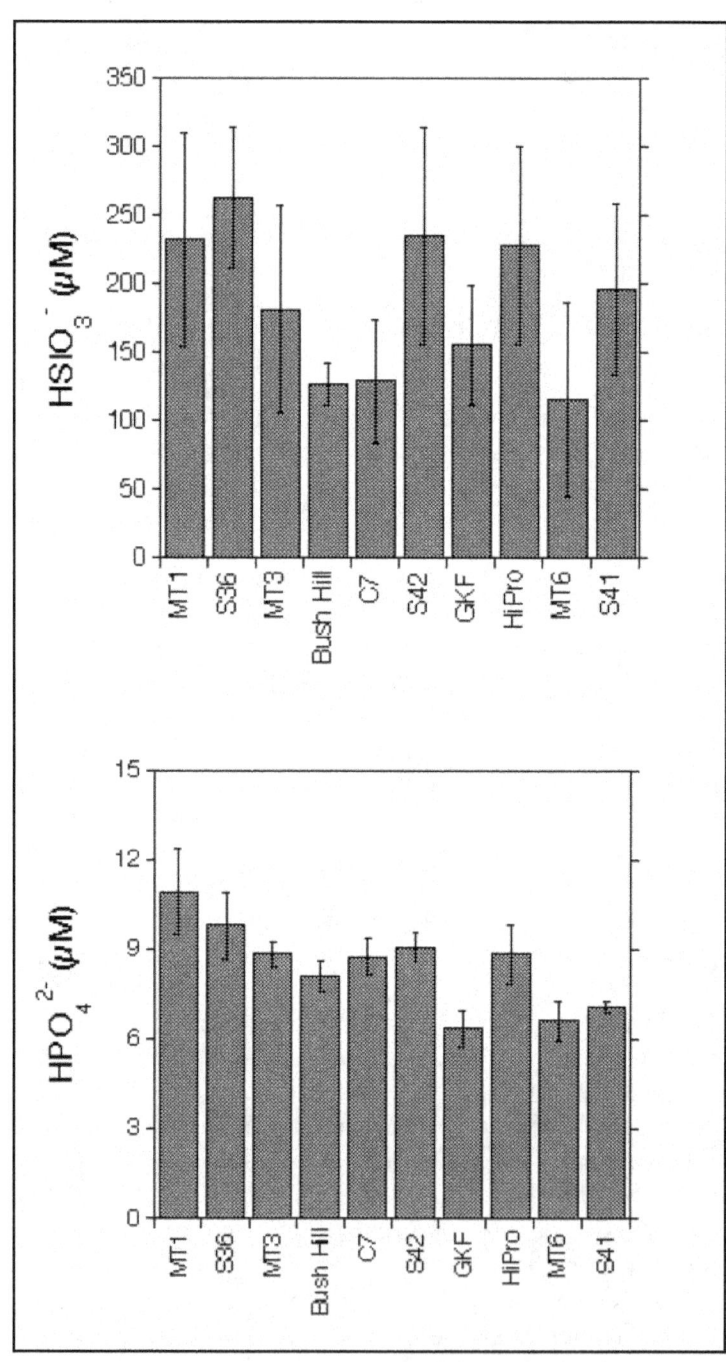

Figure 5.31a. Mean HSiO$_3^-$ and HPO$_4^{2-}$ (μM) concentrations at survey stations (see Figure 4.1 for station locations).

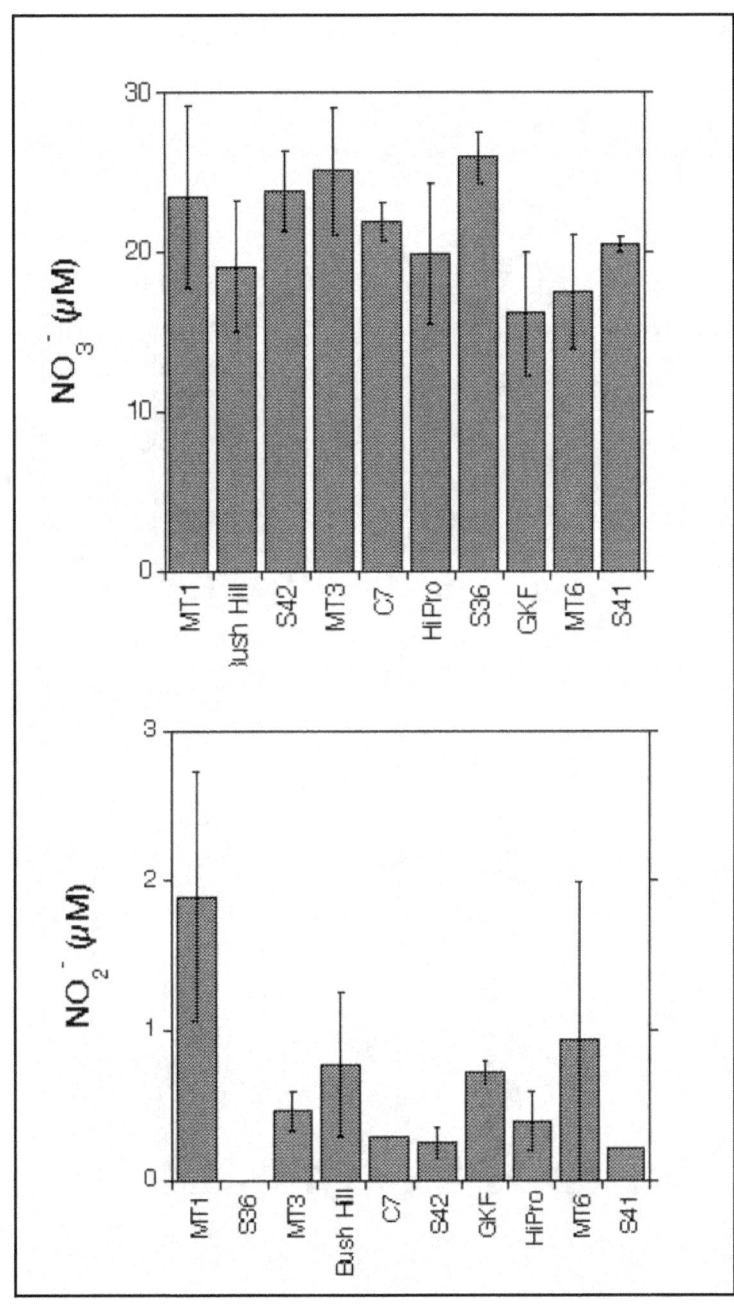

Figure 5.31b. Mean NO_3^- and NO_2^- (μM) concentrations at survey stations (see Figure 4.1 for station locations).

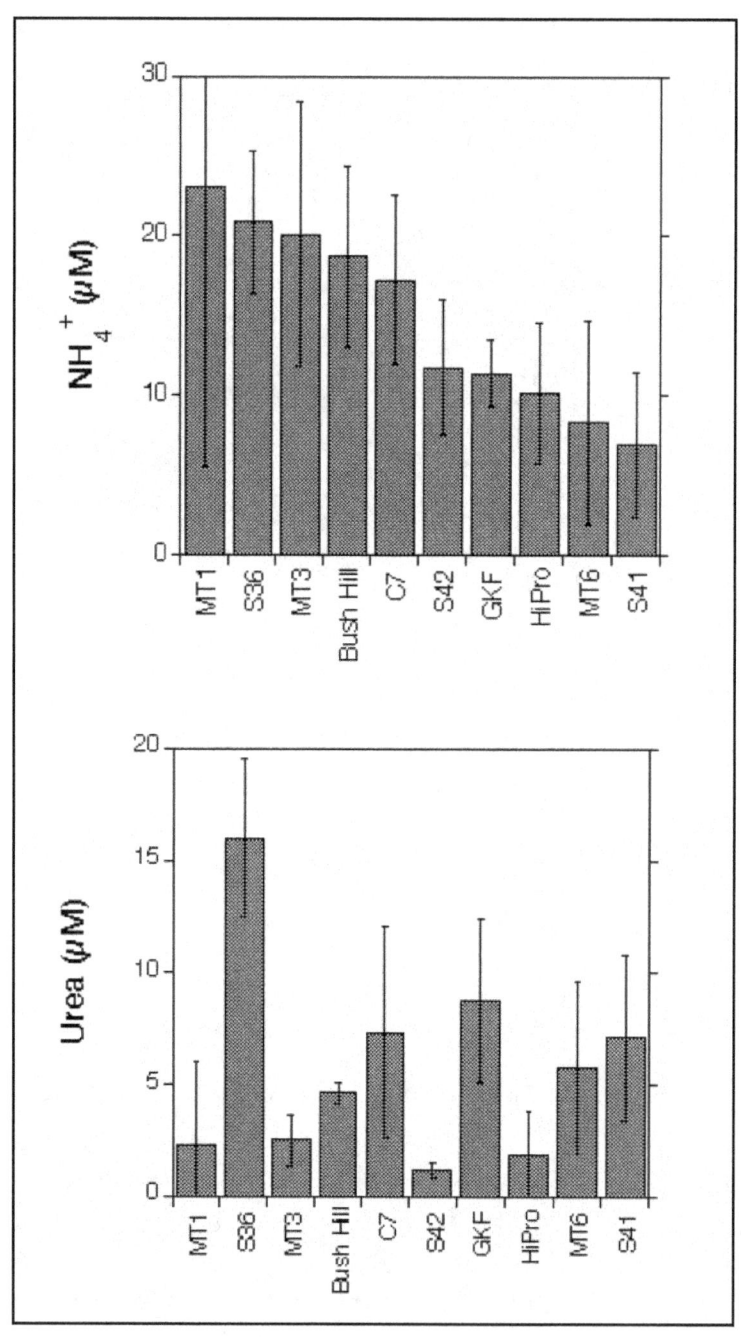

Figure 5.31c. Mean NH_4^+ and urea (μM) concentrations at survey stations (see Figure 4.1 for station locations.

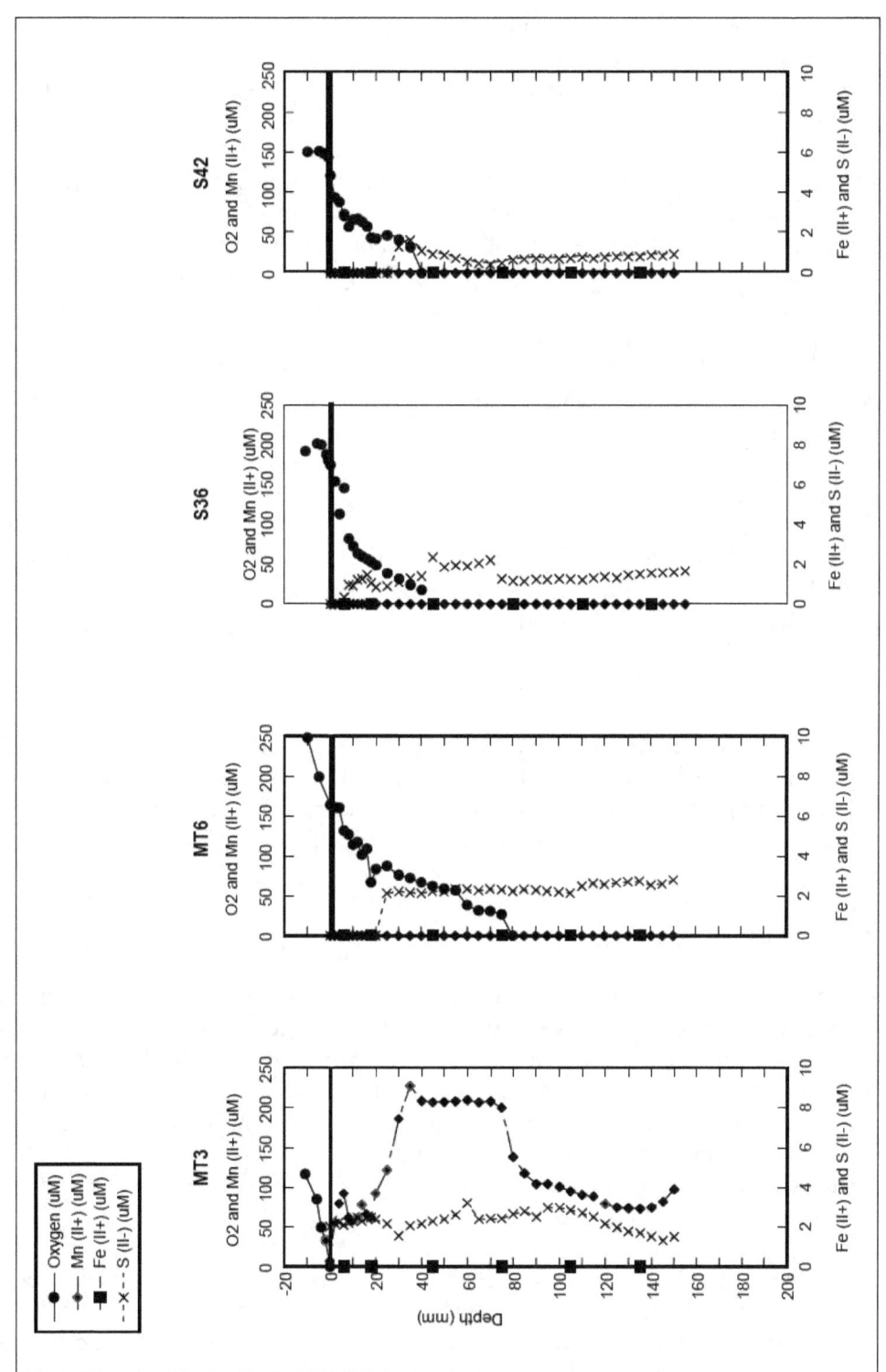

Figure 5.32. Depth-concentration profiles for DGoMB process stations (see Figure 4.2 for station locations).

strong trends with depth, particularly for phosphate, ammonium and urea (Figure 5.33). Depth profiles for DOC were similar at all sites, but evidence for mineralization of organic matter was provided by the $\delta^{13}C$ of DIC at stations MT3 and MT6 (Figures 5.34a,b,c and 5.35). The ^{13}C-depleted value measured at station S42 may be an outlier. Finally, comparison of total inorganic nitrogen (TIN) and phosphate with the expected slope of 16:1 suggests loss of nitrogen to denitrification (Figure 5.36).

The radiochemistry group is processing the radiochemical samples. Four sediment cores were thawed in the laboratory, sectioned at 0.5 cm intervals down to 4 cm, at 1 cm intervals down to 20 cm at 1 cm intervals, and below that, at 2 cm intervals. All samples were initially weighed, dried, then reweighed, in order to calculate the porosity of the sediments. Preliminary gamma counting results for ^{210}Pb, ^{226}Ra, ^{7}Be, ^{137}Cs, and ^{234}Th are available. ^{210}Pb have been alpha counted using a method that yields more accurate results. ^{137}Cs and ^{7}Be activities were low in all the samples and will not yield useful results. $^{210}Pb_{xs}$ profiles are produced by sedimentation and mixing, and require an independent mixing tracer to derive sedimentation rates. Profiles of $^{239,240}Pu$ will be required, since ^{137}Cs activities are too low. $^{239,240}Pu$ analyses are in progress.

Preliminary results indicate mixing depths varying from 1 to 6 cm. The extent of excess-^{210}Pb ($^{210}Pb_{xs}$) penetration into surface sediments (Table 5.4) also varies over an order of magnitude, ranging from 2 to 18 cm for the four stations. This layer, which contains sediments which had accumulated or have been mixed downward over the past century or so roughly coincides with a layer of the greatest porosity gradient.

5.3.5   Biological Studies

All size categories of the sediment-associated biota were sampled on Cruises 1 and 2. These included 1) microbiota, 2) meiofauna, 3) macrofauna, 4) megafauna and 5) demersal fishes. Each fraction was fixed and labeled aboard ship as described above and distributed to respective PI's immediately at the end of the cruise. Analyses of the biological samples are continuing.

5.3.5.1   Microbiota

The bacterial component of the overall project includes assessments of benthic bacterial abundance throughout the study region (survey stations) and benthic bacterial biovolume at selected stations (to convert abundance to biomass in a region-specific manner, rather than using published conversion values). Procedures for determining bacterial abundance and biomass rely on established methods in epifluorescence microscopy in all cases. Microscopic methodologies have been consistent between sampling Cruises in 2000 and 2001, and will be continued in the future, so that the results can be easily compared not only on spatial scales, between stations, but also on temporal scales, between sampling efforts.

Deviations from the original plan include a change in the method for assessing bacterial production. The use of ^{14}C-labeled amino acids was proposed to estimate the rates of bacterial carbon incorporation (biomass maintenance and increase, an indirect measurement of production) and respiration (loss as CO_2) in the presence of labile or readily consumable organic substrates.

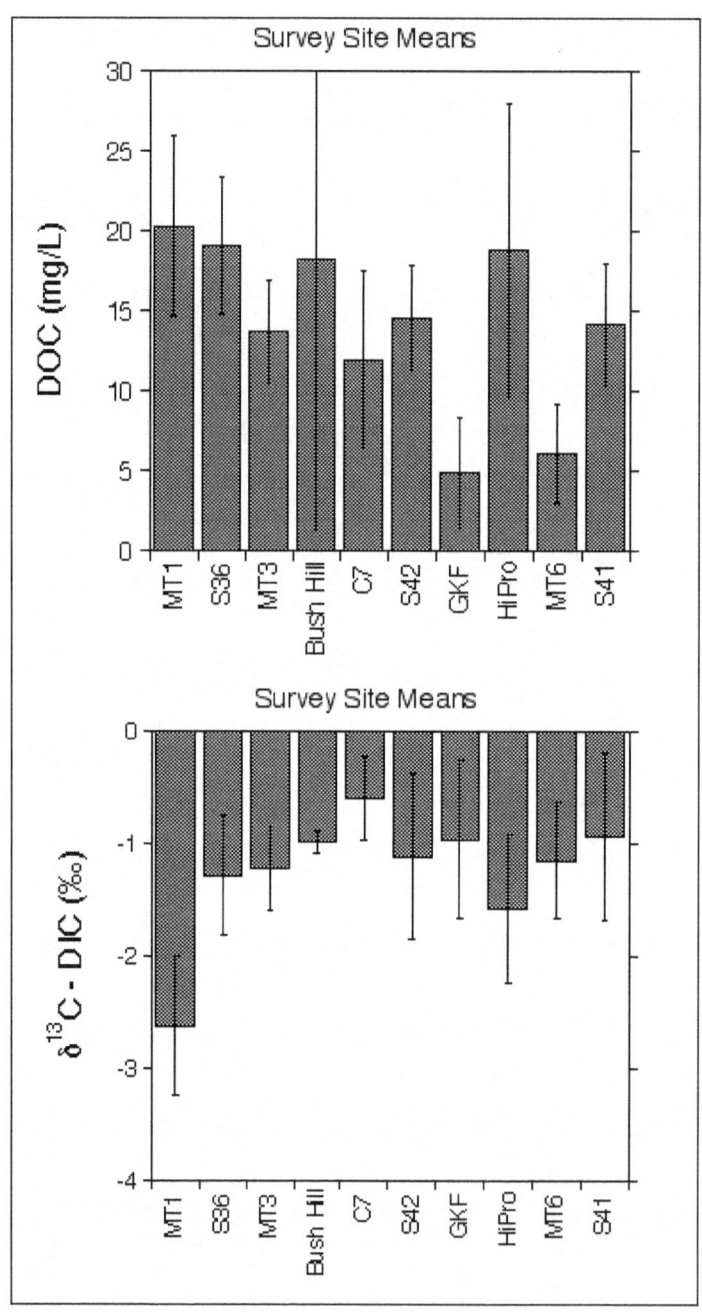

Figure 5.33.   Mean DOC concentrations (mg/L) and DIC stable carbon isotope isotope (‰) values at process stations (see Figure 4.2 for station locations).

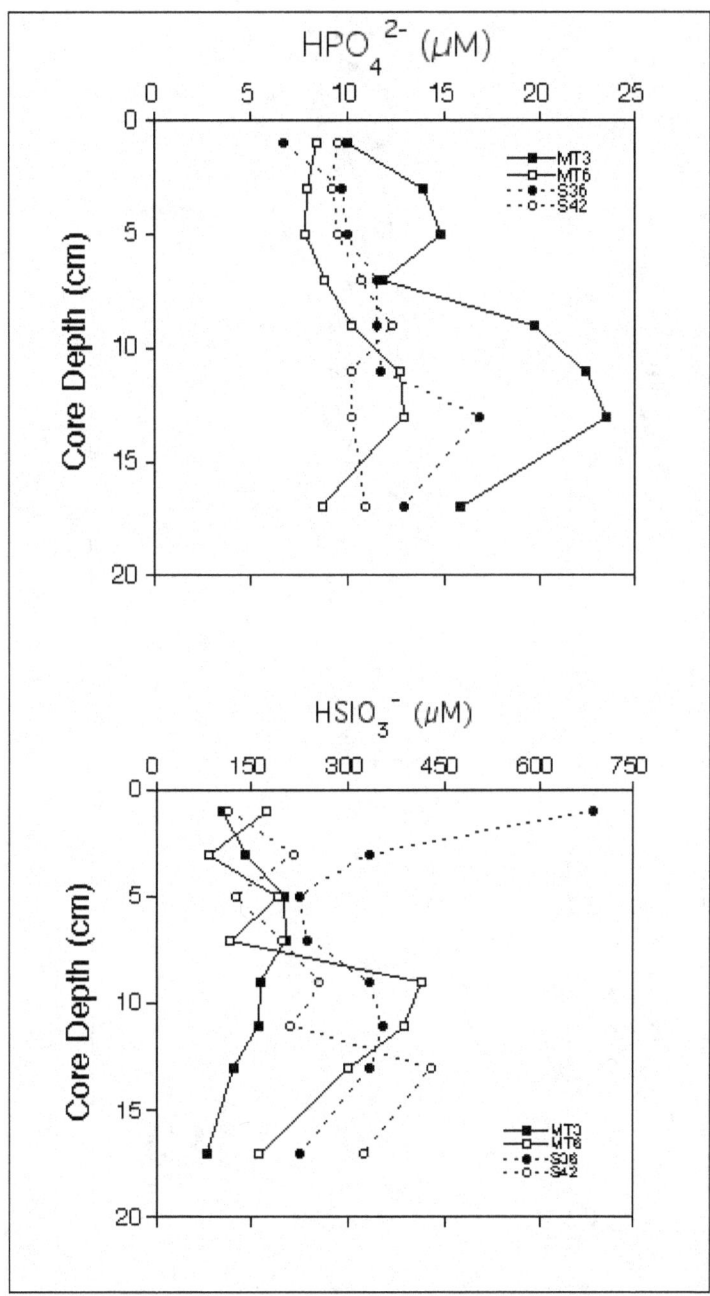

Figure 5.34a. Variation in HSiO₃⁻ and HPO₄⁼ concentrations with depth in the core (see Figure 4.2 for station locations).

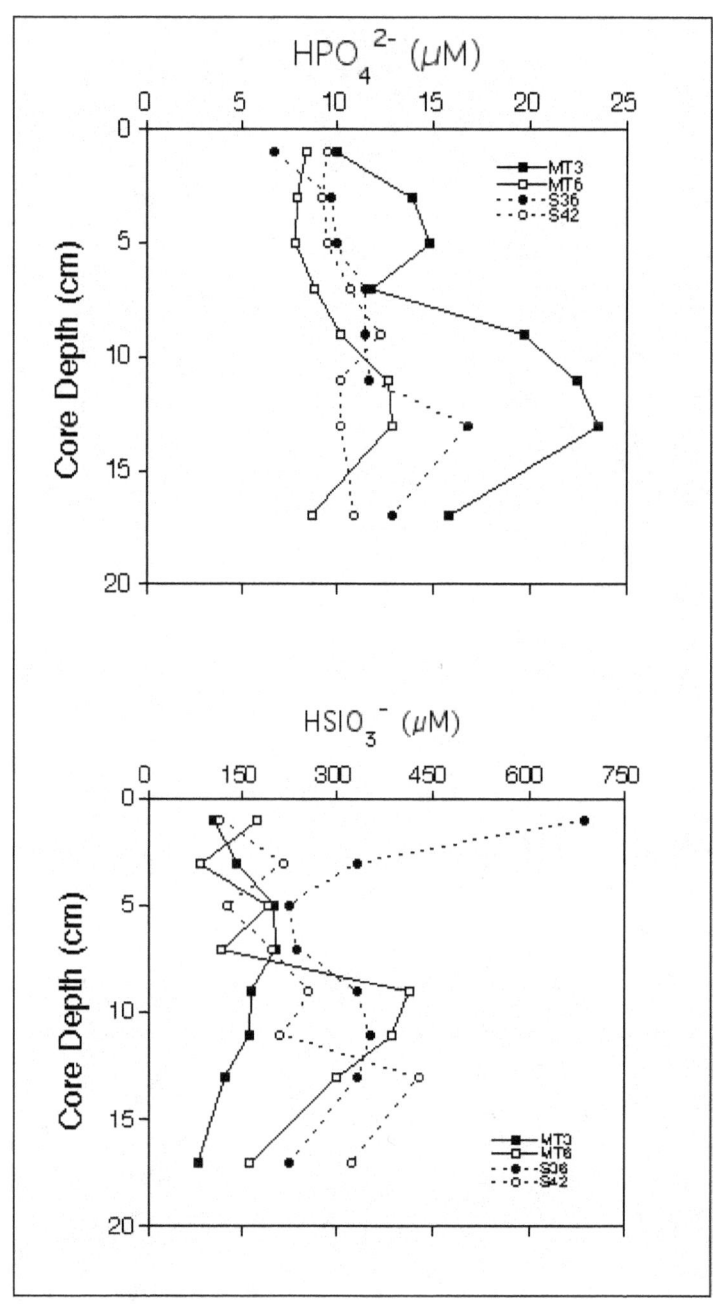

Figure 5.34b. Variation in HSiO$_3^-$ and HPO$_4^=$ concentrations with depth in the core at process stations (see Figure 4.2 for station locations).

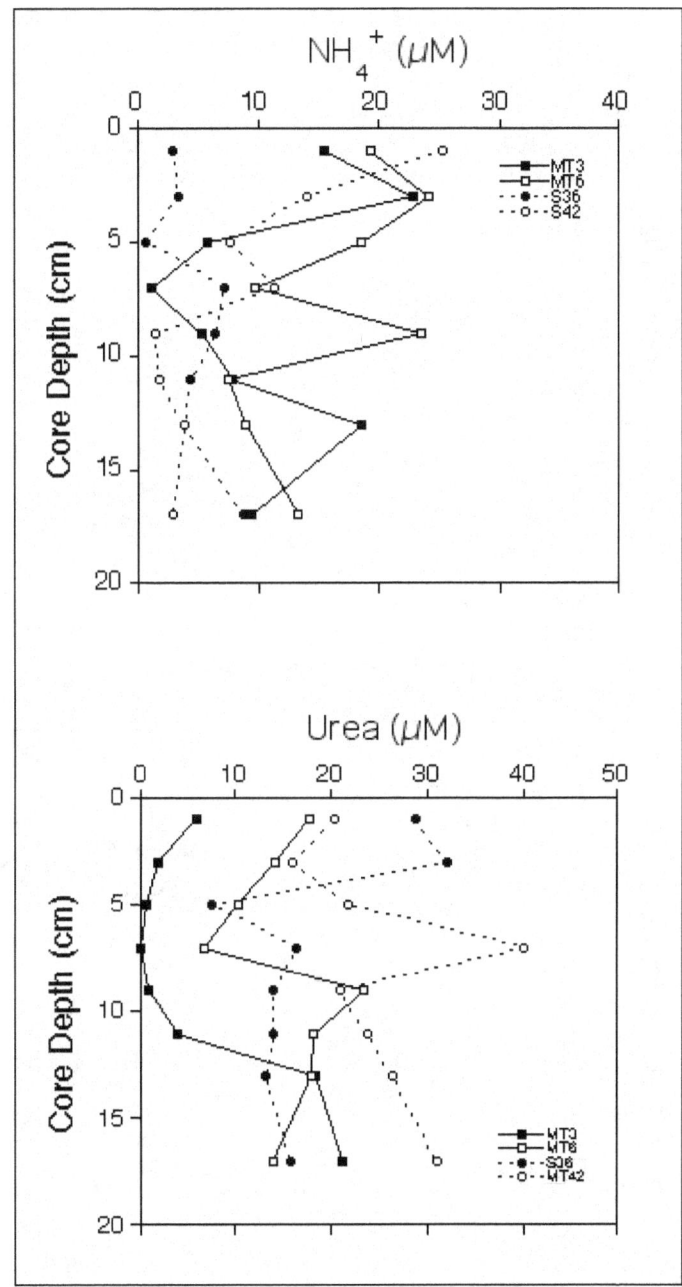

Figure 5.34c. Variation in $HSiO_3^-$ and $HPO_4^=$ concentrations with depth in the core at process stations (see Figure 4.2 for station locations).

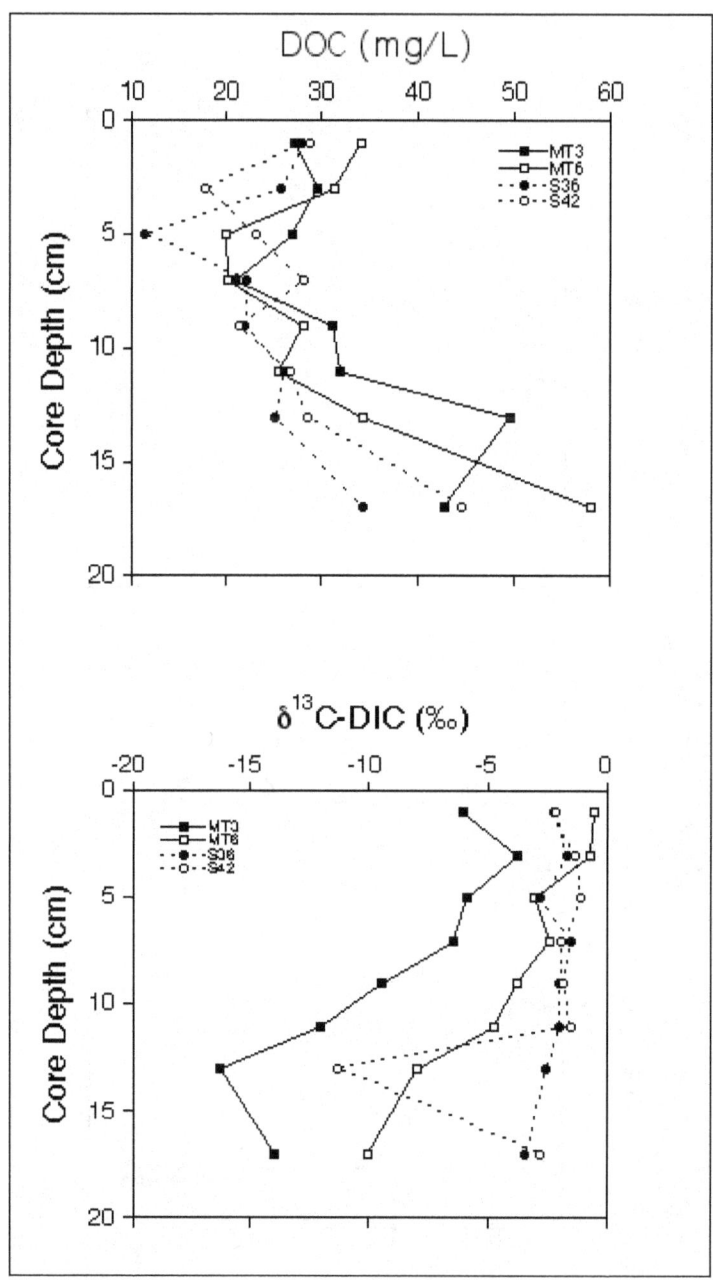

Figure 5.35.   Variations for DOC concentrations (mg/L) and DIC stable carbon isotope composition (‰) with depth in the core at process stations (see Figure 4.2 for station locations).

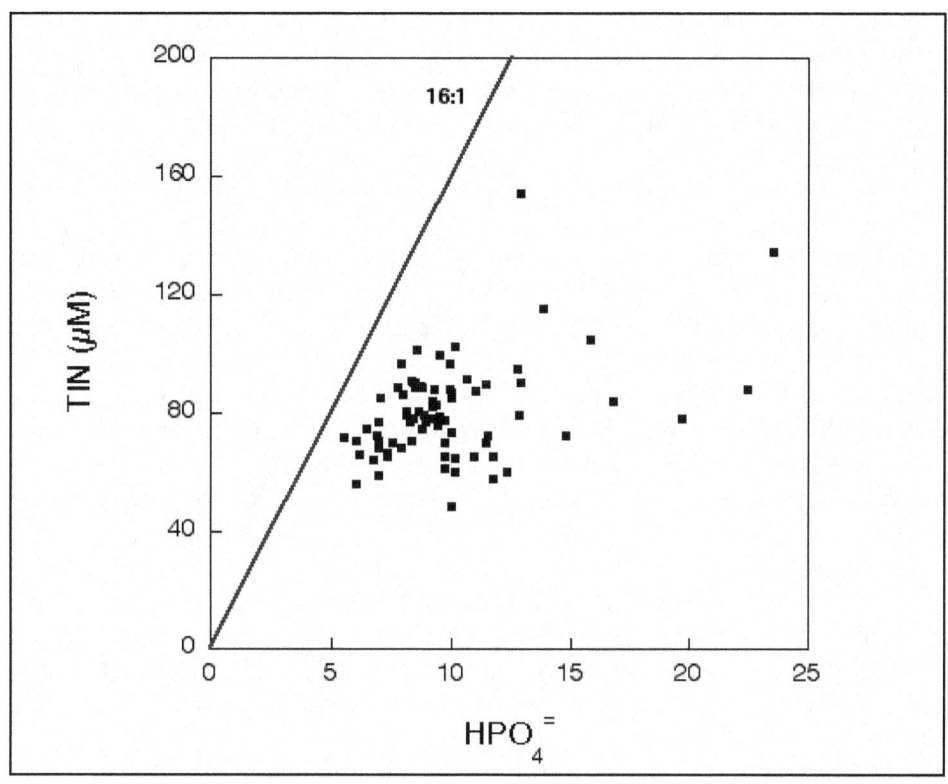

Figure 5.36. Total inorganic nitrogen (TIN; μM) and phosphate (HPO$_4^=$; μM) concentrations. The 16:1 line is shown.

Table 5.4. Summary of preliminary results.

Station #	Boxcore #	Sample ID #	Bioturbation Depth (cm)		$^{210}Pb_{xs}$
			$^{234}Th_{xs}$	$^{210}Pb_{xs}$	layer depth (cm)
MT3	P-2	1	6	6	17
S36	P-2	11	1	4	18
MT6	P-1a	15	1	1	2
S42	P-2	9	2	2.5	10

After additional consultation regarding modeling goals and ways to maximize bacterial and meiofaunal activity measurements, it was decided to use ^{3}H-thymidine to directly measure bacterial growth on the process cruises. This approach incorporates labeled thymidine into the DNA fraction of the resident cells presumably directly reflecting new cell production, regardless of what naturally available organic substrates are being consumed. Measuring bacterial production in this manner thus circumvents assumptions required to convert activity based on labile ^{14}C-substrates to total activity based on the *in-situ* suite of naturally available organic compounds. Incorporation of 3H-thymidine also effectively labels growing cells so that their fate as prey for meiofauna can be tracked, supporting the modeling goal to link one class of organisms to the next. There is precedent for use of the ^{3}H-thymidine approach to measure bacterial activity in deep-sea sediments, so comparable results are available in the literature.

^{3}H-thymidine was originally proposed because the laboratory sample-processing scheme is more complex. Labeled DNA must be extracted and separated from other components of the sample using a more time-intensive protocol than is involved with ^{14}C-amino acid experiments and the team is not experienced in the new methods. However, advice from practitioners ensured success. Because of original interests in bacterial respiration, as well as production, a simple protocol was added that assesses the fraction of the total bacterial community that is actively respiring oxygen. This method relies upon the use of an electron-transport-specific stain (CTC stain) for visual discrimination of oxygen-respiring cells under epifluorescence microscopy. Thus it was added to the cruise activities without too much additional shipboard sample-processing time. The results may allow comment on bacterial respiratory activities, if actual production rates appear low.

The main goal of DGoMB Cruise 1 was to obtain benthic bacterial abundance measurements at each of the survey stations. The plan included sampling subcores from each of five boxcores per station at each of four depths (0, 5, 10, and 15 cm), so that abundance values could be integrated over depth to obtain a station value in terms of number of bacteria per square cm. By determining mean biovolume in selected samples and using a carbon conversion value from the literature, total bacterial abundance can be converted to total bacterial biomass.

Of the 832 samples collected, 565 samples or 68% have been analyzed for bacterial abundance by epifluorescence microscopy, scaled to a cubic centimeter of sediment. Sediment dry weight analyses have also been completed on these samples, if scaling to that parameter ultimately proves desirable. The remaining 32% of the samples have been archived and will not likely be analyzed. They represent primarily the fourth or fifth subcores collected per station and do not provide significant statistical improvement of the mean value already obtained from triplicate samples. Thus, 100% of the samples required to meet the main goal of obtaining depth-integrated values for bacterial abundance per station are completed. Of the 48 samples selected to date (four depths, each in triplicate, from each of the four process stations) for biovolume analyses, 25% have been analyzed. As this work is particularly tedious, complete results should be available by the end of 2001. At that time, abundance measurements will be converted to biomass.

In advance of the biovolume data, a preliminary analysis of the benthic bacterial abundance measurements has been conducted in terms of the proposed hypotheses. In general, bacterial abundance decreased with depth in the sediment at any given station; the only station where a subsurface peak was observed, was station NB5, indicative on little bioturbational mixing (see Section 5.3.3 and Figure 5.24). A plot of mean benthic bacterial abundance at each station (bacteria per cm^2, 0-15 cm depth integration) versus station depth (Figure 5.37; where error bars represent the standard deviation of the mean value from triplicate core data) reveals only a slight trend towards an inverse relationship ($r^2 = 0.095$). This trend becomes slightly stronger ($r^2 = 0.173$), if the stations representing unusual topographic features (WC, B, NB, or AC station designations) are omitted from the analysis (Figure 5.40). As the data set is sizeable (and the most extensive of its kind), additional station or sampling density would not likely improve the trend. However, future analyses based on data conversions to biomass, or log-transformed data, may yield a more compelling test of the hypothesis that water depth determines benthic bacterial community size in the Gulf of Mexico.

There is no support, based on preliminary analyses, for the hypothesis that an east-west gradient in bacterial biomass exists along the sampling sites (Figure 5.38), but the analysis to date is only cursory. In a comparison of basin, non-basin and canyon stations, canyon stations may have slightly lower bacterial abundances, but more data analysis (and perhaps a greater sampling density at such stations in the future) is required to determine whether the trend is significant (Figure 5.39). Following the overall slight inverse relationship between bacterial abundance and water depth, deep stations along the Sigsbee sampling section support lower numbers of bacteria than do the shallow stations, though again, further statistical analyses are required to confirm the significance of the trend (Figure 5.42). Although the data set for testing the hypothesis of higher benthic biomass underlying regions of higher primary production is limited, a trend ($r^2 = 0.545$, the strongest trend among our preliminary analyses) was observed in support of the hypothesis (Figure 5.41). At this time, the testing of the remaining hypotheses is not possible.

Of the 189 samples collected for bacterial abundance determinations on DGoMB Cruise 2, none have been analyzed in deference to processing samples from the ^{3}H-thymidine rate measurement experiments. All bacterial counts (and sediment dry weights) from Cruise 2 will be available by the end of 2001. The extra samples taken for CTC-stain analyses will be processed prior to the total counts, due to sample storage issues, and should be available in October, 2001. Of the samples from the thymidine experiments, 75% of them have been processed in the laboratory. The remaining 25% will be completed by the end of September, 2001. The data will then be analyzed and rates calculated by the end of October, 2001.

Although comment is not possible on absolute rates until all of the samples and related controls have been processed and analyzed, enough of the raw data is available to make the following observations. Injection of ^{3}H-thymidine into whole-core samples of the sediments, the approach most closely mimicking *in-situ* conditions, yielded detectable and, by visual inspection, significant increases in thymidine incorporation into DNA over the course of the shipboard incubation experiments. Rates for each of the four stations should thus be available when all of the analyses are completed; i.e., the method was successful. The various experiments performed on sediment dilutions have so far provided equivocal results with apparently little detectable activity. Additional analyses may allow retrieval of information from these experiments, but at the moment, it is anticipated that future cruise work will center on whole-core injection

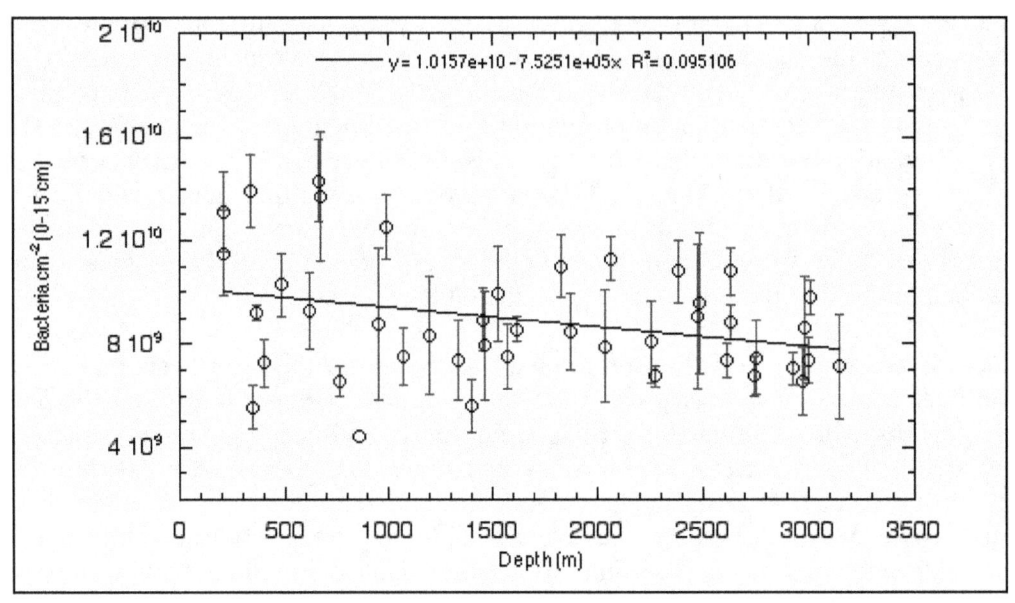

Figure 5.37. Benthic bacterial abundance as a function of depth.

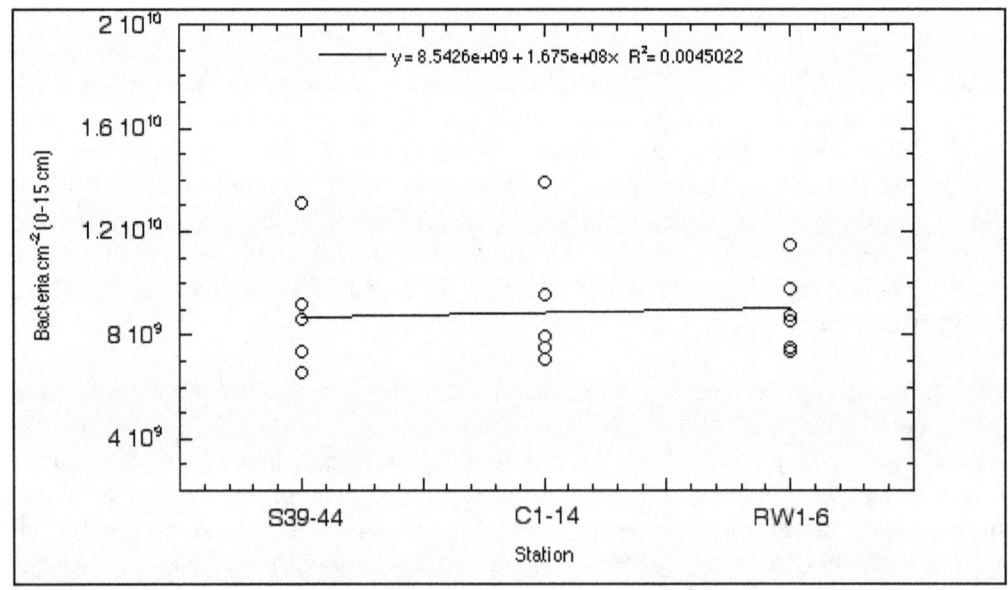

Figure 5.38. Benthic bacterial abundance from the east to west Gulf of Mexico.

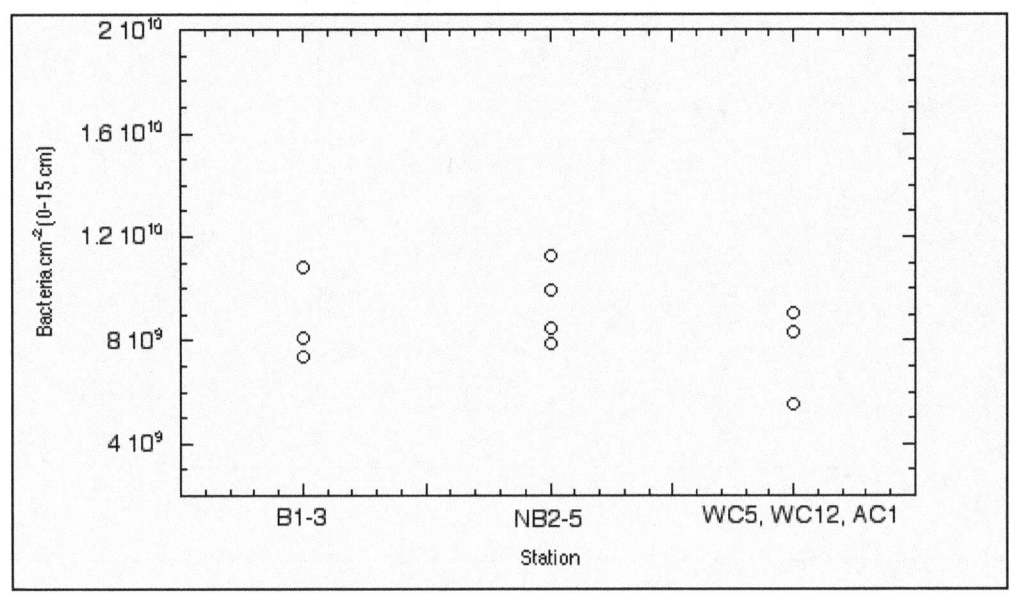

Figure 5.39. Benthic bacterial abundance comparisons for basins, non-basins, and canyons.

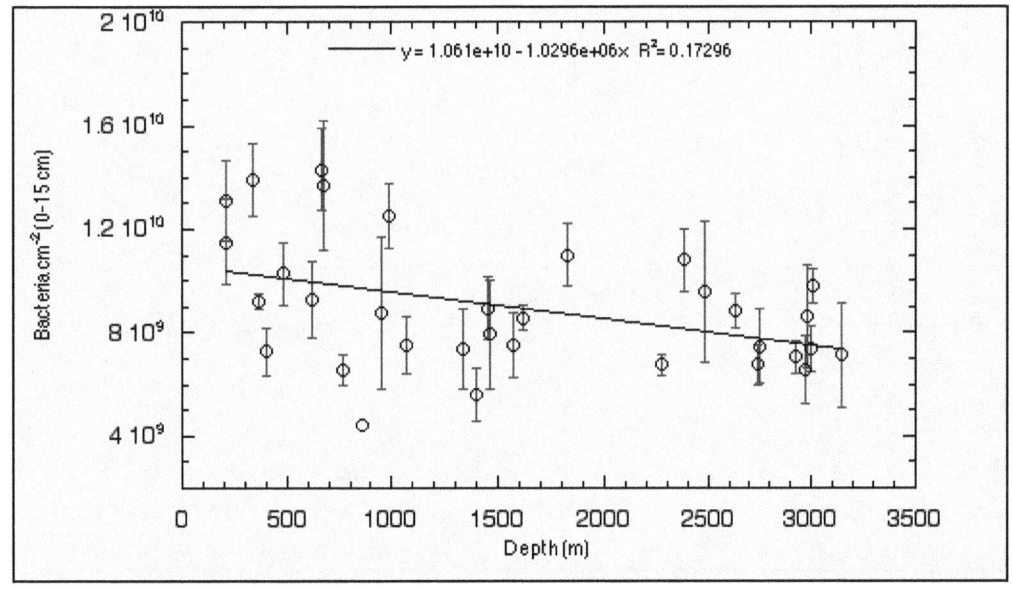

Figure 5.40. Benthic bacterial abundance as a function of water depth (no WC, B, NB, or AC stations).

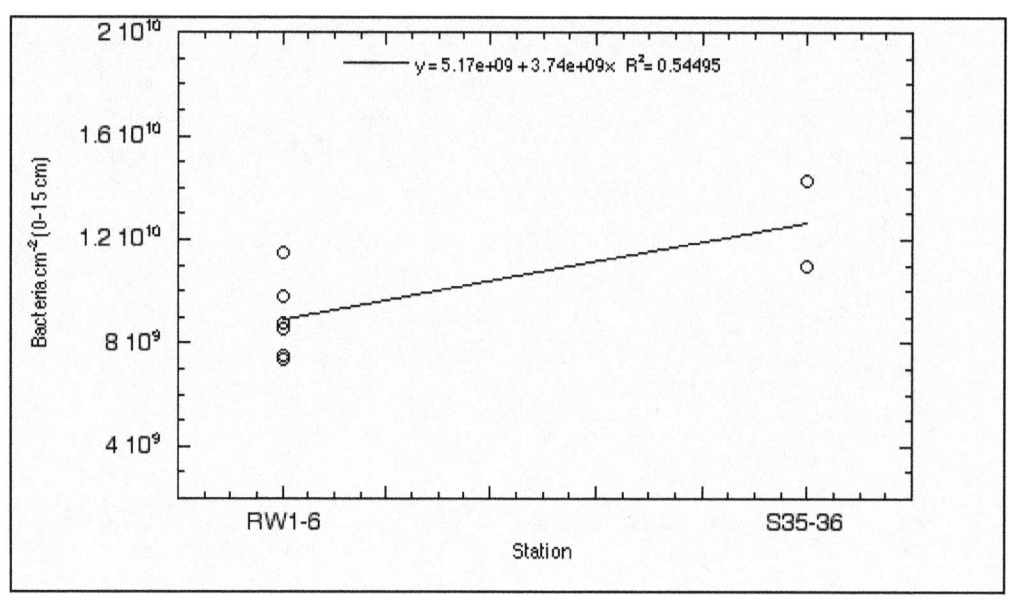

Figure 5.41.   Benthic bacterial abundance related to primary productivity (low vs high).

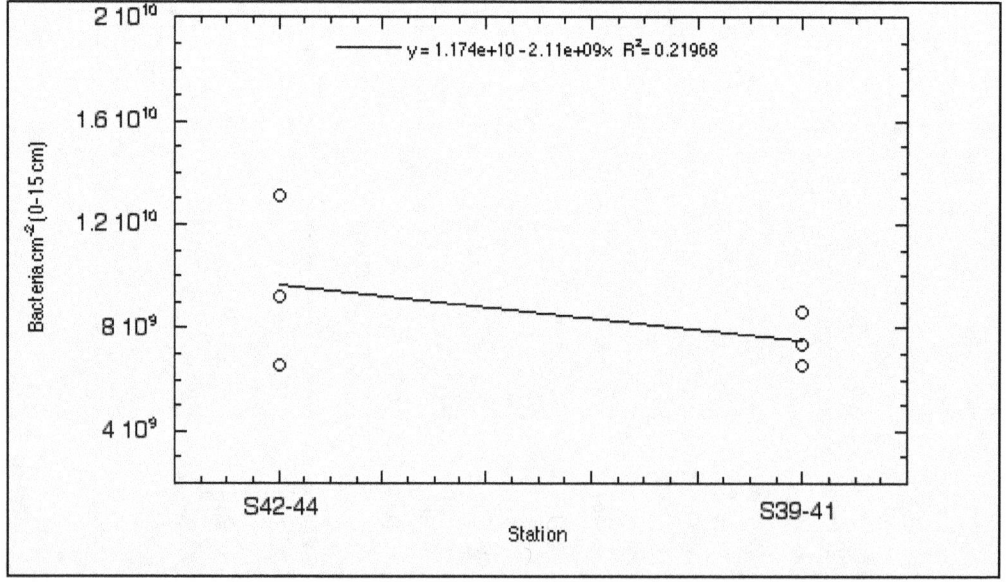

Figure 5.42.   Benthic bacterial abundance related to Sigsbee Escarpment (shallow vs. deep).

approach. If the thymidine approach can be streamlined, then it may be possible to add protocols that use ^{14}C-amino acids as well. Having both types of measurements strengthens any conclusions eventually drawn regarding growth versus respiration.

In designing the thymidine approach, experiments were conducted with and without the application of *in-situ* hydrostatic pressures during the shipboard incubation period. Again, comment on absolute rates cannot yet be made, but a comparison of relative increases in raw data (cpm from the scintillation counter printout over incubation time) makes clear that the only case of a positive pressure effect (faster uptake under pressure) occurred at the deepest of the four process stations (MT6 at 3000 m). At the next deepest station (S36 at 1800 m), the pressure effect appears to be minimal. At the two shallow stations (MT3 at 1000 m and S42 at 750 m), pressure appears to have a negative effect; i.e., rates are faster at atmospheric pressure. As a practical matter, these results indicate that pressure equipment is only needed for deep water stations. As a scientific matter, these preliminary results fit predictions from pure culture work that positive pressure effects (barophily) should not be detected at depths shallower than 2000 m. This data set represents the first field test of this concept across a suitable range of station depths.

5.3.5.2   Benthic Foraminifera

A total of 984 foraminifera were extracted for ATP on the DGoMB Cruise 2 (Table 5.5). When combined with the 324 specimens extracted during the *R/V Atlantis* cruise in October 2000, a total of 1308 foraminifera have been extracted for ATP. Samples were taken at all process stations as well as at an additional two stations during the process cruise (C-7 and Bush Hill). Only the top cm was processed for the survey site cores. At S36 there was an abundant community of arborescent foraminifera (up to 5 cm in height), six of which were analyzed for ATP although none occurred in the foraminiferal biomass core. It is likely that these comprise a major portion of biomass at this station.

Each ATP extract has been analyzed with the luciferin-luciferase reaction and data is being processed. It is expected that final results (i.e., mg C/m^2 per station) will be available by the end of 2002. It is too early to make any predictions about data outcome and the relative contribution of the foraminifera to benthic biomass.

Although the original plan was for five replicate cores to be analyzed per process station, this proved to be unrealistic due to (1) time constraints on coring for "process samples" and (2) shipboard space for additional personnel. As originally agreed, 50 foraminifera were individually extracted for ATP from each of three sediment depth intervals per core. The interval depths changed slightly from the original plan in order to correspond with those being analyzed for meiofauna. The depth intervals analyzed were 0-1, 1-3, and either 9-10 or 14-15 cm, depending on core length. The depth of 9-10 cm was required since some cores were short. In all cases, the deepest interval was located below a change in sediment fabric and the apparent redox boundary. The original depth intervals proposed were 0-1, 4-5, and 9-10 cm.

The temperature of the overlying water in the boxcores was often quite high (>18°C). Given that ambient temperatures at the sites are <10°C, this thermal difference could be detrimental to the foraminifera. Some of the foraminifers may have expired in the time it took for boxcore recovery and subsampling. Water overlying the boxcores was also murky sometimes indicating that the boxcore had been disturbed. If serious discrepancies in *in situ* respiration rates and shipboard analyses on box-cored material occur, the thermal shock and disturbance may account for such differences.

Table 5.5. Foraminifera extracted for ATP.

Station	Depth Interval (cm)	Number Extracted
Process Stations		
MT3	0-1	53
	1-3	50
	14-15	50
MT3 Replicate	0-1	50
	1-3	50
	9-10	50
S42	0-1	50
	1-3	50
	9-10	50
S36	0-1	75
	1-3	50
	14-15	50
"tree" forams from other boxcores		6
MT6	0-1	50
	1-3	50
	9-10	50
Non-Process Stations		
C7	0-1	50
	1-2	50
Bush Hill	0-1	50
	1-2	50
Total for DGoMB 2		984
Atlantis Cruise (10/00)		
Farnella Canyon (*Alvin* dive 3628)	0-1	130
Green Canyon 66 (*Alvin* dive 3629)	0-1	28
Green Canyon 67 (*Alvin* dive 3629)	0-1	40
N. Florida Escarpment (*Alvin* dive 3634)	0-1	100
	2-3	26
Total for *Atlantis* cruise		324

5.3.5.3   Meiofauna

A general linear relationship is observed between meiofauna abundance (n/m^2) and water depth (Figure 5.43). However, there is variability in the regression ($R^2 = 0.4042$), indicating factors other than depth also influence abundance. The main factor appears to be spatial variation of meiofaunal abundance as well as the relationship with depth (Figure 5.44). The deeper stations in the northwestern Gulf of Mexico have high abundance. The highest meiofaunal abundance values are found in relatively shallow depths in the Mississippi Trough and DeSoto Canyon.

Biomass also generally decreased with depth (Figure 5.45); however this relationships is weaker ($R^2 = 0.3267$) than for abundance. The spatial variation from station to station is heterogeneous for biomass (Figure 5.46). However, some stations in the eastern transects were not complete with respect to biomass, and completion of these samples will likely change any conclusions. Highest meiofaunal biomass was observed at stations C4, WC12, and W3. The eastern Gulf will likely have high biomass values associated with the Mississippi Trough and DeSoto Canyon corresponding to high abundance measurements.

The relationship of major taxa diversity to depth is weak (Figure 5.47, $R^2 = 0.126$). Higher diversity was observed in the western Gulf than the eastern Gulf (Figure 5.48). Highest diversity values appear to occur at mid-water depths along transects. Harpactcoid species identifications are not yet sufficiently complete to make preliminary conclusions based species level diversity.

There was a weak linear relationship ($R^2 = 0.2874$) between bacterial abundance and meiofaunal abundance (Figure 5.49). There was significant deviation from the regression and considerable heterogeneity of variance. A relationship between meiofaunal and bacterial abundance would be expected if there were a strong trophic coupling between these two components.

The goal of this program is to provide an understanding of relationships between the biological, chemical, physical and geological factors that are regulating structure and function of benthic communities. Community ecologists have argued for years over whether biological or physical factors in the environment are responsible for shaping benthic communities. Both factors are important. It is only in recent years it has been realized that there are significant interactions between the biotic community and that the physical, chemical and geologic environment. Thus, this program seeks to uncover these interactions.

The importance of depth in shaping meiofaunal communities is one of the primary hypotheses of this program. In general meiofaunal abundance, biomass, and major taxonomic diversity decrease with depth. Depth is evidently important; however other factors also influence ecology in the deep-sea.

Topographic features such as the Mississippi Trough and the DeSoto Canyon appear to have higher abundance and biomass, but lower major taxonomic diversity. These may be areas where POC accumulate, fueling increased productivity. These features are located in the eastern

Gulf where eutrophic conditions in overlying waters could be fueling more productive benthic

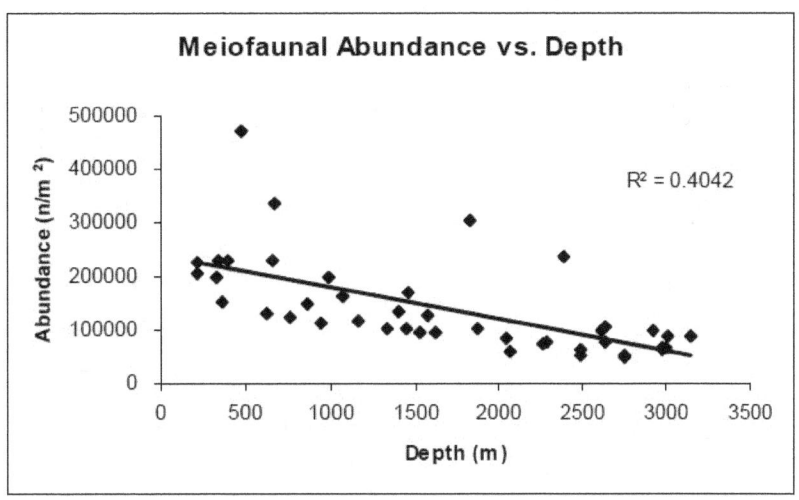

Figure 5.43. Relationship between meiofaunal abundance and water depth.

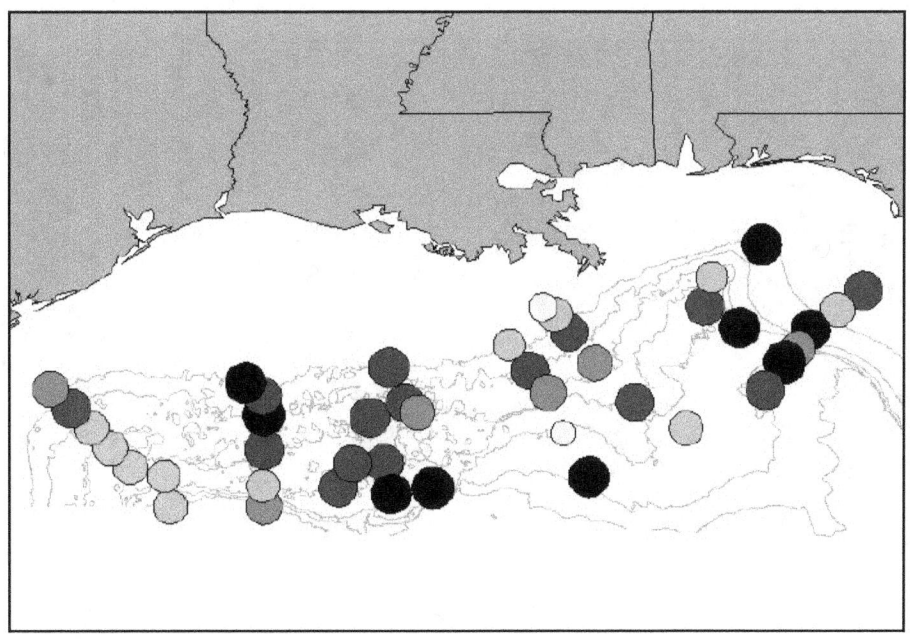

Figure 5.44. Relative meiofaunal abundance at each station.

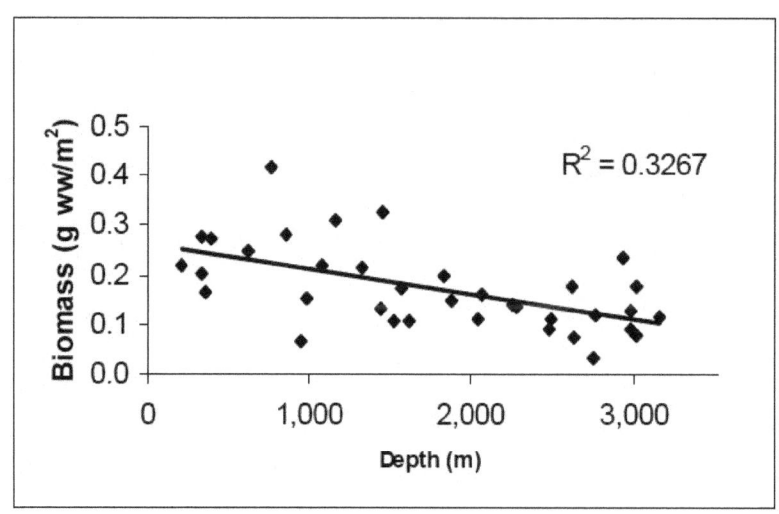

Figure 5.45. Relationship between meiofaunal biomass and depth.

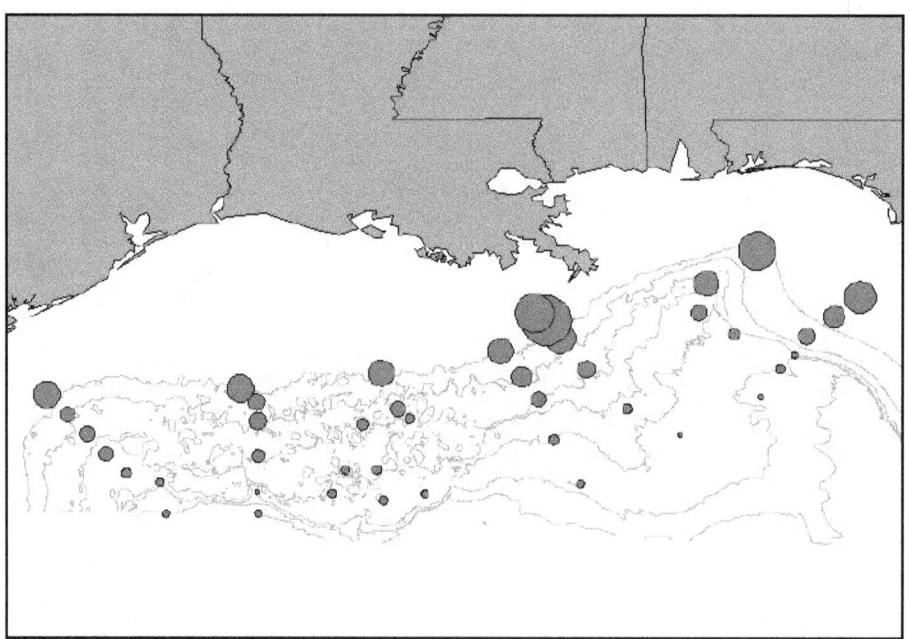

Figure 5.46. Relative meiofaunal biomass (g ww/m^2) at each station. Note, small dots indicate no data.

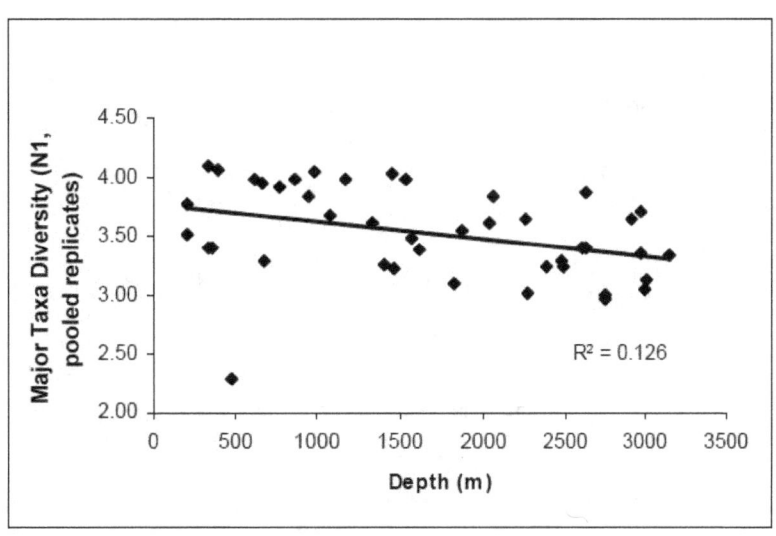

Figure 5.47.　Relationship between major meiofaunal taxa diversity (Hill's number, N1) and depth.

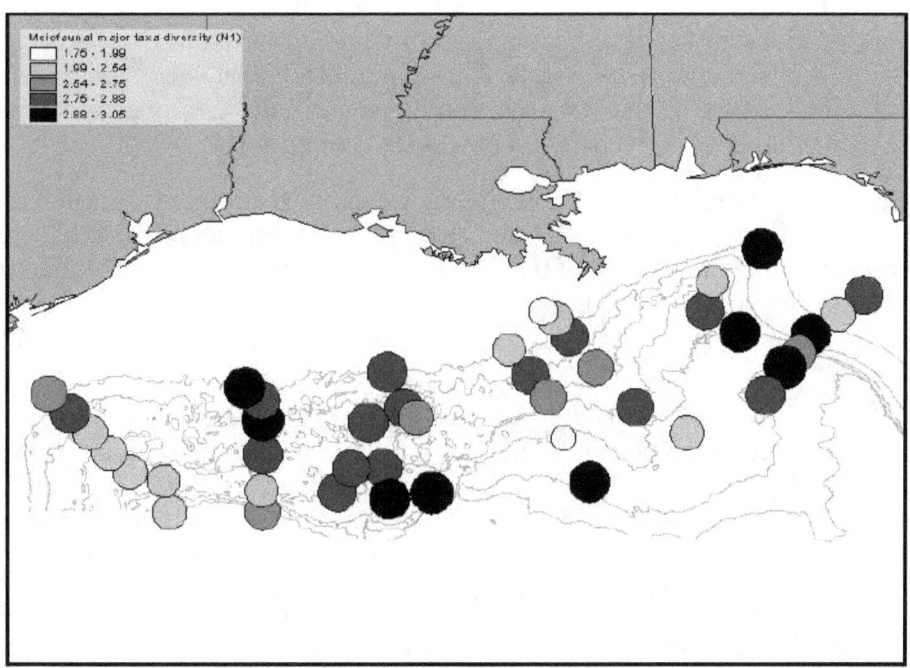

Figure 5.48. Relative major meiofaunal taxa diversity (N1) at each station.

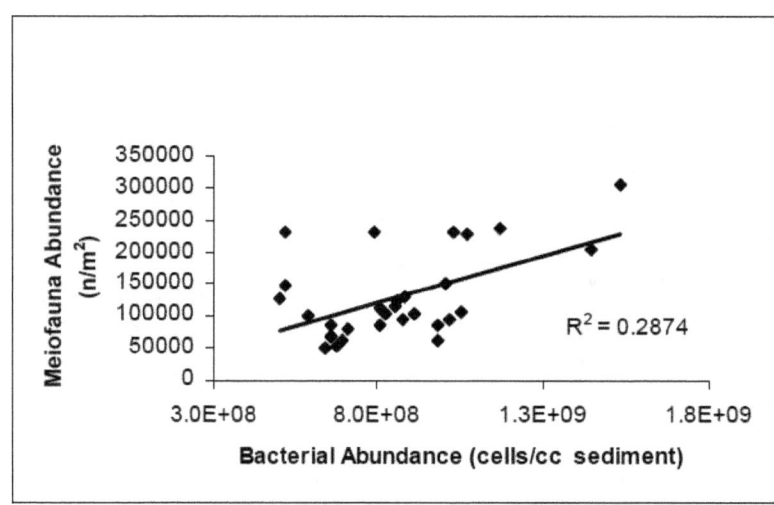

Figure 5.49. Relationship between meiofaunal and bacterial abundance.

communities. It is common for diversity to be lower in trophically enriched environments (Peterson et al. 1996). Higher major taxa diversity was observed in the western Gulf than the eastern Gulf. Conversely, abundance and biomass were lower in the western Gulf. This trend in the more oligotrophic waters in the western Gulf is consistent with the "trophic enrichment" hypothesis.

A weak relationship between bacterial and meiofaunal abundance is surprising. Several explanations of this observation are possible. This may indicate that bacteria are not an important food source for meiofauna in the deep-sea, or conversely that meiofaunal communities are controlled by predation. It is likely that both processes are important.

In regards to the original eight hypotheses, trends in preliminary data for the meiofauna community indicate depth is important, there are east/west differences, and there are differences due to the influence of canyons. Clearly, several environmental factors collectively control meiofaunal community structure and these variables are interrelated.

5.3.5.4   Macrofauna

A total of 215 GOMEX boxcores were taken during DGoMB Cruise 1 to provide detailed information about the communities of organisms that live in continental slope communities. The samples were sieved at sea using a 300 micrometer mesh and then preserved in 10% buffered formalin and sea water solution. In the laboratory they are then sorted to major taxonomic group, switched to an alcohol preservation, and then distributed to various taxonomists around the world for identification to species (list of taxonomists).

The quantitative information on macrofauna from the boxcores is being analyzed to test several of the eight hypotheses that were proposed originally in this project. This is an initial consideration of the data that are presently available. Since considerably more information will eventually be developed, all these initial assessments must be taken with caution. Nonetheless, there is no reason to expect that the general patterns presented here will change as more data are accrued. Regressions of macrofauna animal density as a function of depth for the entire data set indicate that mean density declines with depth from about 10,000 down to about 3,000 ind./m^2 at the base of the escarpment (~3,000 m; Figure 5.50). The variability of these values is extremely high, however, from estimates of more than 30,000 down to less than a 1,000 ind./m^2. Variability seems to decline with depth. As the highest densities were found in eastern GOM at the S locations or in the MT sites (Mississippi Trough), it is worth noting that if these sites are excluded from the analysis, then the extreme highs are eliminated and the mean at the shallow sites goes down to just less than 8,000 ind./m^2 (Figure 5.51). The Mississippi Trough (MT) sites plotted by themselves as a function of depth down the canyon (Figure 5.52) illustrate that the extreme highs nearshore are found at the canyon head. However, the tendency for the canyon to have higher values lessens with depth (MT5 and MT6). The mean at the shallow station was approximately 16,000 ind./m^2, or well above the average mean for the entire set of data. MT5 and 6 are both characterized by quantities of iron stone material mixed into the sediments. It was sampled with the box core and the trawl and it is visible in bottom photographs. It does not form a pavement, however, as has been observed in deeper waters, but appears as a bumpy, red-colored material in irregular patches at the sediment surface.

The sites in the eastern GOM illustrate several features that are unique to that area (Figure 5.53). The samples have been partitioned between those lying east and those lying west of the DeSoto Canyon axis. Those to the east form a series of samples across the west Florida slope and steep escarpment. Those on the west side lie on the eastern margin of the Mississippi cone. While the eastern samples form a general pattern that declines with depth, with a mean trend line that more or less mimics that of the entire sample set, the macrofauna at sites west of the axis do not follow the typical pattern with depth. All of the macrofaunal abundance values are higher than their eastern counterparts and the highest values are at S36 at a depth of 1850 meters. The high density macrofauna at this intermediate depth suggests that the site is unique among the sites sampled to date.

The patterns of macrofaunal abundance can be used to infer the locations where the input of organic matter is accentuated within the study area. In general, the western GOM is characterized by lower densities than the eastern GOM, leading to the assumption that the organic matter available to the deep benthos is less in the west than in the eastern GOM. This is unexpected since the Mississippi River generally flows to the west and the eastern GOM is characterized by the warm relatively unproductive waters of the loop current. The high abundance values in the upper reaches of the Mississippi Trough reflect larger inputs of organic matter that can be assumed to be related to the Mississippi River. This could either be direct input from river-borne material or enhanced primary production that accumulates in the trough where it intersects the continental shelf just west of the delta. The differences in the densities on the two sides of the DeSoto Canyon suggest that in general Mississippi cone sediments are enriched in carbon compared to those off Florida. The cone sediments are primarily terrigenous and it might be assumed richer in organics than the predominantly carbonate sediments off west Florida. The high numbers at S36 near the canyon axis suggest that perhaps this is a location of organic matter accumulation. It is also worth noting that the surface water over and just inshore of S36 is thought to be characterized by unusually high productivity for the GOM, probably due to the incursion of high nitrate water onto the upper slope and continental slope.

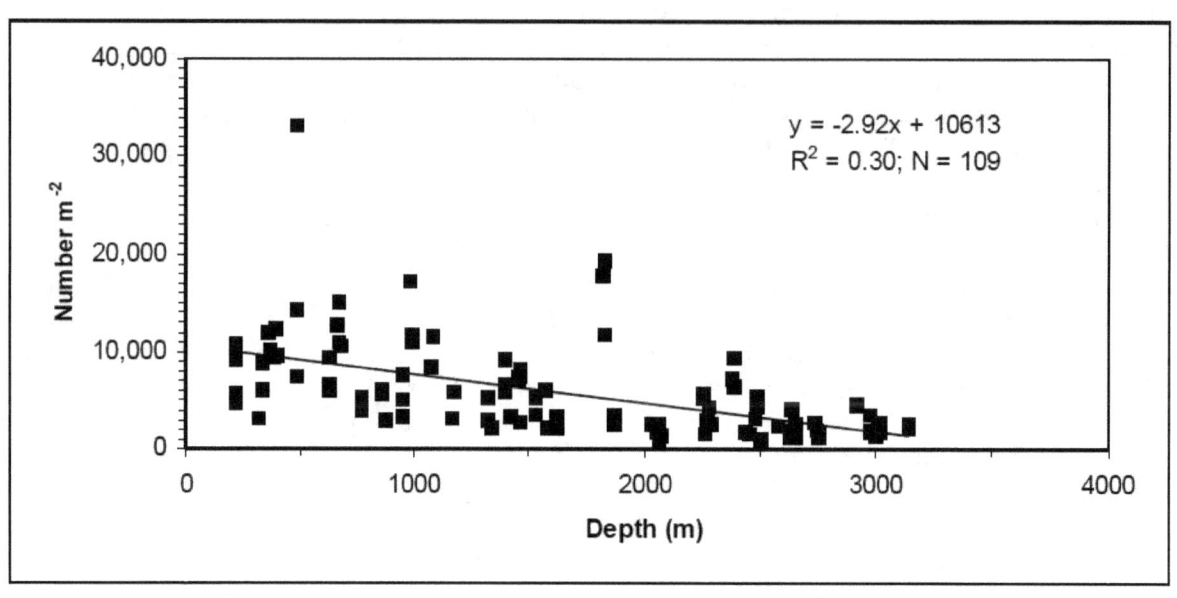

Figure 5.50. Total macrofaunal densities by depth with the regression line and formula, R-squared value, and number of samples involved.

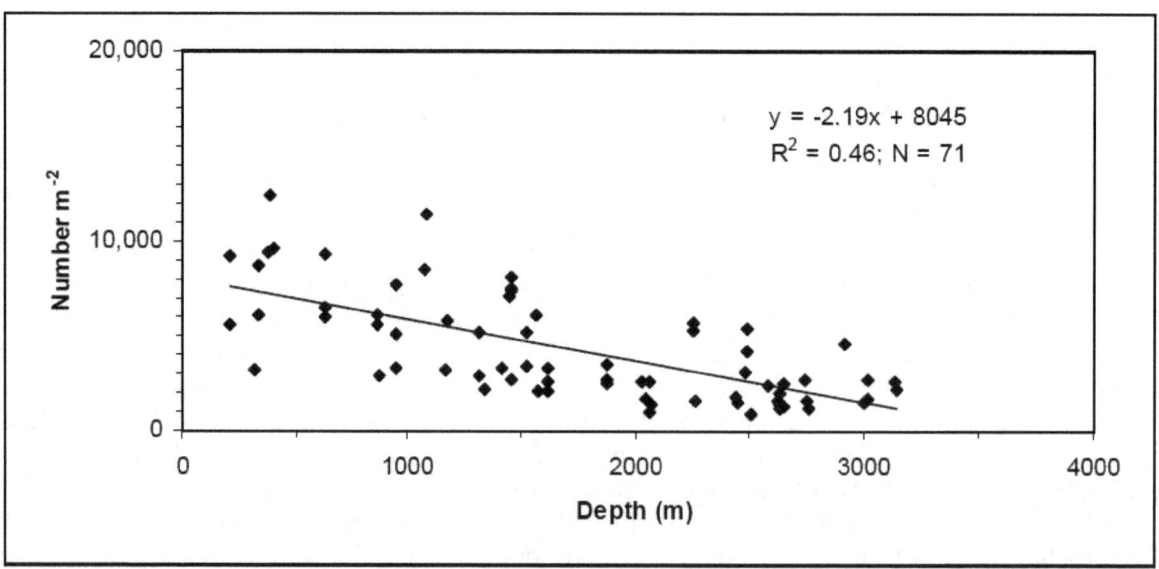

Figure 5.51. Total macrofaunal densities by depth except samples from the Mississippi Trough (MT) and eastern (S) Gulf.

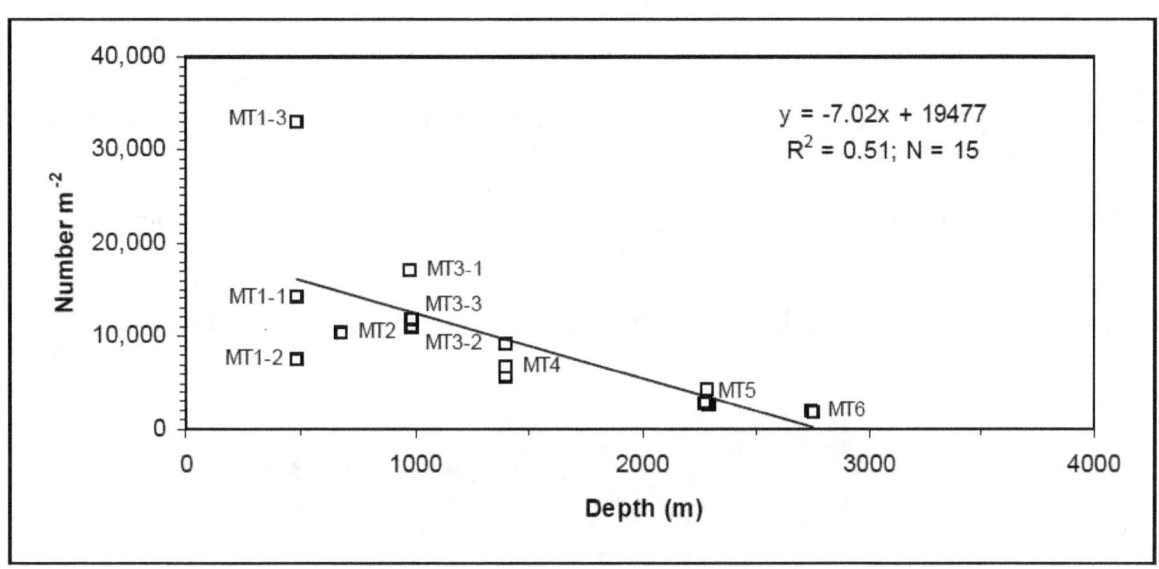

Figure 5.52. Total macrofaunal densities by depth plotting all sorted samples from the Mississippi Trough (MT).

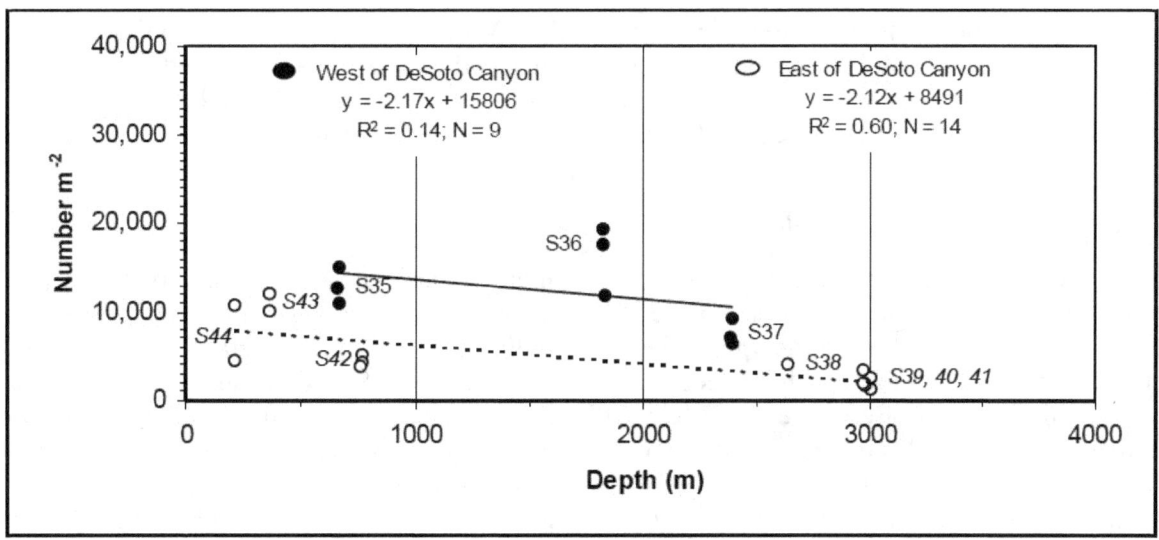

Figure 5.53. Total macrofaunal densities by depth plotting all sorted samples from the eastern Gulf of Mexico (S). Samples from the western side of DeSoto Canyon are indicated by the closed circles (●); those from east of DeSoto Canyon are indicated by open circles (O).

The taxonomic composition of the macrofauna has not proved to be unique with only one exception that appears to also be related to animal densities. While the macrofauna of the entire GOM is dominated by polychaete annelid worms and macrofaunal sized nematode worms, in general, the macrofauna in the shallow head of the Mississippi Trough (MT1) is dominated in all the replicates by tube-dwelling amphipod crustaceans. Macrofauna-sized nematode worms are almost non-existent in the MT1 samples; those that were encountered are small in size. The surface of the sediments is characterized by the numerous tubes that the amphipods inhabit (Figure 5.54). At S36, another site of generally high animal densities, the nematodes were much more abundant and larger. The dominant macrofaunal taxon was the polychaetes, which is typical for fine-grained sediments.

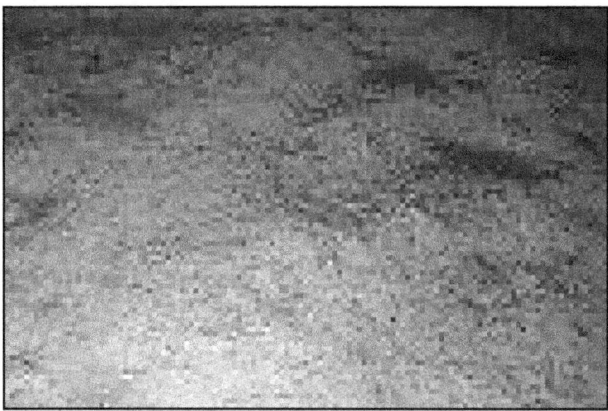

Figure 5.54. Bottom photograph from Station MT1 at the head of the Mississippi Canyon. The odd, lumpy nature of the sediments is caused by dense populations of tube-dwelling amphipods that are characteristic of this unique environment. Depth is approximately 475 m.

5.3.5.5 Megafauna

Trawl samples were split into three components aboard ship: trash, invertebrates and fishes. Each animal was identified to the lowest possible taxon, weighed by taxon (by volume displacement) and preserved as appropriate in 5 gallon plastic tubs. Geographic location of the start and end of each trawl, ship's speed and time on bottom were all recorded and thus estimates can be made of the area covered by each trawl. A comparison can thus be made of animal densities in the trawl samples. The trash was not preserved but was stored wet sealed in 5 gallon plastic buckets. When there was too much for one container, it was photographed, weighed (when possible), discarded over the side (biodegradable material), or stored aboard ship for land disposal. During the cruises completed to date, 6,961 invertebrate specimens of at least 160 species were collected in 36 beam and otter trawl samples. The majority were echinoderms and crustaceans (Table 5.6).

Table 5.6. Larger invertebrate species from trawls.

Taxonomic Group	Number of Species
Porifera (sponges)	4
Cnidaria (corals, sea anemones, etc.)	12*
Nemertea (ribbon worms)	1+
Polychaeta (marine segmented worms)	4*+
Pogonophora (beard worms)	1
Crustacea (shrimp, crabs, etc.)	65
Mollusca (clams, snails, etc.)	48
Brachiopoda (lamp shells)	1
Echinodermata (sea stars, etc.)	27*
Urochordata (sea squirts)	1

* indicates an estimate +indicates a group in which body size usually is too small to be caught in a trawl

Of the species taken, all have been given at least provisional assignments to species. However, at least one species each of sea anemone and tunicate are undescribed--not yet formally named by a biologist. Identification to species of some of the sponges, octocorals and sea anemones at present is not possible due to the need for a thorough revision of certain poorly studied groups. Although the echinoderms have been given provisional identifications, the identifications will be double-checked by Gordon Hendler, Natural History Museum of Los Angeles County.

The maximum number of specimens taken at a single trawl site was at site S-37, where 1,614 specimens of 20 species were collected. Of these, 600 were a single species of sponge, 650 were probably one species of brittle star and another 201 were the soft sea urchin, *Phormosoma placenta*. The most diverse site was MT-5, with 39 species and 477 specimens. Other diverse sites were C-4 (277 specimens, 31 species), NB-5 (321 specimens, 31 species) and S-41 (302 specimens, 31 species). Sites with less than 50 specimens per trawl were C-1, B-2 (May), NB-2, RW-2, W-3 and WC-5.

Three of the crustaceans represented significant range extensions. The shrimp *Sabinea hystrix* and *Benthesicymus carinatus*, and the barnacle *Neoscalpellum debile*, have not been reported previously from the Gulf of Mexico. *Munidopsis geyeri* has not been reported previously from the northeastern Gulf of Mexico.

A list was compiled of all decapod crustacean species known at 200-3000 m in benthic environments of the Gulf of Mexico. For purposes of this study, the Gulf of Mexico was defined as having its southeastern boundary at the Dry Tortugas Islands, Florida. Species reported from "the southeastern Gulf of Mexico", but never collected outside of the Straits of Florida, were not included. For all other species, historic records from the literature, cruise reports (including the DGoMB Cruise 1 sampling) and specimens in collections were compiled. One hundred forty-six species were reported in the area.

A data matrix was constructed by giving a numerical code to each two-by-two degree square of latitude and longitude in the Gulf of Mexico, starting with "1" for the northern tip of the Yucatan Peninsula, Mexico and going clockwise to "27" off the southern tip of Florida

(Table 5.7). Each species known from at least 10 individuals in the Gulf of Mexico, a total of 76 species, was entered into a data matrix by squares in which it occurred. The data matrix contains the total number of stations and individuals taken per square per species, including all historical data. From this data matrix, all squares having at least 10 species per square were compared by presence/absence of species. (Some squares had fewer than 10 recorded species, probably due to a lack of sampling). The results indicate maximum species diversity and abundance from western Louisiana to the DeSoto Canyon. Square 21, containing the head of the DeSoto Canyon, had the greatest number of species (69 out of 76) and specimens.

Data for the larger crustaceans were also analyzed by cluster analysis by site. Except for some similarity by depth range, there were no discernable patterns of distribution of decapod crustaceans by sites. Sites C-4, MT-5 and S35 each had 13 species of large crustaceans, and 148, 42 and 164 crustacean specimens, respectively.

Correlation of numbers and distributions of larger invertebrates with physical factors, geology and distribution of smaller organisms will be incorporated into the final program report. Previous studies have shown distributions related to depth. There is some indication of replacement of decapod crustaceans by other invertebrates, especially echinoderms, at deeper slope depths.

5.3.5.6   Demersal Fish

All of the fish samples that were collected during DGoMB Cruise 1 (summer 2000) are processed, the historical benthic fish database of the Texas Cooperative Wildlife Collection (TCWC) for the northern Gulf of Mexico continental slope was proofed, and data were entered into a MS Excel data base. Taxonomic, numerical, and volumetric data for the fish specimens collected on the first summer cruise were sent to data management and for analysis. The historical fish data base for the study area consists of specimens collected on numerous fisheries surveys in the Gulf of Mexico over the last 60 years, including surveys by the research vessels *Combat, Pelican, Silver Bay, Oregon, Oregon II, Gus III, Alaminos, Gyre*, and numerous chartered commercial shrimp vessels. Most of these records included latitude and longitude coordinates, depth of capture, date of collection, vessel, and time of day.

A total of 1073 individual fishes, representing 121 species and 142 families of benthic fishes, were collected. The families Macrouridae (grenadiers or rattails), with 21 species; Ophidiidae (cuskeels), with 15 species; and Alepocephalidae (slickheads), with eight species dominated the samples. Families of secondary importance are: Halosauridae (halosaurs), with four species, Ipnopidae (tripodfishes), with four species, Moridae (morid cods), with two or three species; and Trichiuridae (cutlassfishes) with two or three species. Discrepancies in number of species within families are due the inability to identify some fishes to species. Cluster analyses revealed that the fish fauna is zoned by depth (Powell, et al. unpubl. ms.). Species richness and abundance were highest on the upper slope (315-785 m) and decreased with depth (Powell et al. unpubl. Ms.).

Table 5.7. Geographic squares in the Gulf of Mexico

Square Number	Degrees North	Degrees West	Description
1	22-24	88-90	N. Yucatan
2	22-24	90-92	NW Yucatan
3	22-24	92-94	SW Yucatan
4	20-22	92-94	Paraiso
5	18-20	92-94	Veracruz
6	18-20	94-96	Veracruz
7	20-22	94-96	Tuxpan
8	20-22	96-98	Tuxpan
9	22-24	96-98	Tampico
10	24-26	96-98	N. Mexico
11	24-26	94-96	N. Mexico
12	26-28	96-98	S. Texas
13	26-28	94-96	S. Texas
14	28-30	94-96	Galveston
15	26-28	92-94	Lake Charles
16	28-30	92-94	Lake Charles
17	28-30	90-92	Morgan City
18	26-28	90-92	Morgan City
19	28-30	88-90	Miss. Delta
20	26-28	88-90	Miss. Delta
21	28-30	86-88	Pensacola
22	26-28	86-88	Pensacola
23	28-30	84-86	Apalichicola
24	26-28	84-86	Apalichicola
25	28-30	82-84	Crystal River
26	26-28	82-84	Tampa
27	24-26	82-84	SW Florida

Notes: Squares 19 and 20 supposedly are the zoogeographic "cut-off" or "boundary" area. In square 27, locations must be north of 24° 30'N, the southeastern boundary of the Gulf of Mexico. (Anything taken south of the Dry Tortugas is not considered to be in the Gulf of Mexico).

The TCWC has over 3,000 samples of fishes captured at depths greater than 300 m from the northern Gulf of Mexico between 84° and 96° W longitude. Proofing the data base was time consuming because about one quarter of the samples had missing data fields, including latitude, longitude, and depth. These data had to be located in survey data records such as Springer and Bullis (1956), Bullis and Thompson (1965), and Chittenden and Moore (1976); in cruise records of the *Alaminos* and *Gyre*; and in field notes housed in the TCWC. Also, because dates of capture and initial identifications ranged over a 60 year period, many of the identifications and much of the nomenclature had to be updated. It took several passes through the 3,000 records to rectify the data. The proofing process reduced the fish records to 2,296 for which missing data fields could be reconstructed and for which specimens could be reliably identified at least to genus.

Based on DGoMB Cruise 1 and the holdings of the TCWC, the northern slope of the Gulf of Mexico has a diverse fish fauna of 364 species representing 108 families; however, 74 species representing 12 families, are epipelagic or mesopelagic, and likely were caught in the water column prior to or after the sampling gear reached the bottom. The families Macrouridae, with 37 or 38 species; Ophidiidae, with 24 or 25 species; and Alepocephalidae, with 14 or 15 species are represented by the most species and individuals. Families of secondary importance are Rajidae (skates), with nine or ten species; Ipnopidae, with seven or eight species, Triglidae (searobins), with seven or eight species; Squalidae (dogfish sharks), with six species, and Scyliorhinidae (catsharks), with five or six species.

Species composition varied with depth of capture. A total of 149 species representing 64 families were captured between 300 m and 500 m; however, 30 species representing 12 families were epipelagic or mesopelagic and were probably captured in the water column. The families represented by the most species were Macrouridae, with 18 species; Triglidae, with six species; Rajidae, with six species; and Scorpaenidae (scorpion fishes), with five species. Families of secondary importance were Squalidae, with four species; Ophidiidae, with four species; Moridae, with four species; and Ogcocephalidae (batfishes), with three species.

Between 500 and 1000 m, 208 species representing 72 families were captured; however, 48 species representing 12 families, were epipelagic or mesopelagic and were probably captured in the water column. The families represented by the most species were Macrouridae, with 26 or 27 species; Ophidiidae, with 10 species; and Rajidae, with seven species. Families of secondary importance are Synaphobranchidae (cutthroat eels), with six species; Alepocephalidae, with five species; and Nettastomatidae (duckbill eels), with four species.

Between 1000 and 2000 m, 114 species representing 43 families were captured; however, 24 species representing nine families were epipelagic or mesopelagic and were probably captured in the water column. Families represented by the most species were Macrouridae, with 22 species; Ophidiidae with 13 species; and Alepocephalidae, with 10 species. Families of secondary abundance were Ipnopidae, with four species, and Rajidae, Halosauridae, and Synaphobranchidae, with three species each.

Between 2000 m and 3000 m, 71 species representing 33 families were captured; however, 25 species representing 10 families were epipelagic or mesopelagic and were probably captured in the water column. Families represented with the most species were Ophidiidae, with 11 species, Ipnopidae with six species; and Alepocephalidae, with four species.

The historical data base includes the great majority of the benthic fishes either known or thought to inhabit the slope of the northern Gulf of Mexico (McEachran and Fechhelm 1998, unpubl. ms.). These data reveal, as did Powell et al. (unpubl. ms.), that the fish fauna is zoned by depth. The families Macrouridae, Triglidae, Rajidae, and Ophidiidae dominate the upper slope (300 to 500 m). The families Macrouridae, Ophidiidae, and Rajidae dominate the middle slope (500 to 1000 m). The families Macrouridae, Ophidiidae, and Alepocephalidae dominate the lower slope (1000 to 2000 m). The families Ophidiidae, Alepocephalidae, and Ipnopidae dominate the lower slope-continental rise (2000 to 3000 m). Although macrourids were the most diverse family in three of the four depth strata, the taxonomic composition within the family varies with depth. The genera *Hymenocephalus* and *Malacocephalus*, and species *Caelorinchus caelorhincus* and *C. caribbaeus* are most common on the upper and mid slope. The genus *Coryphaenoides* and species *Cetonurus globiceps*, *Sphagemacrurus grenadae*, and *Squalogadus modificatus* are most abundant on the mid to lower slope. Species composition of Ophidiidae, to a lesser degree, also varies with depth.

The demersal fish data is further examined in the light of the hypotheses being tested. In each table below, CPUE (number/hr) is a measure of abundance, 'Species' is the number of demersal fish species taken, H' diversity is the Shannon-Wiener information function, and % overlap is the percentage similarity between the region where the region in question and the next region (i.e., directly below, the overlap between the Shelf and the Upper Slope fauna is 3.2%; Table 5.8).

Table 5.8. Fish characteristics by capture and location.

Depth Zones (n=34)	Shelf	Upper slope	Mid-slope	Lower slope	Rise
CPUE	52.8	170.9	74.8	5.0	5.5
Species	16	53	37	18	17
H' Diversity	0.80	1.45	1.13	1.16	1.09
% overlap	3.2	9.7	8.1	15.4	

The Upper Slope has the highest abundance, species number, and diversity. The 5 zones indicated in the table are well-defined and the overlap at all levels is small (the greatest, 15.4%, is where one would expect the least difference -- Lower Slope to Rise). This suggests that the largest faunal differences are due to differences in water depth.

Because the fauna is zoned with depth, two comparisons were conducted to test east/west trends in the data (Table 5.9). In the shallow water comparison (shelf/upper slope), the Canyon samples were deleted (Table 5.10). Abundance was highest in the Canyon site and least at the West sites. Diversity was lowest in the Canyons and Central sites. Each region was rather distinct, as shown by the generally lower values in percent overlap (the last value of overlap, 16.9%, is for East-West). These data do not support the hypothesis of a regular east/west trend on fish distributions, particularly because the Canyon is so different.

Table 5.9. East to west faunal comparison (shelf/upper slope depths) including the Canyon.

Shelf / Upper Slope (n=11)	East	Canyon	Central	West
CPUE	148.0	234.0	196.0	65.3
Species	42	27	15	36
H' Diversity	1.32	1.14	0.81	1.28
% overlap	33.4	13.4	9.9	16.9

Table 5.10. East to west faunal comparison (lower slope/rise depths).

Lower Slope/Rise (n=15)	East	Central	West
CPUE	8.1	4.0	3.4
Species	21	10	17
H' Diversity	1.23	0.94	1.13
% overlap	30.8	24.1	51.1

The Canyon site is not as distinct on the lower slope and rise (and is furthermore explicitly dealt with below), so we only recognized a central zone (Table 5.10). The low species number and diversity in the Central region is interesting because it was unexpected. East and West are more similar (PS = 51.1%) than either is to the nearer Central region. These data weakly support the hypothesis.

The basin/non-basin comparison showed little difference in overall community parameters, although the non-basin values were a bit higher than the basin ones (Table 5.11). Abundance was relatively low and species were few, as would be expected for this more western region. There is some difference between the two regions in respect to faunal composition, as indicated by the percent overlap of 33.1%. This is weak support for the hypothesis.

Table 5.11. Basin to non-basin faunal comparison.

Lower slope (n=6)	Basin	Non-basin
CPUE	2.3	4.0
Species	6	8
H' Diversity	0.73	0.86
% overlap	31.3	

The comparisons of canyon and non-canyon sites were made at depth, the shallower situation having been addressed (Table 5.12). Community parameters were quite similar in and out of the canyons (MT stations), but the species composition was different. Percent overlap was only 12.5%. But this is also a part of the central region, where, as noted above, the number of species was rather low, and this could influence the percent overlap. This is weak support for the hypothesis that canyon and non-canyon sites are different.

Table 5.12. Canyon to non-canyon faunal comparison (lower slope/rise depths).

Lower Slope/Rise (n=3)	Canyon	Non-Canyon
CPUE	3.6	5.3
Species	6	6
H' Diversity	0.75	0.72
% overlap	12.5	

The spatial distribution information is shown on maps (Figures 5.55-5.58). A re-analysis of the older Pequegnat data in terms of the several megafaunal groups represented is planned. These data include information on echinoderms, crustaceans, polychaetes and various miscellaneous species in addition to fishes.

Too few stations were made in and out of both basins and canyons to be able, with the fish data, to come to firm conclusions. It would be useful to compare results from other faunal groups, when the data become available, to see if better support for some hypotheses can be found. For this reason, it is important to complete biogeographic studies based on a number of groups.

5.3.5.7   ADCP Detection of Mobile Near-Bottom Fauna

On DGoMB Cruise 2, four deployments of the free-vehicle ADCP were made. From these deployments 29, 16, 70, and 26 hours of usable ADCP backscatter data were collected (see Table 5.13). The water depths in which the ADCP was recording data were 935 m in the first deployment, 755 m in the second deployment, 1,823 m in the third deployment, and 2,740 m in the fourth deployment (see Table 5.13). For each deployment, the downward looking ADCP was moored 35 m off the bottom and data were logged every 15 minutes by two meter depth bins. Measurements collected within 4 m of the ADCP's transducers (35-4 = 31 m off bottom) were too close to the instrument to give accurate data, and at and below approximately 28 m from the instrument (35-28 = 7 m off bottom), the bottom echo was too high to allow accurate data. Thus, there were a total of 11 usable depth bins (from 35-6 = 29 m off bottom to 35-26 = 9 m off bottom).

Table 5.13. Backscatter averaged from the 14-m depth bin (21 m off bottom) in four deployments.

	Date/Time (local time)	Location	Water Depth	Average Backscatter (read data as counts)
Deployment 1 MT-3	6/3/01 - 6/4/01 12:00 pm-3:00 pm	Lat 28°13.3N Long 89°30.0W	935 m	129
Deployment 2 S-42	6/6/01 - 6/7/01 6:15 pm-2:00 pm	Lat 28°15.0N Long 86°25.0W	755 m	146
Deployment 3 S-36	6/9/01 - 6/12/01 9:45 am-7:30 am	Lat 28°55.2N Long 87°40.1W	1,823 m	120
Deployment 4 MT-6	6/12/01 - 6/14/01 11:00 pm-12:30 am	Lat 27°00.0 N Long 88°00.0W	2,740 m	111

Mean backscatter intensity was higher in the shallower ADCP deployments. The highest intensities were seen in deployment two, where the water depth was 755 m, and the lowest in deployment four, where water depth was 2,740 m. Higher current velocities in general correspond to lower backscatter intensities. Summary data from the four deployments is shown in Table 5.13. There was no apparent phase change seen in the data collected during the four deployments to indicate diel vertical migration of scavengers or zooplankton. However, at least 3

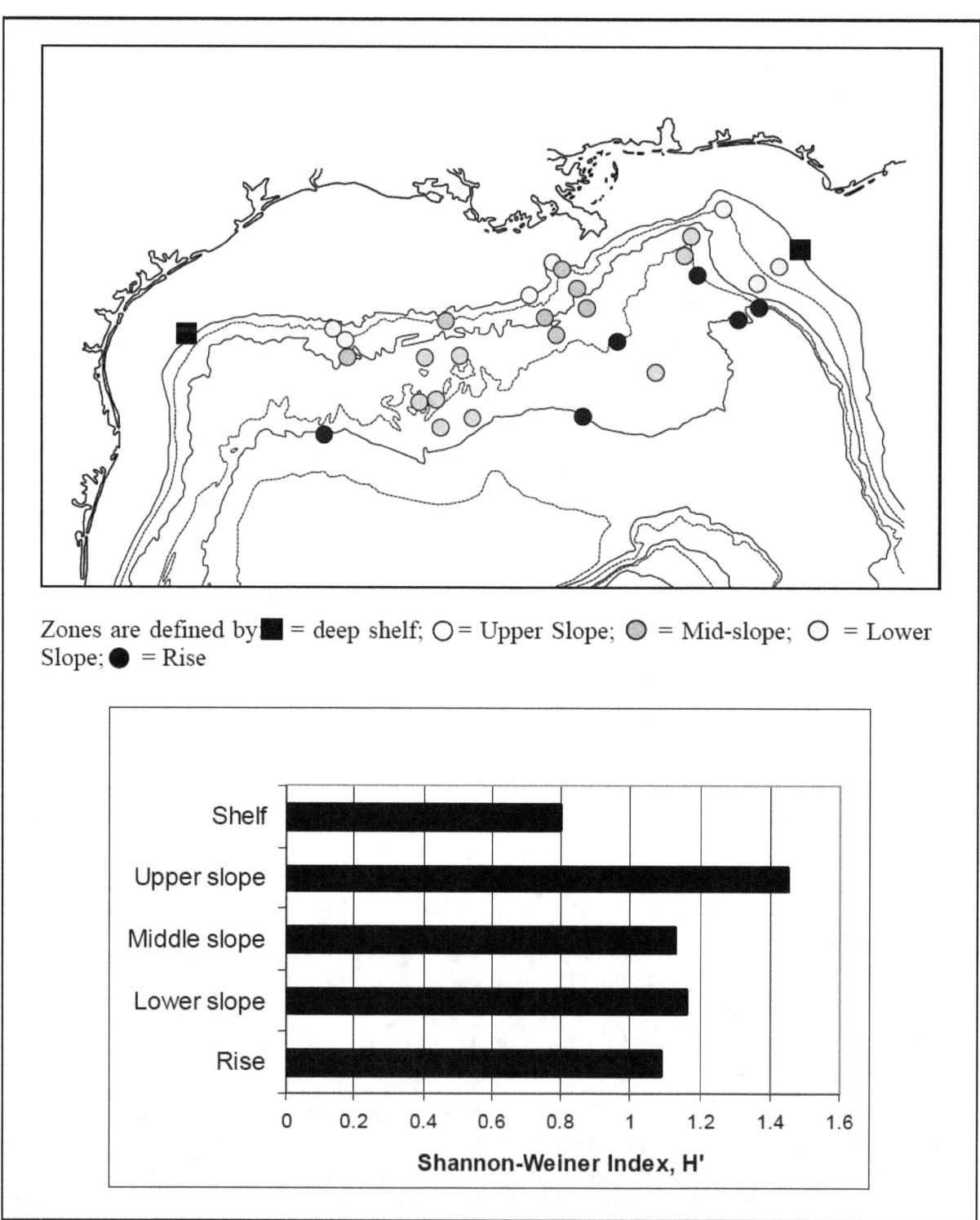

Zones are defined by ■ = deep shelf; ○ = Upper Slope; ◉ = Mid-slope; ○ = Lower Slope; ● = Rise

Figure 5.55. Zonation and diversity (H') in demersal fishes.

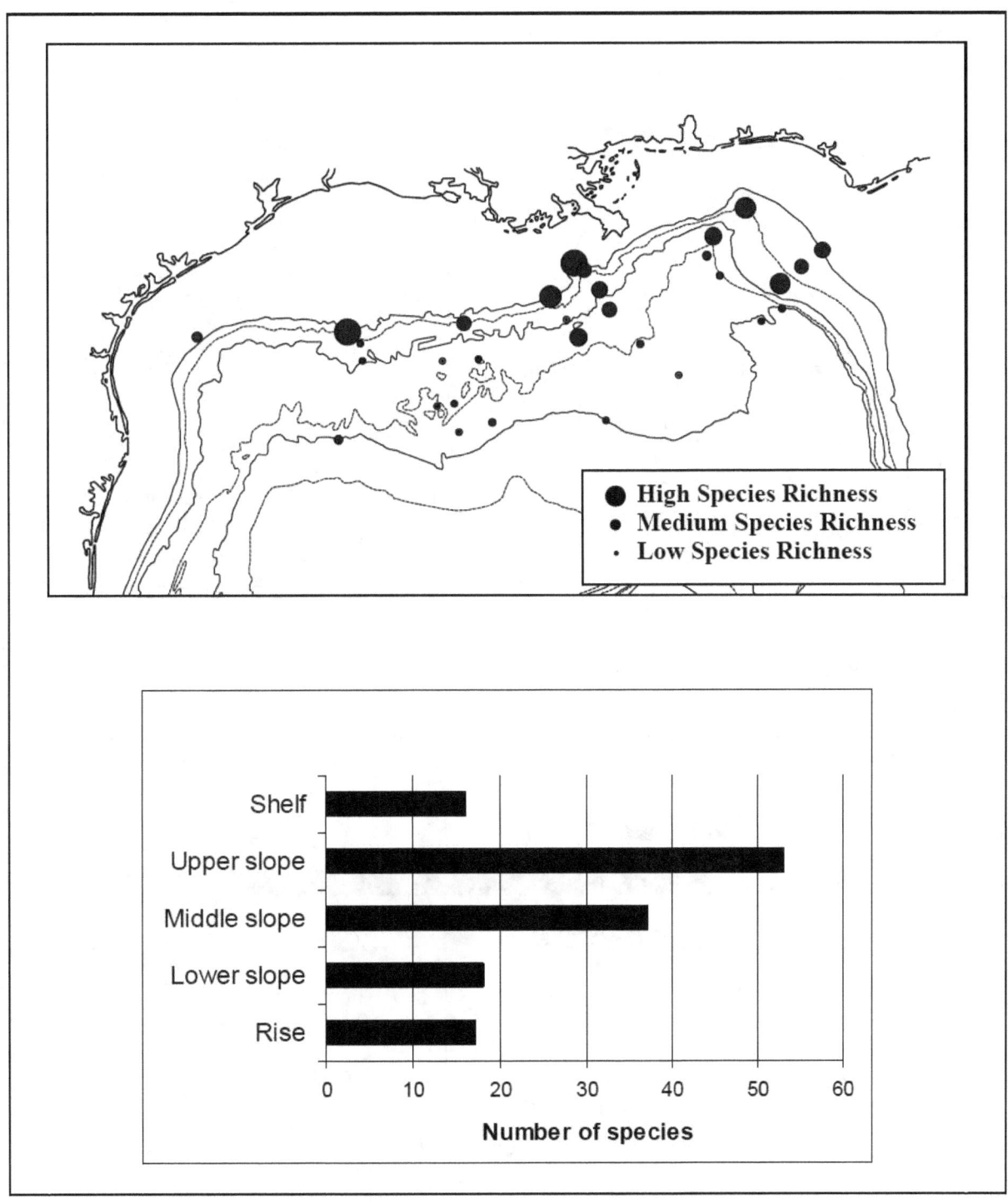

Figure 5.56. Species richness in demersal fishes.

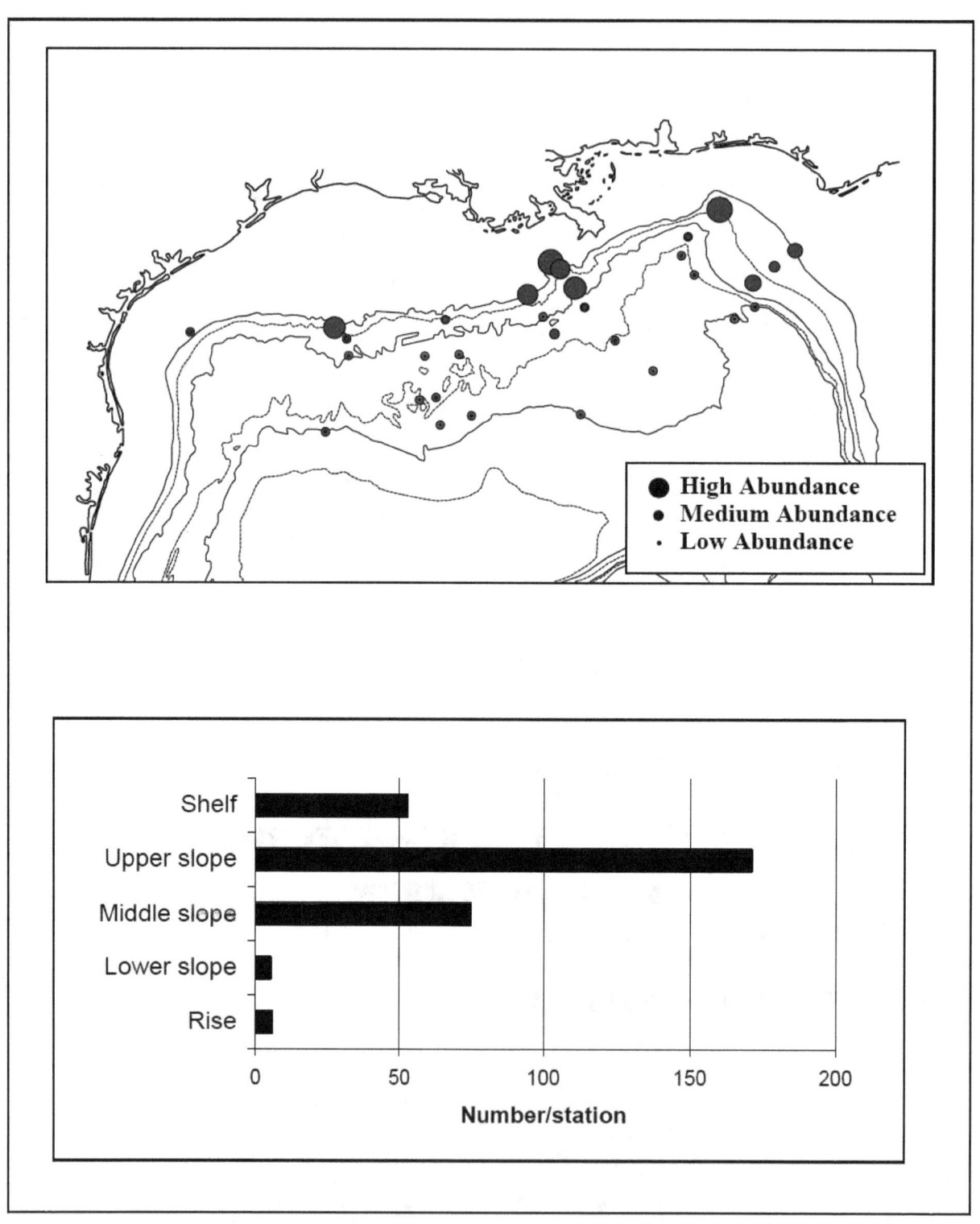

Figure 5.57. Abundance of demersal fishes by depth zone.

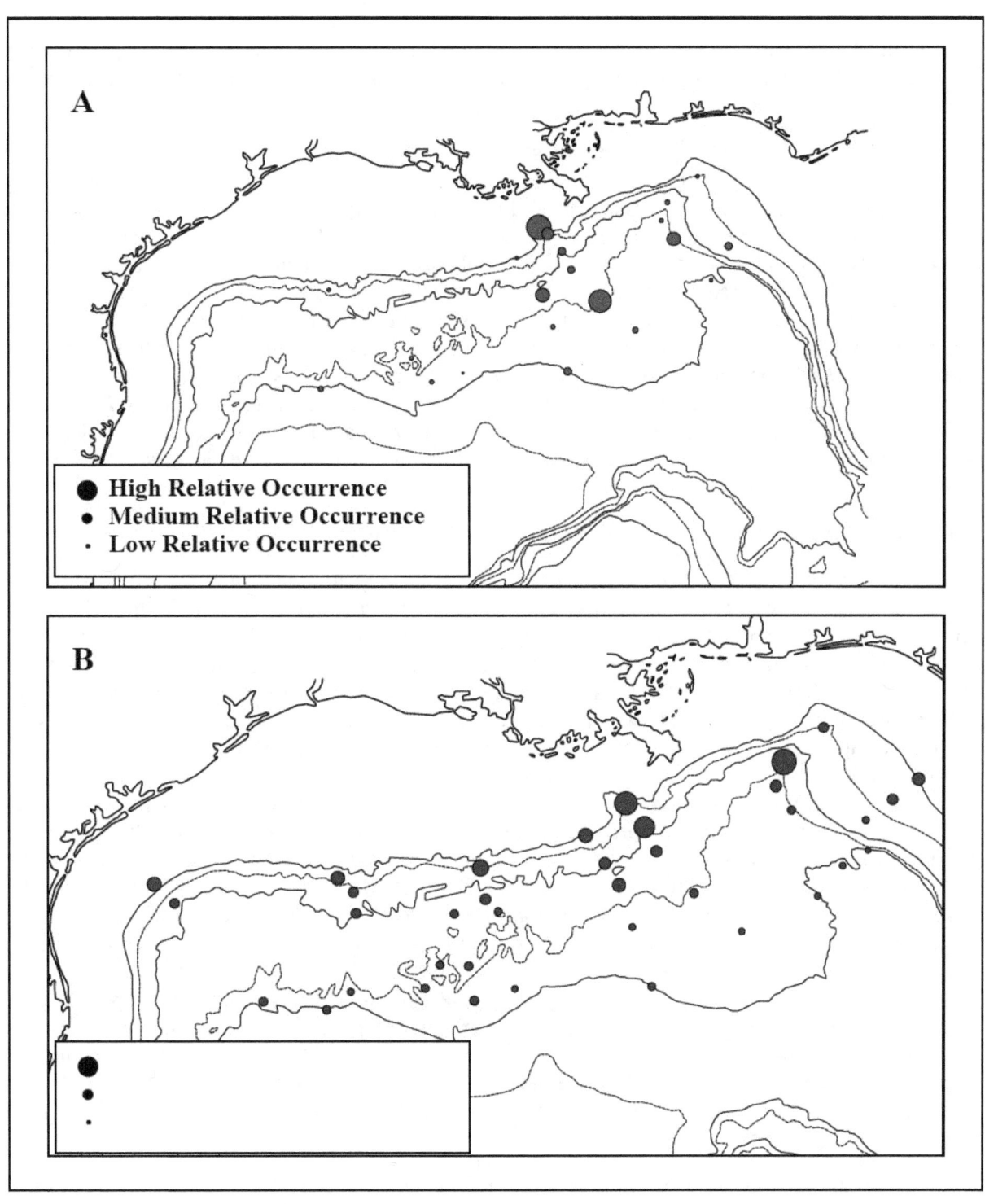

Figure 5.58. Maps of relative occurrences of A) trawl-caught trash and B) relative abundance of macrofaunal sized nematodes (CPUE is catch per unit efforts).

of the four depths sampled were below depths at which light should penetrate to give a day/night cue. Light penetration data from the Optical Backscatter Sensor (OBS) on the CTD will later be obtained to check for a possible diel light signal.

To analyze the ADCP measurements, the initial binary data were transcribed into ASCII format using the program BBlist (downloaded from the RDInstruments website). Preliminary graphs of backscatter intensity versus time and current velocity versus time for each of the depth bins from 6-26 m were then created to look for patterns in the data. The time series for deployments 2 and 3 is shown in Figure 5.59. Analysis continues using PV-Wave and programs created by Steve DiMarco and Rebecca Scott to convert the intensity which was collected in relative counts to decibels and to use 40 hour lowpass filters to smooth the data. This will allow inner comparison of data among the four deployments as well as comparison with moored data from near surface time series. Completion of the ADCP data analysis from DGoMB Cruise 2 is expected at the end of February, 2002. For the next and final field season (summer 2002), it is planned to return to two of the deployment sites and open a baited trap midway through the ADCP deployment period. The trap will be opened using timed burnwires and used to look for any associated changes in backscatter intensity.

5.4   Community Function/Processes and Model Development

Process studies began on DGoMB Cruise 2. Few results are finalized from that field work, but a summary of preliminary observations can be presented to illustrate the trends that are emerging. Total sediment community oxygen consumption (SCOC) is estimated from incubations of sediments with overlying water. The decline in oxygen concentration in the chambers as a function of time is used as a measure community respiration (SCOC). *In situ* incubations were conducted at two lander sites and ship-board laboratory incubations were carried out at five sites at *in situ* temperatures. Additional data have been generated by sending DGoMB researchers out with the *Johnson Sea-Link* submersible to sites on the continental slope. The locations are not DGoMB sites, but they add to the database for the slope environment in the GOM. In addition to these slope sites, shallow water continental shelf incubations were conducted at locations of studies by the MMS-supported GOOMEX program off Port Aransas, Texas and in the fine carbonate sands adjacent to the coral banks at the Flower Gardens National Sanctuary. Two SCOC values at two abyssal plain sites have been taken from the literature (Hinga et al. 1979; eastern GOM abyssal plain) and Rowe et al. (in press, western GOM abyssal plain). So far, therefore, a total of 14 values can be presented as representative of the GOM continental margin in the region of oil and gas development on the continental slope. To this, five (5) continental shelf sites and two (2) deep abyssal plain sites have been added. This database thus allows us to characterize the general nature of SCOC in the western Gulf of Mexico. This database does not include numerous values available near or adjacent to the Mississippi River plume as they tend to be affected by a number of processes associated with the river that are atypical of the GOM as a whole.

The SCOC from the western GoM continental shelf down across the slope to the abyssal plain can be characterized by a log-log relationship with depth (Figure 5.60). The units of measure are mmoles O_2 m^{-2} d^{-1}. Thus, rates decline from about 30 mmoles O_2 m^{-2}d^{-1} on the shelf down to less than 1 on the abyssal plain. This would account for a turnover of organic carbon by

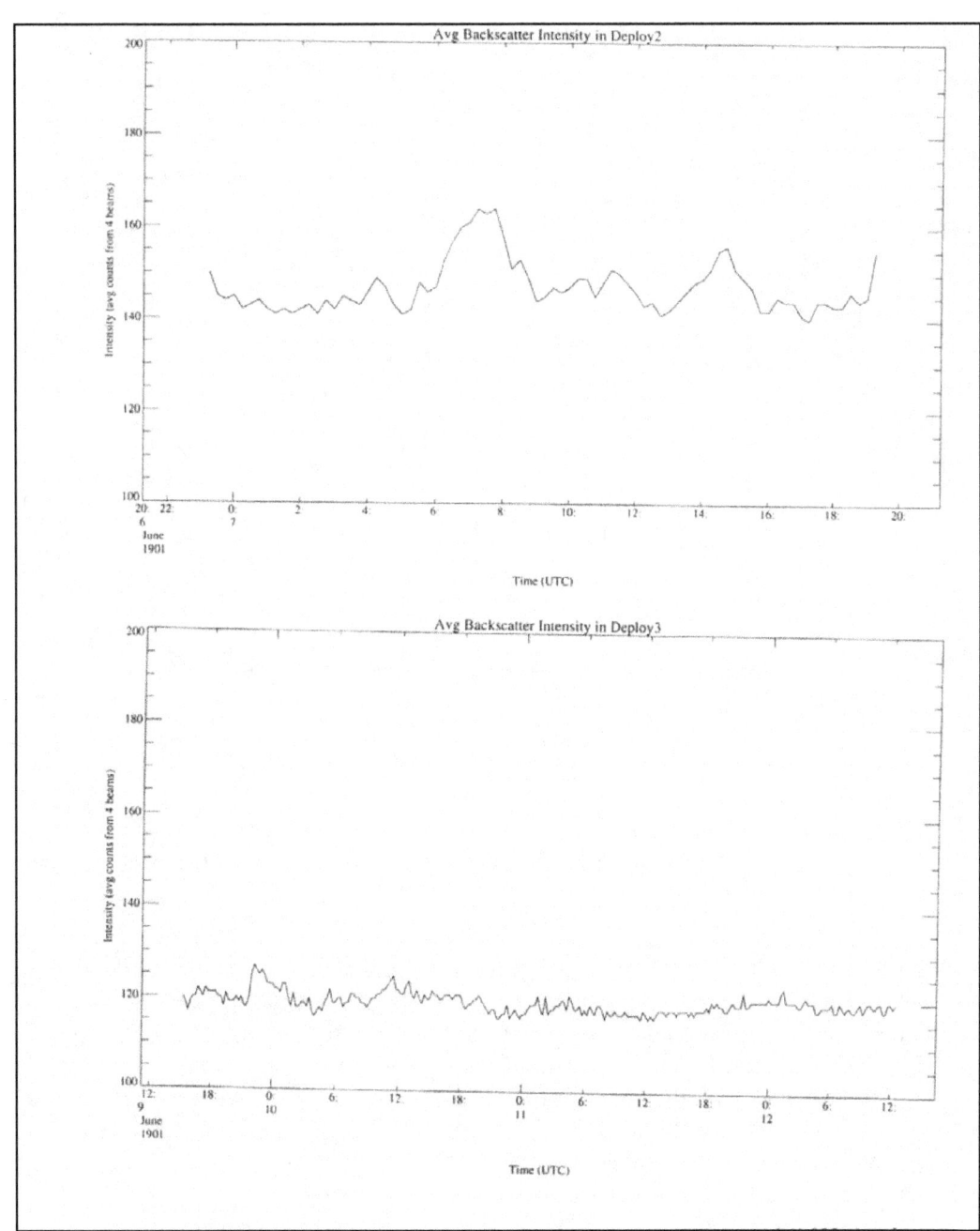

Figure 5.59.   Raw ADCP backscatter intensity from deployments 2 (755 m) and 3 (1,823 m) at the 14 m depth bin (21 m off bottom).   The intensity was read in counts and was averaged for the ADCP's four beams.

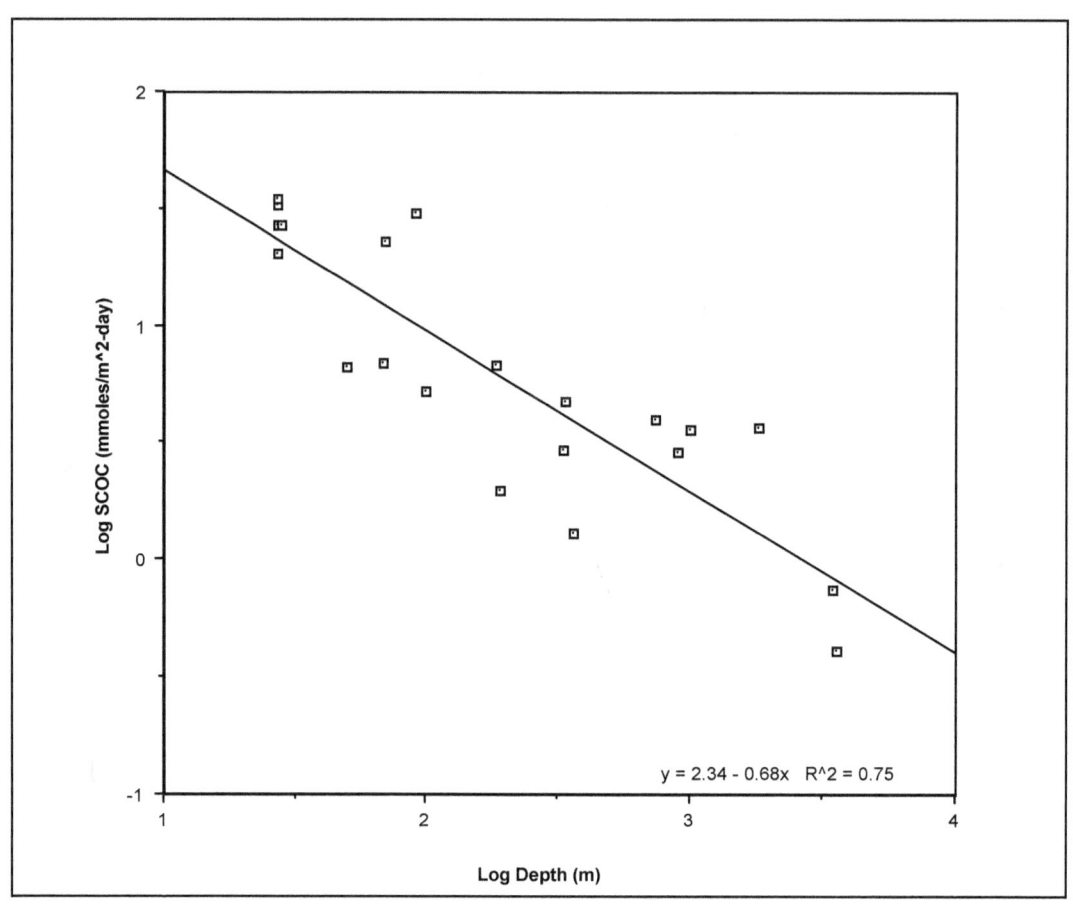

Figure 5.60. The SCOC from the western GOM continental shelf down across the slope to the abyssal plain is characterized by a log-log relationship with depth.

these communities of about 300 down to less than 10 mg C m^{-2} d^{-1} over the depth range of the data available. These values are typical for most continental margins where similar studies have been conducted. It is worth noting at this point that the variation at any particular depth down the slope is high. This is because a wide range of divergent types of habitats have been included in the study to get as broad a range of conditions as possible. Ensuing studies will be attempting to use the characteristics of the biota to explain why the rates of SCOC vary from site to site. Contrasting different SCOC values among the different environments will constitute an important approach to differentiating between habitats.

5.5   Task 4 - Data Interpretation, Synthesis, and Reporting

A preliminary interpretation of data is provided in Section 6.0.

6.0 PRELIMINARY OBSERVATIONS AND SUMMARY

The progress in the present program to date has been focussed along narrow sub-disciplinary lines, as reported in Section 5.0 The study however has been designed to be interdisciplinary, composed of parallel measurements of a wide variety of environmental variables that could play roles in or have effects upon the communities of organisms that live in association with the deep ocean floor in the northern GoM. In the reports presented in Section 5.0, little attempt has been made to compare or synthesize results because they are incomplete and preliminary. The individual investigators have not yet had the opportunity to make comparisons among the on-going parallel studies. The purpose of this section is to call attention to those areas of overlap and interaction that are beginning to emerge from the data sets, even though most of them are as yet preliminary. It is important to point out these relationships now because the field program and the thrust of the process studies is intended to be iterative. The choice of sites, the activities at each site, the details of the experimental protocols, and the on-board sampling will be rehashed as the information in Section 5.0, and the synthesis attempted here, are considered and discussed among the principal investigators.

A long-held paradigm in deep-sea biology is that depth, or some correlate with it, has over-riding control over benthic community structure and dynamics. As a result all the biological size groups have been plotted against depth, but with somewhat different results. The abundance of metazoans (meiofauna and macrofauna) living within the sediments correlated negatively with depth, but with rather wide variations at any depth along the gradient (Figures 5.43 and 5.50). The bacteria densities did not decline in nearly as consistent a fashion with depth, however (Figure 5.37). When anomalously high values were excluded from the different regressions, the coefficients all increased measurably (Figures 5.51 and 5.52). In each case, the anomalous values came from many of the same sites for each group: the Mississippi Trough and the DeSoto Canyon. This coherence between the high values in each group suggests that these sites are all characterized by exceptionally high inputs of organic detritus. The gulf, we might conclude, can be partitioned into regions of high biomass and low biomass. Thus other factors besides depth influence deep ocean biomass. The decline in sediment community oxygen consumption (SCOC), as measured by in situ incubations (Figure 5.60), declined with depth as expected, but values at the mid-slope experimental site in the Mississippi Trough (MT3) were above the regression line, reinforcing the suggestion in standing stocks that the trough is an enriched region. The SCOC regression did not include sites that were within methane seep communities. The effect of seeps will be considered when more samples near seeps have been analyzed.

The stations were distributed on the survey to provide broad geographic coverage with a wide variety of environmental and biological standing stock data. As anticipated, those data fields can be mapped across broad horizontal regions of the continental slope. For many of the data fields, no such information has ever existed before. Thus, this program will be generating maps of entirely new biogeographic information that will eventually be published in the peer-refereed literature. In general, deep-ocean studies sample along transects across depth gradients. While this provides useful analyses of the responses of variables to depth, they do not provide information that can be mapped: DGoMB data on the other hand will be amenable to mapping across the entire northern GoM. The usefulness of these maps is already emerging in on-going DGoMB analyses. For example, the degree of bioturbation, as indicated by the variation in the physical properties of sediments in short cores, is minor over vast areas of the western GoM

(Figures 5.19-5.24) but is intense over much of the eastern GoM. Trace organic contaminants, while well below values that might affect the biota, have a distribution that can be contoured in a pattern that implies that the source is the Louisiana continental shelf or the Mississippi River (Figures 5.27 and 5.28). Meiofaunal densities are clearly highest on the upper slope, but the head of the Mississippi Trough jumps out as being far higher than any other area (Figure 5.44). The fish fauna is partitioned by depth, with different combinations of relatively distinct assemblages characterizing the outer shelf, the upper slope, the deep slope and the upper rise, all around the northern GoM (Figure 5.55). As each of the different data sets become available, they will each be displayed as maps, providing similar insightful conclusions.

This project is based on hypotheses that will be used to predict what to expect of bottom communities in different environments. Although it is hypothesis based, it is also model driven. That is, evolving conceptual models are used to direct an evolving set of process measurements that are being used to construct a budget of the carbon stocks and carbon cycling through the components of the food web of organisms living on or near the sea floor. One cruise to measure processes has now been completed (June 2001). Some of the results are now available and have been reported on in Section 5.0. This section of this Interim Report 2 will attempt to identify the areas in which these processes appear to agree and interact and the instances in which relationships are as yet obscure.

The choice of the sites where processes would be studied was based on results of the survey of standing stocks. It was reasoned that rates of metabolic processes would be highest, input of organic matter would be highest, growth rates would be elevated, etc., at those sites with the highest biomass and greatest densities of organisms. And the opposite was also assumed: the lowest rates would be found at the sites where abundances and biomass were the lowest. Based on these assumptions, the four contrasting sites chosen were MT3 and S36, as representatives of sites with high biomass, and MT6 and S42, as representatives of sites with low biomasses and thus low rates. In making these choices, we searched for and found conformity between the standing stocks of the different size groups being measured: bacteria, meiofauna, macrofauna, megafauna and fishes. The sites were chosen based on discussions among the PIs at Interim Meeting No. 1, in February, 2001. Maps and locations of these sites can be found in the cruise report of the survey cruise in 2000, in the results of the !st Interim Meeting, in the Cruise Plan for the first processes cruise, June, 2001, and in the report on that cruise.

This portion of the work is model driven, but the models being applied are in a constant state of evolution. The earliest conceptual model presented as basis for this study was derived from a study of the NW Sigsbee Abyssal Plain, at a depth of 3.65 km (Rowe et al. in press). That linear and branched food web analysis (Figure 1) has now been modified for heuristic purposes. This new version (Figure 6.1) places organic matter at the center of the system, thus illustrating its hypothetical importance as the over-riding forcing function in the processes that characterize the system. The main source of organic matter is sinking POC, but other sources are possible (import from pelagic food webs and methane seeps). The major fates of organic matter are remineralization into metabolic CO_2 by each of the size groups and long-term burial within the sediments.

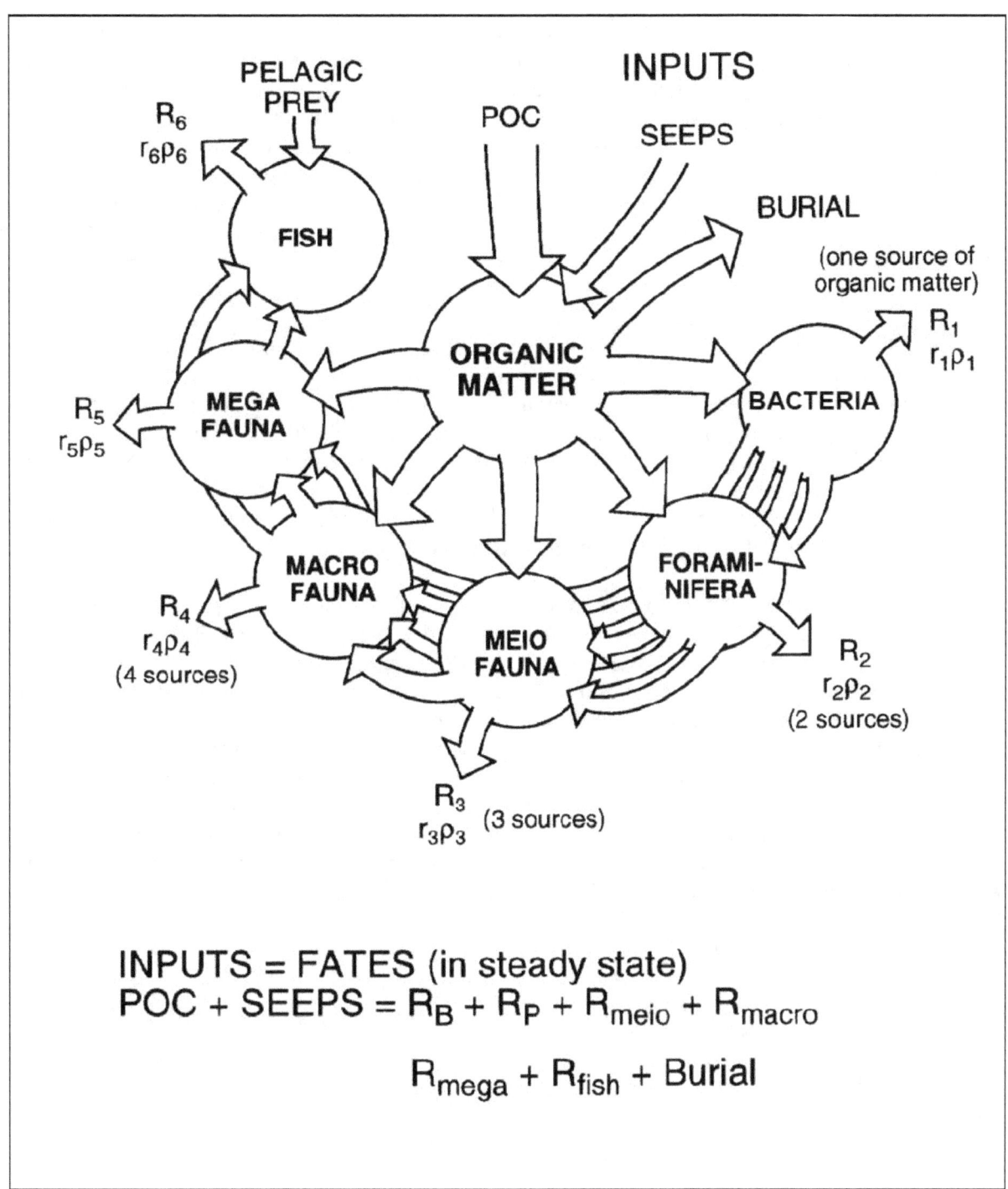

Figure 6.1. Conceptual model of a hypothetical deep benthos foodweb illustrating that the input of organic carbon controls the web's structure and dynamics.

Model output is now also available from the Sigsbee study referred to above (Rowe et al. in press). The surface concentration of pigments is known to vary seasonally by a factor of two. If this degree of variation is transferred to the rate of POC input needed to support the sediment biological fates, then the sea floor values will vary accordingly. As Rowe et al. point out, there is a temporal lag in maximum biomass for each size group, as the organic pulse is transferred up the food web (Figure 6.1). These recognizable patterns in standing stocks have been modeled in other systems, but validating the seasonality has not yet been possible. It has been observed that POC input varies by season, but how this affects biomass is unknown. The values we present are only theoretical so far.

The general pattern of metabolic intensity does appear to follow the pattern we predicted. For example, the oxygen concentration gradient is steepest at MT3 and the least at MT6. This pattern is similar to that found for bioturbational mixing, as reflected in the radionuclide distributions, with the caveat that biomass should be proportional to POC input. If bioturbation is a function of biomass, and the biomass is highest at MT3, then why is oxygen penetration the least at MT3? This appears to be a contradiction. Shouldn't oxygen penetration be greatest where mixing is the greatest? We assume at this point that our presumption that mixing is a function of biomass is true, but that the oxygen declines precipitously because metabolic consumption, which is also accentuated by high POC input, outpaces oxygen penetration.

The most important data to date is our increasing ability to predict sediment community oxygen consumption (SCOC) rates as a function of depth (Figure 5.60). This illustrates the overall decline in metabolic processes as a function of depth. While the line is significant and confirms the steep rate at which community metabolism declines with depth and distance from shore, the variation around the line is large, almost an order of magnitude. A next step will be to determine the internal consistency between the various different approaches to estimating community metabolism and the rates of the separate individual components within the assemblage of organisms. This cross checking is now underway. These rates will eventually be the ground truth against which the model-generated values are compared. The regression is very preliminary and will be supplemented by lander deployments to be made during ensuing field work described in the earlier chapters of this document.

7.0 LITERATURE CITED

Bayne, B.L. K.R. Clarke, and J.S. Gray. 1988. Background and rationale to a practical workshop on biological effects of pollutants. Mar. Ecol. Prog. Ser. 46:1-5.

Boothe, P.N. and B.J. Presley. 1989. Trends in sediment trace element concentrations around six petroleum drilling platforms in the northwestern Gulf of Mexico. In: F.R. Engelhardt, J.P. Ray and A.H. Gillam, eds. Proceedings of the 1988 International Conference on Drilling Wastes, Calgary, Canada, 5-8 April. Elsevier Applied Science, New York. pp. 3-21.

Boothe, P.N. and B.J. Presley. 1985. Distribution and behavior of drilling fluids and cuttings around Gulf of Mexico drilling sites. Report to the American Petroleum Institute, Washington, DC 140 pp.

Bullis, H.R., Jr. and J.R. Thompson. 1965. Collections by the exploratory fishing vessels *Oregon*, *Silver Bay*, *Combat*, and *Pelican* made during 1956 to 1960 in the southwestern North Atlantic. U.S. Fish. Wildl. Serv. Spec. Sci. Rep. Fish. 510:1-30.

Carney, R.S. [ed.]. 1998. Workshop on environmental Issues Surrounding Deepwater Oil and Gas Development: Final Report. U.S. Department of the Interior, Minerals Management Service, Gulf of Mexico Region. New Orleans, LA. 163 pp. OCS Study 98-0022.

Chittenden, M.E., Jr. and D. Moore. 1976. Composition of the ichthyofauna inhabiting the 100 m bathymetric contour of the Gulf of Mexico, Mississippi River to the Rio Grande. Sea Grant Publ. No. TAMU-SG-76-210. 156 pp.

Coull, B.C., R.L. Ellison, J.W. Fleeger, R.P. Higgins, W.D. Hope, W.D. Hummon, R.M. Rieger, W.E. Sterrer, J. Thiel, and J.H. Tietjen. 1977. Quantitative estimates of the meiofauna from the deep-sea off North Carolina, USA. Mar. Biol. 39:233-240.

Ferraro, S.P. and F.A. Cole. 1990. Taxonomic level and sample size sufficient for assessing pollution impacts on the Southern California Bight macrobenthos. Mar. Ecol. Prog. Ser. 67:251-262.

Gooday, A.J. 1986. Meiofaunal foraminiferans from the bathyal Porcupine Seabight (northeast Atlantic): size, structure, standing stock, taxonomic composition, species diversity and vertical distribution in the sediments. Deep-Sea Res. 33:1345-1373.

Green, R.H. and P. Montagna. 1996. Implications for monitoring: study designs and interpretation of results. Can. J. Fish. Aquat. Sci. 53:2629-2636.

Haedrich, R.L. and J.E. Maunder. 1985. The echinoderm fauna of the Newfoundland continental slope. Proc. 5th Int. Echinoderm Conf., Galway, September 1984.

Haedrich, R.L. and N.R. Merrett. 1988. Summary atlas of deep-living demersal fishes in the North Atlantic. J. Nat. Hist. 22:1325-1362.

Haedrich, R.L., G.T. Rowe, and P.T. Polloni. 1980. The megabenthic fauna in the deep-sea south of New England. Mar. Biol. 57:165-179.

Heip, C., R.M. Warwick, M.R. Carr, P.M.J. Herman, R. Huys, N. Smol, and K. Van Holsbeke. 1988. Analysis of community attributes of the benthic meiofauna of Frierfjord/ Langesundfjord. Mar. Ecol. Prog. Ser. 46:171180.

Hinga, K., J. Sieburth, and G. Heath. 1979. The supply and use of organic material by the deep-sea benthos. J. Mar. Res. 37:557-579.

Kennicutt, M.C. II, P.N. Boothe, T.L. Wade, S.T. Sweet, R. Rezak, F.J. Kelly, J.M. Brooks, B.J. Presley, and D.A. Wiesenburg. 1996. Geochemical patterns in sediments near offshore production platforms. Can. J. Fish. Aquat. Sci. 53:2554-2566.

Kirk, R.E. 1982. Experimental Design: Procedures for the Behavioral Sciences. 2nd edition. Brooks/Cole Publishing Co., Belmont, California. 911 p.

LGL Ecological Associates, Inc. and Texas A&M University. 1988. Northern Gulf of Mexico Continental Slope Study. Year 4 Final Report. U.S. Department of the Interior, Minerals Management Service, Gulf of Mexico Region, New Orleans, LA. Volume I, Executive Summary; Volume II, Syntheses Report; Volume III, Appendices. OCS Study 88-0052, 88-0053, 88-0054.

Lin, S. and J.W. Morse. 1991. Sulfate reduction and iron sulfide mineral formation in Gulf of Mexico anoxic sediments. American Journal of Science 291:55-89.

Linke, P. 1992. Metabolic adaptations of deep-sea benthic foraminifera to seasonally varying food input. Mar. Ecol. Progr. Ser. 81:51-63.

Long, E.R. and L.G. Morgan. 1990. The potential for biological effects of sediment-sorbed contaminants tested in the National Status and Trends Program. NOAA Tech. Memo. NOS OMA 52, U.S. Department of Commerce, National Oceanographic and Atmospheric Administration, Seattle, WA.

MacDonald, I.R. [ed.]. 1998. Stability and Change in Gulf of Mexico Chemosynthetic Communities. Interim Report. Prepared by the Texas A&M University Geochemical and Environmental Research Group for the U.S. Department of the Interior, Minerals Management Service, Gulf of Mexico Region, New Orleans, LA. 96 pp. OCS Study 98-0034.

MacDonald, I.R., Wm. W. Schroeder, and J.M. Brooks. 1996. Chemosynthetic Ecosystem Study. Final Report. Prepared by the Texas A&M University Geochemical and Environmental Research Group for the U.S. Department of the Interior, Minerals Management Service, Gulf of Mexico Region, New Orleans, LA. 360 pp.

McEachran, J.D. and J.D. Fechhelm. 1998. Fishes of the Gulf of Mexico. Vol. 1. Myxiniformes to Gasterosteiformes. Univ. Texas Press, Austin. 1112 pp.

McEachran, J.D. and J.D. Fechhelm. Unpublished manuscript. Fishes of the Gulf of Mexico. Vol. 2. Scorpaeniformes to Tetraodontiiformes.

Melo-Gonzalez, N., F.E. Muller-Karger, S.Cerdeira-Estrada, R. Perez de los Reyes, I. Victoria del Rio, P. Cardenas-Perez, and I. Mitrani-Arenal. 2000. Near-surface phytoplankton distribution in the western Intra-Americas Sea: The influence of El Nino and weather events. J. Geophys. Res. 105:14,029-14,043.

Merrett, N.R. and R.L. Haedrich. 1997. Deep-Sea Demersal Fish and Fisheries. Chapman & Hall, London. 282 pp.

Montagna, P.A. 1995. Rates of meiofaunal microbivory: a review. Vie et Milieu 45:1-10.

Montagna, P.A. and D.E. Harper. 1996. Benthic infaunal long-term response to offshore production platforms in the Gulf of Mexico. Can. J. Fish. Aquat. Sci. 53:2567-2588

Muller-Karger, F.E., J.J. Walsh, R.H. Evans, and M.B. Meyers. 1991. On the seasonal phytoplankton concentration and sea surface temperature cycles of the Gulf of Mexico as determined by satellites. J. Geophys. Res. 96:12645-12665.

Neff, J.M., R.J. Breteler, and S.R. Carr. 1989. Bioaccumulation, food chain transfer and biological effects of barium and chromium from drilling muds by flounder, *pseudo pleuronectes americanus* and lobster, *Homarus americanus*. In, Drilling Wastes, F.R. Engelhardt, J.P. Ray and A.H. Gillam (eds.). Elsevier, London.

Pequegnat, W.E., B.J. Gallaway, and L.H. Pequegnat. 1990. Aspects of the ecology of the deep-water fauna of the Gulf of Mexico. American Zoologist 30:45-64.

Peterson, C.H., M.C. Kennicutt II, R.H. Green, P. Montagna, D.E. Harper, Jr., E.N. Powell, and P.F. Roscigno. 1996. Ecological consequences of environmental perturbations associated with offshore hydrocarbon production: a perspective on long-term exposures in the Gulf of Mexico. Can. J. Fish. Aquat. Sci. 53:2637-2654.

Powell, S., R.L. Haedrich, and J.D. McEachran. Unpublished manuscript. The deep-sea fish fauna of the northern Gulf of Mexico.

Presley, B.J., R.J. Taylor, and P.N. Boothe. 1992. Trace metal concentrations in sediments of the Eastern Mississippi Bight. Marine Environ. Res. 33:267-282.

Rapport, D.J. and W.G. Whitford. 1999. How ecosystems respond to stress. BioScience 49(3): 193-203.

Rapport, D.J., R. Constanza and A.J. McMichael. 1998. Assessing ecosystem health. TREE 13(10): 397-402.

Rowe, G., A. Lohse, G. Boland, E. Escobar Briones, G. F. Hubbard and Jody Deming. Trophic structure and dynamics in the benthos of the Sigsbee Deep, Northern Gulf of Mexico. American Fisheries Society Special Publication, The Gulf of Mexico: Fish and Fisheries Issues (in press).

Rowe, G. 1971. Benthic biomass and surface productivity. In: Fertility of the Sea, vol. 2, ed. by J. Costlow. Gordon and Breach, New York.

Rowe, G. 1998. Organic carbon cycling in abyssal benthic food chains: Numerical simulations of bioenhancement by sewage sludge. J. Mar. Syst. 14:337-354.

Rowe, G.T. and R.L. Haedrich. 1979. The biota and biological processes on the continental slope. in Doyle and Pilkey (eds.), The Continental Slope. Amer. Assoc. Petrol. Geol., Spec. Pub. No. 27: 49-59, Tulsa.

Rowe, G.T., G.S Boland, E.G. Escobar, M.E. Cruz-Kaegli, A. Newton, D. Piepenburg, I.D. Walsh, and J.W. Deming. 1997. Sediment community biomass and respiration in the Northeast Water Polynya, Greenland: A numerical simulation of benthic lander and spade core data. J. Mar. Systems 10:497-515.

Smith, K.L., Jr and R. Kaufmann. 1999. Long-term discrepancy between food supply and demand in the deep eastern Pacific. Science 284:1174-1177.

Smith, K.L., Jr. 1992. Benthic boundary layer communities and carbon cycling at abyssal depths in the central North Pacific. Limnol. Oceanogr. 37:1034-1056.

Snelgrove, P.V.R. and R.L. Haedrich. 1985. Structure of the deep demersal fish fauna off Newfoundland. Mar. Ecol. Prog. Ser. 27:99-107.

Snider, L.J., B.R. Burnett, and R.R. Hessler. 1984. The composition and distribution of meiofauna and nanobiota in a central North Pacific deep-sea area. Deep-Sea Res. 31:1225-1249.

Springer, S. and H.R. Bullis, Jr. 1956. Collections made by the Oregon in the Gulf of Mexico. U.S. Fish. Wildl. Serv. Spec. Sci. Rep. Fish. 196:1-134.

TerEco Corporation. 1976. Ecological Aspects of the Upper Continental Slope of the Gulf of Mexico. Prepared under contract 08550-CT4-12 for the U.S. Department of the Interior, Bureau of Land Management, Gulf of Mexico Region, New Orleans, LA. 560 pp.

TerEco Corporation. 1983. The Ecological Communities of the Continental Slope and Adjacent Regions. Prepared under contract AA851-CT1-12 for the U.S. Department of the Interior, Minerals Management Service, Gulf of Mexico Region, New Orleans, LA. 675 pp.

Trefry, J.H. and B.J. Presley. 1982. Manganese fluxes from Mississippi Delta sediments. Geochem. Cosmochem. Acta 46:1715-1726.

Warwick, R.M. 1988. Analysis of community attributes of the macrobenthos of Frierfjord/ Langesundfjord at taxonomic levels higher than species. Mar. Ecol. Prog. Ser. 46:167-170.

The Department of the Interior Mission

As the Nation's principal conservation agency, the Department of the Interior has responsibility for most of our nationally owned public lands and natural resources. This includes fostering sound use of our land and water resources; protecting our fish, wildlife, and biological diversity; preserving the environmental and cultural values of our national parks and historical places; and providing for the enjoyment of life through outdoor recreation. The Department assesses our energy and mineral resources and works to ensure that their development is in the best interests of all our people by encouraging stewardship and citizen participation in their care. The Department also has a major responsibility for American Indian reservation communities and for people who live in island territories under U.S. administration.

The Minerals Management Service Mission

As a bureau of the Department of the Interior, the Minerals Management Service's (MMS) primary responsibilities are to manage the mineral resources located on the Nation's Outer Continental Shelf (OCS), collect revenue from the Federal OCS and onshore Federal and Indian lands, and distribute those revenues.

Moreover, in working to meet its responsibilities, the **Offshore Minerals Management Program** administers the OCS competitive leasing program and oversees the safe and environmentally sound exploration and production of our Nation's offshore natural gas, oil and other mineral resources. The MMS **Minerals Revenue Management** meets its responsibilities by ensuring the efficient, timely and accurate collection and disbursement of revenue from mineral leasing and production due to Indian tribes and allottees, States and the U.S. Treasury.

The MMS strives to fulfill its responsibilities through the general guiding principles of: (1) being responsive to the public's concerns and interests by maintaining a dialogue with all potentially affected parties and (2) carrying out its programs with an emphasis on working to enhance the quality of life for all Americans by lending MMS assistance and expertise to economic development and environmental protection.

www.ingramcontent.com/pod-product-compliance
Lightning Source LLC
Chambersburg PA
CBHW051958280526
45793CB00005B/770